D1393669

*0007107840*

# Accounting for Tastes

658.8 BECK

Gary S. Becker

# Accounting

## for Tastes

HARVARD UNIVERSITY PRESS

Cambridge, Massachusetts

London, England

1996

Copyright © 1996 by Gary S. Becker
All rights reserved
Printed in the United States of America

*Library of Congress Cataloging-in-Publication Data*

Becker, Gary Stanley, 1930–
    Accounting for tastes / Gary S. Becker.
        p.    cm.
    Includes bibliographical references and index.
    ISBN 0-674-54356-4 (alk. paper)
    1. Consumers' preferences.   2. Consumer behavior.   3. Consumption
(Economics)—Social aspects.   4. Human capital.   I. Title.
    HF5415.32.B43   1996
    658.8′343—dc20                                            95-50824

To Judy, Cathy, Mike, Cyrus, and Fred—
We helped account for their tastes

# Preface

In writing this book I received help from several persons. I am especially indebted to Michael Grossman, Kevin M. Murphy, and George J. Stigler, co-authors of several previously published essays included in this collection. George came to me in the mid-1970s with a quotation from Alfred Marshall's *Principles of Economics* claiming that "good" music was not an exception to the law of diminishing marginal utility even though "the more good music a man hears, the stronger is his taste for it likely to become." This started me thinking about how to incorporate consumption capital into utility theory, which led eventually to our celebrated paper on *De Gustibus*.

But the behavioral dynamics in that paper were unsatisfactory, and Laurence R. Iannoccone in his dissertation on religion as habit (University of Chicago, 1984) worked out a much more satisfactory dynamical analysis of habitual behavior. His discussion stimulated Kevin Murphy and me to begin joint work on incorporating addiction into economic analysis. Thus began a long collaboration that has been one of the most rewarding experiences of my intellectual life. Kevin's ability to see problems quickly and to devise solutions shows genuine brilliance, and I have benefited enormously from working with him. This book uses four of our joint papers—two of them are also with Mike Grossman.

Michael Aronson, my editor at Harvard University Press, as usual has been very helpful. He provided valuable comments on an earlier draft of the introductory chapter, and suggested the title of the book after we struggled with several alternatives. Jamie Johnson provided excellent research assistance in proofreading, checking references, and many other tasks required to prepare a book for publication. Kate Schmit was a useful but not obtrusive editor, Roberto Marques skillfully drew the charts, and

Jodi Simpson constructed the index. Myrna Hieke, who has assisted me on several previous projects, was again invaluable in typing the manuscript and in many other tangible and intangible ways.

# Contents

# Personal Capital

# Preferences
# and Values

**1**

## 1. Introduction

Preferences or tastes play a crucial part in virtually all fields of study in economics and other social sciences, such as economic growth and capital accumulation, welfare analysis, effects of advertising, tax incidence, monopoly pricing, occupational choices, voting, peer pressure, and cultural influences. But with a few exceptions, economists and political scientists typically pay little attention to the structure of preferences, while sociologists and anthropologists do not embed their analyses of social forces and culture in a powerful analytical framework.

Much of modern economics still proceeds on the implicit assumption that the main determinants of preferences are the basic biological needs for food, drink, shelter, and some recreation. That may not be a bad approach for the very poorest countries, where families spend over half their incomes on food and another quarter on shelter, and where adult males manage only a few hours of true leisure each week. But even in these societies, culture and symbols usually have great influence over behavior.

It should be obvious that basic needs for food, shelter, and rest have little to do with the average person's choice of consumption and other activities in modern economies. The furniture people buy, the type of housing they want, much of the food they consume, especially in restaurants, the type of leisure activities they choose, all are determined by considerations that have almost nothing to do with basic biological needs. Rather, these choices depend on childhood and other experiences, social interactions, and cultural influences.

The economist's normal approach to analyzing consumption and leisure choices assumes that individuals maximize utility with preferences that depend at any moment only on the goods and services they consume at that time. These preferences are assumed to be independent of both past and future consumption, and of the behavior of everyone else. This approach has proved to be a valuable simplification for addressing many economic questions, but a large number of choices in all societies depend very much on past experiences and social forces.

For example, whether a person smoked heavily or took drugs last month significantly affects whether he smokes and uses drugs this month. How a person votes depends very much on the way friends and others in the same peer group vote. Successful advertising for a product increases the desire for that product. The clothing people wear depends crucially on what others wear.

The challenge in extending the normal approach to preferences is to retain its power and most of its simplicity while expanding the analysis to deal with the effects of experiences and social forces. This book retains the assumption that individuals behave so as to maximize utility while extending the definition of individual preferences to include personal habits and addictions, peer pressure, parental influences on the tastes of children, advertising, love and sympathy, and other neglected behavior.

This extension of the utility-maximizing approach to include endogenous preferences is remarkably successful in unifying a wide class of behavior, including habitual, social, and political behavior. I do not believe that any alternative approach—be it founded on "cultural," "biological," or "psychological" forces—comes close to providing comparable insights and explanatory power. The goal of this book is to convince readers that these claims are much more than an author's exaggerated sense of the importance of the work to which he has been committed for many years. This chapter sets out the general principles that provide the foundation for the analysis, and uses them to discuss many issues involved in explaining behavior and in evaluating public policies.

## 2. Extending Preferences

My approach incorporates experiences and social forces into preferences or tastes through two basic capital stocks. *Personal capital, P,* includes the relevant past consumption and other personal experiences that affect current and future utilities. *Social capital, S,* incorporates the influence of past actions by peers and others in an individual's social network and control system.

A person's personal and social capital form part of his total stock of human capital. Although the human capital literature has focused on education, on-the-job training, and other activities that raise earnings, capital that directly influences consumption and utilities are sometimes even more important. Fortunately, the methodology that has been developed to study the effects of investments in human capital on earnings is applicable to investments in personal and social capital, although rates of return on such capital cannot be directly measured since utilities cannot be observed.

After incorporating these new types of (human) capital stocks, the utility function at any moment depends not only on the different goods consumed but also on the stock of personal and social capital at that moment. Utility at time $t$ equals

$$(1.1) \qquad\qquad u = u(x_t, y_t, z_t, P_t, S_t),$$

where $x$, $y$, and $z$ are different goods.

The utility function itself is independent of time, so that it is a stable function over time of the goods consumed and also of the capital stocks. However, the relevant class of goods includes not only ordinary goods, like apples and clothing, but also advertisements (see Chapter 10), education, and other determinants of preferences not ordinarily considered as "goods."

If present choices affect future levels of personal and other capital, utility functions in the future do not change, but utility levels do change. Of course, to the extent that these capital stocks change over time, the subutility function that depends only on goods and services would be unstable since it would tend to shift whenever these capital stocks change. The extended utility function in equation (1.1) is stable only because it includes measures of past experiences and social forces. When extended utility functions are made the foundation of behavior, the study of preferences becomes a vital and exciting contributor to the understanding of economic and social life.

In a more fundamental approach, utility does not depend directly on goods and consumer capital stocks, but only on household-produced "commodities," such as health, social standing and reputation, and pleasures of the senses. The production of these commodities in turn depends on goods, consumer capital, abilities, and other variables. The utility at any time is then only a function of commodities produced at the same time, and not of any commodities produced in the past. Nevertheless, the past, present, and future are still linked through the capital stocks that determine the productivity of commodity production. Present accumulation of personal and social capital changes household productivity in the future.

Current choices are made partly with an eye to their influence on future capital stocks, and hence on future utilities and choices. For example, in deciding whether to take children regularly to church, parents consider how churchgoing affects their own and their children's religiosity in the future. Or Mary may choose to date Tom rather than Bill—even though Bill is handsomer and smarter—because she believes Tom has better character and will make a better husband if they married later on.

The direct linkage between present and future utilities—not whether the utility functions are considered stable or unstable—is what distinguishes this analysis from the more conventional one. But the stability of extended utility functions does suggest that individuals may have different subutility functions only because they "inherit" different levels of personal and social capital. The influence of childhood and other experiences on choices can explain why rich and poor, whites and blacks, less and more educated persons, or persons who live in countries with totally different traditions have subutility functions that are often radically different. But their extended utility functions might be quite similar.

George Stigler and I in "De Gustibus Non Est Disputandum" (see Chapter 2) explicitly considered extended utility functions, not subutility functions, for the utility functions that remained the "same" over time and are the "same" for different individuals included addictive, social, and advertising capital as arguments.

Our assumption that extended preferences are stable was intended not as a philosophical or methodological "law," but as a productive way to analyze and explain behavior. We were impressed by how little has been achieved by the many discussions in economics, sociology, history, and other fields that postulate almost arbitrary variations in preferences and values when confronted by puzzling behavior. We hoped that making these puzzles explicit would hasten the development of more rewarding approaches.

The examples in "De Gustibus" were chosen because they seemed to pose special challenges to the theory of choice. However, I now believe that personal and social capital are crucial not only for understanding addictions and the other behavior discussed there, but also for most other behavior in the modern world, and probably in the distant past as well.

Extended utility functions can also form a stable foundation for welfare analysis that uses Pareto-optimality and other criteria. Subutility functions of goods do not provide a stable foundation because these functions "shift" over time in response to advertising, addictions, and other behavior that changes personal and other capital. Whether particular public policies and other actions raise or lower utilities may then crucially depend on how the changes in utility are evaluated. Does one use the subutility functions that exist before the actions or those produced by the actions (see the further discussion in Section 6 below and in Chapter 10)?

## 3. Personal Capital

Current behavior may raise future personal capital, or this capital may fall over time because of psychological and physiological "depreciation" of the effects of past behavior. The capital stock next period equals the formation of personal capital this period plus the undepreciated portion of the capital from this period.[1]

This formulation is sufficiently flexible to include many kinds of behavior. For example, investment may depend on smoking, attending church, or playing tennis because these types of consumption build up stocks of habitual capital. Childhood abuse and other experiences may influence teenage and adult choices through affecting the accumulation of capital from childhood. Divorce, unemployment, advertising, and other experiences may also help determine choices through affecting the accumulation of personal capital.

This book assumes that forward-looking persons recognize that their present choices and experiences affect personal capital in the future, and that future capital directly affects future utilities. Then current choices depend not only on how they affect current utility, but also on how they affect future utilities.

The demand for goods and experiences which increase future personal capital is stimulated when this capital raises utility, and it is depressed when personal capital lowers utility. For example, the evidence that smoking harms future health, which began to accumulate in the 1960s, caused a large reduction in the demand for smoking. Initial declines in smoking caused large further reductions because smoking is habitual, and because pressure to stop came from peers who were also smoking much less. Many people jog and participate in other exercise only because they believe that physical activity improves their capacities to enjoy life.

---

1. Formally,

(1.2)
$$P_{t+1} = x_t + (1 - d_p)P_t$$

where $d_p$ is a constant depreciation rate and $x$ is the amount invested in personal capital.

Investments in personal capital raise the accumulation of personal capital, but changes in personal capital also affect the dynamic demand for activities that contribute to these investments. Greater personal capital stimulates the demand for investment activities if they are complements to personal capital in the extended utility function in equation (1.1). For then increases in personal capital raise the marginal utility from these activities (a full analysis is more complicated; see the formal treatment in Chapter 3).

These complementarities are especially important in understanding habitual and addictive activities. "Reinforcement," one of the defining characteristics of an addiction, means that an increase in current use of a drug or other good raises the demand for consumption of that good in the future. In the technical language of consumption theory, "reinforcement" means that past and present consumption are complements, which is the same as stating that addictive capital and consumption of addictive goods are complements.

Complementarities and reinforcement in habitual behavior help explain why, for example, the desire to smoke is greater when a person has been smoking heavily for a while, why eating corn flakes regularly for breakfast increases the future demand for this cereal, why telling lies and acting violently increases the tendency to lie and commit violence, why saving becomes habitual, even when people become old and have few years to spend their wealth, why growing up in a religious family greatly increases the likelihood that a person is religious as an adult, or why living with a wife for many years generates such strong dependencies that the husband may experience a mental and physical breakdown after she dies.

A very different example considers what is called in politics the "tyranny of the status quo"—that it is very difficult to eliminate regulations and other public policies which have been in effect for many years. The habits and other attitudes of beneficiaries and even of those harmed adjust to a policy, and after a while both sides may treat programs that have been around for a while as natural and morally justified. For this reason, reversals of policies that have survived for a long time usually are politically unpopular.

That human beings are creatures of habit has been noticed for thousands of years. Aristotle claimed that "Moral virtue . . . is formed by habit" (*Nicomachean Ethics*, 1962, II.I.33). Adam Smith partly explains the affection for family members by habit: "After himself, the members of his own family . . . are naturally the objects of his warmest affections . . . He is more habituated to sympathize with them" (Smith, 1976, VI.ii.12).

I believe the main reason habitual behavior permeates most aspects of life is that habits have an advantage in the biological evolution of human traits. For as long as habits are not too powerful they have social as well as personal advantages (see Becker and Madrigal, 1995). The importance of habitual behavior justifies the attention I give to the formation of habits and addictions in this book.

Individuals help guide their destinies by exercising control over future stocks of personal capital that determine future utilities and preferences. Therefore, individuals, in effect, help to choose their own preferences, if "preferences" are taken to mean not the extended preference function of goods *and* capital, but the (sub)utility function that depends only on goods, which is the function economists usually consider.

For example, a woman who fears and loathes men, perhaps because she was sexually abused as a child, may try to change her attitudes toward men by undergoing psychotherapy treatment and by taking other actions, or she may decide to accept these feelings and seek relations only with other women. In either case, she helps determine her future attitudes to men and women, conditional of course on the earlier sexual abuse and other childhood experiences.

Of course, individuals are not omnipotent, and they sometimes make mistakes while trying to influence their future preferences. The assumption of forward-looking behavior does not imply perfect foresight, or even accurate calculation of the probabilities of future events. Rather, it implies only that individuals try as best they can to anticipate the future consequences of their present choices. Therefore, they may be unhappy about who they are not only because of childhood and other experiences beyond their control, but also because of the effect of their own mistakes on their present "tastes."

A young man may drink heavily because he does not anticipate that he will become addicted to alcohol (Orphanides and Zervos, 1995, provide a formal analysis of maximizing behavior when there is uncertainty about becoming addicted). Of course, if he turns out to be wrong and he does become addicted later on in life, he would wish he had not drunk so much as a young man. He might decide to fight his addiction by joining Alcoholics Anonymous and in other ways; on the other hand, continuing to drink heavily could be a way of maximizing utility if his preferences "shifted" greatly in favor of alcohol.

A woman may eventually regret that she went to a psychiatrist to help her overcome her hatred of men because she continues to dislike sexual and other relations with them. At some point, she may stop her therapy and radically alter her behavior to seek the companionship of other women.

Uncertainty about the outcomes from their choices is just one reason why individuals only *partly* control their own destinies. Parents have enormous influence over the experiences of their children, especially during the formative early years, and these childhood experiences can greatly influence adult preferences and choices. For example, adults who had hardworking and caring parents tend to work harder and care more about their children than adults who had abusive parents, or parents who were addicted to drugs.

And from childhood on, other influences besides our parents also shape our preferences. Companies in the United States spend well over $100 billion annually on advertisements that try to change preferences by influencing personal capital. Schools and the media affect values and other attitudes, and governments influence choices through their own advertising and "propaganda" (see, e.g., Lott, 1990). In particular, the sharp increase in labor force participation of women and other groups during World War II despite lower after-tax real wages may have been partly due to government appeals to patriotism (see Mulligan, 1995).

Of course, most people are not simply puppets who are manipulated by others. Even small children look "cute" and helpless, learn how to make parents feel guilty, and develop other expressions and behavior that can induce their parents to treat them better. Adults may avoid advertisements they strongly dislike, and they expose themselves to others that lower utility only if they receive compensation (see the discussion in Chapter 10). Residents of totalitarian states learn to ignore or minimize the impact of ubiquitous government propaganda.

## Discounting the Future

The usual assumption in economics is that discount rates on future utilities are constant and fixed to each person, although they may differ between persons. This assumption is a good initial simplification, but it cannot explain *why* discount rates differ by age, income, education, and other personal characteristics, or why they change over time for the same individual, as when a person matures from being a child to being an adult.

The weight a person places on future utilities in determining present decisions is affected by how well she can imagine what future utilities will be like. The capacity to anticipate future utilities is not rigidly fixed, although it probably has a biological component (see the interesting analysis by Rogers, 1994). People change the weight they attach to future utilities by spending more time, effort, and goods in creating personal capital that helps them to better imagine the future.

It has been claimed for hundreds of years by philosophers, economists, and many others that most people undervalue future utilities because they have difficulty in imagining the future. That may well be true, but people train themselves to reduce and sometimes more than fully overcome any tendency toward undervaluation. The analysis in this book allows people to maximize the discounted value of present and future utilities partly by spending time and other resources to produce "imagination" capital that helps them better appreciate future utilities (see Becker and Mulligan, 1994).

They may choose greater education in part because it tends to improve the appreciation of the future, and thereby reduces the discount on the future. Parents teach their children to be more aware of the future consequences of their choices (Akabayashi, 1995, studies the conflict between parents and children over the weight attached to the future). Addictions to drugs and alcohol reduce utility partly through decreasing the capacity to anticipate future consequences. Religion often increases the weight attached to future utilities, especially when it promises an attractive afterlife.

Imagination capital not only affects the discount on future utility, but it also alters preferences over goods by affecting present and future choices. Someone who places greater weight on the future consequences of current choices is more likely to engage in activities that raise future utilities, perhaps partly at the expense of current utility. Such a person is less likely to become addicted to harmful substances like drugs, alcohol, and cigarettes, and is more likely to develop a belief in the afterlife, and to acquire beneficial habits like exercise and coming to work on time. As a result, individuals who are more future-oriented develop habitual and other preferences that have more beneficial future consequences.

I assume that individuals choose their discount rates within a framework in which preferences are *consistent* over time. That is, the choices an individual *would like* to make in the future, if he knew now what would happen in the interim, are exactly the same as the choices he *will actually* make then. The assumption of consistent preferences is clearly not a literal description of much actual behavior, and is not necessary to develop an analysis of endogenous preferences, but it is an extremely useful simplification of behavior.

I believe that even extreme forms of addictive behavior, such as heavy smoking or drinking, involve forward-looking, consistent utility maximization (see Chapters 3 and 5), although some philosophers and economists assume that addictive behavior is inconsistent, the result of the existence of conflicting selves within the same person (see, e.g., Elster, 1984; Schelling, 1984b; and Posner, 1995). However, behavior over time may *appear* to be inconsistent only because changes in the stock of personal capital have been neglected. The assumption of consistency focuses the analysis of conflict not on multiple selves within the same individual, but on the far more important conflict between different individuals and organizations. Such conflict is analyzed in Chapters 10, 11, and 12, and in Becker and Madrigal (1995).

## 4. Social Capital

Men and women want respect, recognition, prestige, acceptance, and power from their family, friends, peers, and others. Consumption and other activities have a major social component partly because they take place in public. As a result, people often choose restaurants, neighborhoods, schools, books to read, political opinions, food, or leisure activities with an eye to pleasing peers and others in their social network.

I incorporate the influences of others on a person's utility through the stock of social capital, $S$ (see the pioneering analysis of social capital in Coleman, 1990). Since this capital captures the effects of the social milieu, an individual's stock of social capital depends not primarily on his own choices, but on the choices of peers in the relevant network of interactions.

A simple formulation[2] has next period's social capital of person $i$ equal to the consumption of social goods by all persons in $i$'s network plus the undepreciated portion of his current social capital. A more general formulation would distinguish investments in social capital of leaders and followers (see Becker and Murphy, 1994), and it need not be an additive function of their behavior.

An increase in social capital can either raise or lower utility. The peer pressure on a teenager to smoke or join a violent gang may lower his utility, whereas a family's utility is higher when neighbors will help if a burglar tries to break into its house. This dependence of a person's social capital on the behavior of others may create important externalities. Heavy

---

2. The formation of social capital can be expressed as

(1.3) $$S_{t+1}^i = X^i + (1 - d_s)S_t^i$$

where $d_s$ is the depreciation rate on social capital, and $X^i (= \sum x^j)$ is the effect of choices by the $j$ members of $i$'s network on his social capital.

drinking by peers imposes a cost when it pressures a person into drinking heavily too. Similarly, the diligence of neighbors in looking out for crime benefits everyone in their neighborhood (see Coleman, 1990, pp. 249–260).

Once a social network is given, people have little control over the production of their social capital, for that is mainly determined by the actions of peers and relevant others. What a person does hardly affects the total investment in her social capital ($X$ in equation 1.3 in footnote 2) if many persons are in her network. Therefore, an individual's social capital is much less under her control than either her personal or imagination capital.

But while individuals do not have much *direct* influence over their social capital, they often have an enormous *indirect* influence over it, since they try to become part of social networks that benefit rather than hurt them. The noted anthropologist Mary Douglas claims that "the real moment of choosing is . . . choice of comrades and their way of life" (1983, p. 45). Thompson, Ellis, and Wildavsky observe that "Rational people support their way of life. It follows that what is rational depends on the way of life . . . there cannot be any one set of actions rational for everyone" (1990, p. 98). This endogeneity of social networks creates a tendency for social capital to raise rather than lower utility.

Still, the choices available may be limited by market prices and other circumstances. A teenager enrolled in a particular school may have little choice over the peer pressure she feels. The equilibrium degree of segregation between blacks and whites, rich and poor, and other groups is determined by market and other forces that are partly beyond the control of any individual.

An increase in a person's social capital increases her demand for goods and activities that are complements to the capital and reduces the demand for those that are substitutes. Although the stock of ordinary consumer durables and purchases of the durables are usually substitutes in preferences, social capital and investments in this capital are often strong complements. A teenager may begin to smoke, join a gang, and neglect his studies mainly because his friends smoke, are gang members, and do not pay attention to school. Individuals may follow others by rooting for the home football and baseball teams, or by buying books they do not understand—such as Stephen Hawking's *A Brief History of Time* (see Max, 1992).

If only one person in a social network is given an incentive to change the amount invested in her social capital, the capital of the others in a large network is only slightly affected. Then investments by the person affected also may change only a little, even when her investments and the stock of social capital are complements in preferences. If she stops working she has more leisure time to play tennis, but she may not play much more if none of her working friends have additional free time.

However, investments in social capital may greatly change when most members of the same network are affected. Suppose the desire to play tennis depends on how many other people play, and the cost of playing falls because the number of tennis courts increases. Given the initial stock of players, the number of players may increase only a little at first, but the greater number of players then increases the desire to play by others. This complementarity between the desire to play and the number who play increases playing over time, either explosively or until it converges to a new and possibly much higher level.

The horizontal axis in Figure 1.1 graphs a typical individual's stock of social capital, while the vertical axis graphs complementary investments in the capital. The initial equilibrium has a stock of $S^*$ and investments of

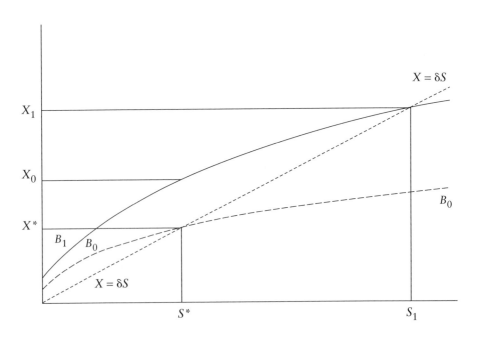

FIGURE 1.1

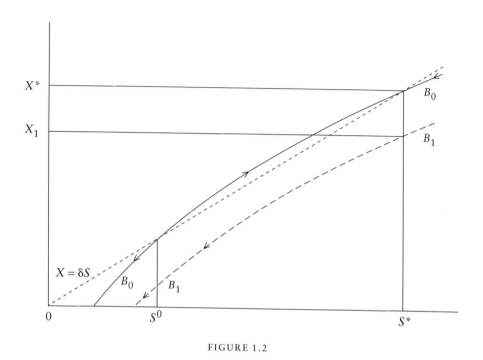

FIGURE 1.2

$X^*$, where the curve $B_0$, determined by preferences, gives the amount an individual invests as a function of his stock of social capital. A common change to all members of the social network, such as a fall in the cost of investments that shifts the desire to invest upward from the curve $B_0$ to the curve $B_1$, initially raises investment only from $X^*$ to $X_0$. The greater investment increases next period's stock, which further raises investment because of the complementarity. Investments and the stock continue to rise over time until they reach a new equilibrium at $X_1$ and $S_1$, which is much above the initial level of $X^*$ and $S^*$.

Cumulative effects on consumption can be much more dramatic when complementarity between investments and capital stock causes multiple equilibria, as in Figure 1.2. With the relation between investments and the capital stock given by $B_0$, this figure has three possible equilibria: at $S = 0$, $S = S^0$, and $S = S^*$. Only the first and third are stable—the equilibrium at $S^0$ is unstable since the stock eventually falls to zero if it is even slightly below $S^0$, and the stock eventually increases to $S^*$ if it is even slightly above $S^0$.

Behavior dependent on social forces may be quite unstable and sensitive to even modest shocks to the group. Even small changes in initial conditions can ultimately have enormous effects on behavior, such as when rather small differences in family backgrounds cause teenagers either to take or avoid drugs, to work hard at school or neglect their studies. In Figure 1.2, a rise perhaps in the price of drugs that shifts the desire to invest downward from the curve $B_0$ to the curve $B_1$ initially reduces drug use only from $X^*$ to $X_1$, but then drug consumption drops quickly until everyone in the group becomes drug-free and $S$ falls to zero.

Reactions to common changes are still larger when the formation of social capital also depends on habits. A teenager may take drugs partly because he took them in the past and partly because his friends do. A reduction in the price of drugs may initially stimulate drug consumption only a little. But over time each member of the group increases drug use for two reasons: they used more in the recent past, and their friends are also using more. The interaction between habits and social forces can produce explosive changes in drug use that lead either to heavy addiction or drug-free behavior (see Chapter 6).

## CULTURE

Culture and traditions are shared values and preferences handed down from one generation to another through families, peer groups, ethnic groups, classes, and other groups. Clifford Geertz said that "culture is best seen not as complexes of concrete behavior patterns . . . but as a set of control mechanisms—plans, recipes, rules, instructions . . . for the governing of behavior" (quoted in Elkins and Simeon, 1979, p. 129). Like other kinds of social capital, culture may change over time, but it changes slowly—presumably, the depreciation rate on cultural capital is small because these "control mechanisms" are not easily altered.

Individuals have less control over their culture than over other social capital. They cannot alter their ethnicity, race, or family history, and only with difficulty can they change their country or religion. Because of the difficulty of changing culture and its low depreciation rate, culture is largely "given" to individuals throughout their lifetimes.

Culture exercises a sizable influence over preferences and individual behavior, whereas behavior has only a slow return influence on culture. Differences in cultures cause considerable differences in preferences over goods, as with the taboo against eating pork among religious Jews and

Moslems, or the tradition of filial obedience in Chinese and some other cultures. The economists' traditional assumption of "given" and stable preferences over goods seems to be much more consistent with the influence of culture on preferences than with the influence of personal capital or other kinds of social capital.

But some anthropologists and sociologists go much too far when they claim that culture so dominates behavior that little room is left for choice. The economist James Duesenberry reflected this view when he asserted in a comment on a paper of mine that "economics is all about choices, while sociology is about why people have no choices" (1960, p. 233). The anthropologist Mary Douglas recognizes in her statement quoted earlier that people make fundamental choices about overall lifestyles. And within each lifestyle, they help choose their type and quantity of personal capital.

The types of cultures that are sustainable depend in important ways on individual choices and personal capital. Thus cooperation can be sustained more easily without sanctions against uncooperative behavior when individual behavior is habitual (see Becker and Madrigal, 1995). For if individuals are habitual, and if they were cooperative in the past, they might continue to be cooperative even if they could gain an advantage from uncooperative behavior.

The evidence on communism provides an obvious counterexample to the claims about the tyranny of culture over behavior. Many cultures tried the communist recipe for organizing the economy, including Chinese, Russian, Central European, African, and Latino cultures. Communist ideology proclaimed that selfish behavior in Western nations was due to capitalism, and that communism could reorient workers and consumers to care more about the State's welfare and less about their own. Yet every communist regime, regardless of culture, failed to achieve any lasting reorientation. Since pay was not sensitive to how hard people worked, they invariably chose to work little, no matter what the culture. And since such behavior became habitual, many persons in the former communist nations have not yet acquired good work habits.

Sen proposes to incorporate cultural and ethical values into behavior by distinguishing utility based on "personal welfare" from "commitment" that involves a "ranking of preference rankings to express our moral judgments" (1977, p. 337)—he calls this ranking of personal welfare rankings a "meta-ranking." My use of "meta-preference" in Chapters 6 and 10 differs from Sen's, for it is simply another way to describe the extended utility function in equation (1.1).

In this book, moral and cultural judgments affect choices by influencing the personal and social capital included in a single extended utility function. Second-order meta-preference rankings may help to articulate the moral judgments that underlie behavior, which appears to be Sen's purpose in introducing them. However, I do not believe that higher-order rankings are either necessary or useful in understanding behavior since ethics and culture affect behavior in the same general way as do other determinants of utility and preferences. In particular, considerations of price and cost influence ethical and moral choices—such as whether to act honestly—just as they influence choices of personal goods.

### 5. The Influence of Economic Activity on Preferences

In neoclassical economic analysis, preferences—along with technologies and government policies—determine economic outcomes, including prices and wages, rates of growth in output, and the distribution of incomes. The endogeneity of preferences highlighted in this book implies that the economy also affects tastes regarding goods, leisure, and other activities. In other words, preferences both influence economic outcomes and are in turn influenced by the economy.

The classical economists, Marx, and other writers during the nineteenth century well appreciated that economic processes affect preferences. Adam Smith took the division of labor as the main source of economic progress, but he also believed that "The man whose whole life is spent in performing a few simple operations . . . has no occasion to exert his understanding . . . He naturally loses, therefore, the *habit* [emphasis added] of such exertion . . . [which] renders him . . . not only incapable of relishing or bearing a part in any rational conversation, but of conceiving any generous, noble, or tender sentiment" (1937, pp. 734–735).

Marx said, "By acting on the external world and changing it, [the worker] at the same time changes his own nature" (1906, pp. 197–198, quoted by Gintis, 1974). Gintis's article on endogenous preferences is pioneering, but it is marred by an excessive ideological slant.

De Tocqueville remarked that "The principle of self-interest produces no great acts of self-sacrifice . . . but it disciplines a number of persons in habits of regularity, temperance, moderation, foresight, self-command; and if it does not lead men straight to virtue by the will, it gradually draws them in that direction by their habits" (1969, part II, p. 527).

According to Stigler (1949), the classical economists believed that private property and individual responsibility have their most important effects on self-reliance and other desirable attitudes and preferences.

Whether or not this belief is correct is less important for present purposes than that modern economics has lost a lot by completely abandoning the classical concern with the effects of the economy on preferences and attitudes.

This book combines the classical and modern links between preferences and the economy. Initial stocks of personal and social capital, along with technologies and government policies, do help determine economic outcomes. But the economy also changes tastes and preferences by changing personal and social capital.

To illustrate how the economy and preferences interact, suppose single persons marry only after falling in love, and that they are likely to fall in love with people they meet at school, church, parties, exercise clubs, and other gatherings. This gives them an incentive to choose schools, clubs, friends, and neighborhoods partly with the goal of improving their chances of falling in love with "desirable" persons (see Chapter 12). In this way the importance of falling in love would greatly affect the allocation of single individuals by neighborhood and other categories.

The endogeneity of preferences makes it difficult to determine whether preferences or opportunities are responsible for particular economic outcomes. Do some economies grow more rapidly than others mainly because individuals in growing economies have work and other habits that are conducive to growth, or are good habits created by more rapid growth for other reasons?

Preferences and the rates of economic growth are correlated partly because tastes, such as a lower rate of preference for present utilities, are more conducive to rapid economic growth. However, the endogeneity of preferences implies that growth and preferences are related also because economic outcomes help form tastes. In particular, workers in economically advanced countries tend to come to work on time and value promptness not only because time is more valuable in richer countries but also because people develop a habit for promptness after living in a society that puts a premium on being prompt.

Government entitlement programs and other government policies sometimes have sizable effects on preferences. Welfare discourages the independence and self-reliance of recipients, while social security weakens the ties that bind together older parents and their children (see Chapter 8) and encourages retired people to believe they deserve government support (see Romer, 1994). Civil rights legislation that banned segregation of blacks in buses, schools, and elsewhere eventually led southern whites and blacks to feel more comfortable with participating in activities together.

## 6. Endogenous Preferences and Welfare Criteria

The endogeneity of preferences would appear to play havoc with traditional approaches to welfare evaluations of economic outcomes. If advertising increases the utility consumers received from goods that are advertised, should the effect on consumer welfare be measured by changes in utility from the preferences prior to the advertising, by changes in utility from the preferences afterward, or by some combination of these changes (this issue is the focus of Dixit and Norman, 1978)?

These difficulties, however, are intrinsic not to the endogeneity of preferences but to inadequate incorporation of this endogeneity into welfare criteria. If the relevant utility function for welfare analysis includes personal and social capital, the effect on utility of advertising and public policies can be evaluated without any ambiguity (see Chapter 10).

Consider how to approach the welfare evaluation of civil rights legislation. Suppose that whites initially suffer a big drop in utility from being forced to mix with blacks in schools, on teams, in buses, and in other ways. Over time, however, they get habituated to integration and eventually do not mind it very much, and may even prefer integration. A welfare analysis should consider not only the initial effects on utility when whites and perhaps blacks too intensely dislike integration, nor only the ultimate effects when both groups might like integration, but the discounted value of both initial and later changes in utilities that incorporates the transition between the initial and later attitudes toward integration (see the brief comment in Philipson, 1993, p. 331). If the discounted utility of whites falls, the legislation hurts them even if ultimately they like integration. Similarly, the legislation helps whites if their discounted utility increases, even though initially they hate integration.

In other words, initial preferences should have no priority over final preferences in welfare analysis when policies change preferences. Sunstein sees this clearly: "If legal rules have inevitable effects on preferences, it is hard to see how a government might even attempt to take preferences 'as given'" (1993, p. 22). Aaron also recognizes that "The idea that values can change leads to thinking about how public policy might alter values and thereby change responses to public policies" (1994, p. 6).

But it is misleading to claim that welfare analysis then has no solid foundation: "When preferences are functions of legal rules, the rules cannot be justified by reference to the preferences. Social rules and practices cannot be justified by practices that they have produced" (Sunstein, 1993, p. 22). For the effects on discounted utility incorporate initial attitudes, final attitudes, and transitional attitudes into a single consistent welfare criterion.

Many persons appear to recognize that participating in public programs may greatly change their preferences. A sizable fraction of those eligible for welfare and other transfer programs do not enroll (see Moffitt, 1992), perhaps because they anticipate that receiving these benefits would actually lower their utility through the development of dependency and other bad habits.

Still, one might be skeptical about basing welfare analysis even on discounted utilities when preferences are heavily dependent on childhood upbringing, peer pressure and other social interactions, and lucky or unlucky experiences. Should preferences be "sovereign" when individuals take drugs, drink heavily, or abuse others because their parents were on crack, were drunkards, and abused their children and each other? In particular, the utilitarian criterion of maximizing a weighted sum of utilities—used in the optimal tax and other welfare literature—makes even less sense once the endogeneity of preferences is recognized. This criterion requires resources to be redistributed away from individuals who are ineffective "utility-producing machines" and toward those who are effective "machines," but why redistribute away from individuals who cannot easily produce utility because they had miserable childhoods?

Uneasiness about using preferences as the foundation of welfare analysis is related to the discussions in recent years of the alleged conflict between *actual* preferences and *desired* preferences. This distinction recognizes that many people dislike their preferences and wish they were different: individuals may be unhappy because they are addicted to drugs, or they pursue women who apparently have no interest in them, or they are prejudiced against blacks, or they watch too much television. Hirschman points out that "men and women have the ability to step back from their 'revealed' wants, volitions, and preferences, to ask themselves whether they really want these wants and prefer these preferences"; individuals "form meta-preferences that may differ from their preferences . . . [and] there is a close link between preference change and the concept of metapreference" (1992, p. 144; also see Sen, 1977).

I do not distinguish between actual and desired preferences, but in my approach individuals would be unhappy with their preferences if they do not like the personal and social capital they "inherited" from the past. In effect, they *wish* their actual preferences over goods and other activities were different. But they do not act on this wish because actual capital stocks constrain their utility-maximizing choices, no matter how much they may regret the amount and kind of capital they inherited from the past. Their utility would be lower, perhaps much lower, if their "desired" preferences alone guided choices. Even though a person may greatly regret he acquired a taste for crack because both his parents took crack, he might be miserable if he ignored his background and abstained from taking the drug.

But conflicts between actual and desired stocks of personal and social capital would have a large influence over choices if individuals try to depreciate inherited capital that lowers their utility and invest in capital that raises their utility. Still, a person can regret that he inherited certain types of personal and social capital, and yet he may invest in that capital because he is addicted to particular types of behavior, or because of other reasons also consistent with utility-maximizing behavior.

## 7. Is Behavior Rational?

Although this book assumes that individuals maximize utility in a consistent way, and that they consider the effects of their actions on future as well as present utilities, individuals may occasionally do otherwise: they may have imperfect memories, they may discount the future "excessively," they may make erroneous calculations and be influenced by how questions are framed, and their perceptions may be distorted by drugs, anesthesia, or Ulysses' sirens. Psychologists and others in recent years have placed great emphasis on these cognitive limits on individual "rationality" (see, e.g., Kahneman and Tversky, 1986, or Akerlof, 1991).

Such cognitive imperfections are sometimes important, but in recent years they may have received excessive attention at the expense of more significant weaknesses in standard models of rational choice for explaining behavior in real, as opposed to experimental, situations. These models typically assume that preferences do not directly depend on either past experiences or social interactions. But childhood and other experiences, and the attitudes and behavior of others, frequently place more far-reaching constraints on choices than do mistakes and distortions in cognitive perceptions.

To highlight these neglected constraints, the book does not emphasize cognitive imperfections, but rather the influence of personal and social capital on choices. Preferences and constraints no longer have independent influences on behavior since personal and social capital are constraints that operate through preferences.

The behavior analyzed in these essays can be said to be "rational" because individuals are still assumed to make forward-looking, maximizing, and consistent choices. But the type of rationality modeled here is quite different, and much more relevant, than that found in standard models because behavior is influenced by habits, childhood and other experiences, and culture, peer pressure, and other social interactions.

Indeed, the choices implied by this broader approach will often bear little resemblance to the choices produced by traditional models of rational behavior. The following chapters demonstrate the explanatory power of the broader approach by analyzing a variety of individual and aggregate choices that are crucially affected by past experiences and social interactions.

# De Gustibus Non Est Disputandum

The venerable admonition not to quarrel over tastes is commonly interpreted as advice to terminate a dispute when it has been resolved into a difference of tastes, presumably because there is no further room for rational persuasion. Tastes are the unchallengeable axioms of a man's behavior: he may properly (usefully) be criticized for inefficiency in satisfying his desires, but the desires themselves are *data*. Deplorable tastes—say, for arson—may be countered by coercive and punitive action, but these deplorable tastes, at least when held by an adult, are not capable of being changed by persuasion.

Our title seems to us to be capable of another and preferable interpretation: that tastes neither change capriciously nor differ importantly between people. On this interpretation one does not argue over tastes for the same reason that one does not argue over the Rocky Mountains—both are there, will be there next year, too, and are the same to all men.

The difference between these two viewpoints of tastes is fundamental. On the traditional view, an explanation of economic phenomena that reaches a difference in tastes between people or times is the terminus of the argument: the problem is abandoned *at this point* to whoever studies and explains tastes (psychologists? anthropologists? phrenologists? sociobiologists?). On our preferred interpretation, one never reaches this impasse: the economist continues to search for differences in prices or incomes to explain any differences or changes in behavior.

The choice between these two views of the role of tastes in economic theory must ultimately be made on the basis of their comparative analyt-

By George J. Stigler and Gary S. Becker; originally published in *American Economic Review*, 67, no. 2 (1977): 76–90.

ical productivities. On the conventional view of inscrutable, often capricious tastes, one drops the discussion as soon as the behavior of tastes becomes important—and turns his energies to other problems. On our view, one searches, often long and frustratingly, for the subtle forms that prices and incomes take in explaining differences among men and periods. If the latter approach yields more useful results, it is the proper choice. The establishment of the proposition that one may usefully treat tastes as stable over time and similar among people is the central task of this essay.

The ambitiousness of our agenda deserves emphasis: we are proposing the hypothesis that widespread and/or persistent human behavior can be explained by a generalized calculus of utility-maximizing behavior, without introducing the qualification "tastes remaining the same." It is a thesis that does not permit of direct proof because it is an assertion about the world, not a proposition in logic. Moreover, it is possible almost at random to throw up examples of phenomena that presently defy explanation by this hypothesis: Why do we have inflation? Why are there few Jews in farming?[1] Why are societies with polygynous families so rare in the modern era? Why aren't blood banks responsible for the quality of their product? If we could answer these questions to your satisfaction, you would quickly produce a dozen more.

What we assert is not that we are clever enough to make illuminating applications of utility-maximizing theory to all important phenomena—not even our entire generation of economists is clever enough to do that. Rather, we assert that this traditional approach of the economist offers guidance in tackling these problems—and that no other approach of remotely comparable generality and power is available.

To support our thesis we could offer samples of phenomena we believe to be usefully explained on the assumption of stable, well-behaved preference functions. Ultimately, this is indeed the only persuasive method of supporting the assumption, and it is legitimate to cite in support all of the existing corpus of successful economic theory. Here we shall undertake to give this proof by accomplishment a special and limited interpretation. We take categories of behavior commonly held to demonstrate changes in tastes or to be explicable only in terms of such changes, and show both

---

1. Our lamented friend Reuben Kessel offered an attractive explanation: since Jews have been persecuted so often and forced to flee to other countries, they have not invested in immobile land, but in mobile human capital—business skills, education, etc.—that would automatically go with them. Of course, someone might counter with the more basic query: but why are they Jews, and not Christians or Moslems?

that they are reconcilable with our assumption of stable preferences and that the reformulation is illuminating.

## 1. The New Theory of Consumer Choice

The power of stable preferences and utility maximization in explaining a wide range of behavior has been significantly enhanced by a recent reformulation of consumer theory.[2] This reformulation transforms the family from a passive maximizer of the utility from market purchases into an active maximizer also engaged in extensive production and investment activities. In the traditional theory, households maximize a utility function of the goods and services bought in the marketplace, whereas in the reformulation they maximize a utility function of objects of choice, called commodities, that they produce with market goods, their own time, their skills, training and other human capital, and other inputs. Stated formally, a household seeks to maximize

(2.1) $$U = U(Z_1, \ldots Z_m)$$

with

(2.2) $$Z_i = f_i(X_{1i}, \ldots X_{ki}, t_{1i}, \ldots t_{\ell i}, S_1, \ldots S_\ell, Y_i), i = 1 \ldots m$$

where $Z_i$ are the commodity objects of choice entering the utility function, $f_i$ is the production function for the $i$th commodity, $X_{ji}$ is the quantity of the $j$th market good or service used in the production of the $i$th commodity, $t_{ji}$ is the $j$th person's own time input, $S_j$ the $j$th person's human capital, and $Y_i$ represents all other inputs.

The $Z_i$ have no market prices since they are not purchased or sold, but do have "shadow" prices determined by their costs of production. If $f_i$ were homogeneous of the first degree in the $X_{ji}$ and $t_{ji}$, marginal and average costs would be the same and the shadow price of $Z_i$ would be

(2.3) $$\pi_i = \sum_{j=1}^{k} \alpha_{ji}\left(\frac{p}{w_1}, \frac{w}{w_1}, S, Y_i\right) p_j + \sum_{j=1}^{\ell} \beta_{ji}\left(\frac{p}{w_1}, \frac{w}{w_1}, S, Y_i\right) w_j$$

---

2. An exposition of this reformulation can be found in Michael and Becker (1973). This exposition emphasizes the capacity of the reformulation to generate many implications about behavior that are consistent with stable tastes.

where $p_j$ is the cost of $X_j$, $w_j$ is the cost of $t_j$, and $\alpha_{ji}$ and $\beta_{ji}$ are input-output coefficients that depend on the (relative) set of $p$ and $w$, $S$, and $Y_i$. The numerous and varied determinants of these shadow prices give concrete expression to our earlier statement about the subtle forms that prices take in explaining differences among men and periods.

The real income of a household does not simply equal its money income deflated by an index of the prices of market goods, but equals its full income (which includes the value of "time" to the household)[3] deflated by an index of the prices, $\pi_i$, of the produced commodities. Since full income and commodity prices depend on a variety of factors, incomes also take subtle forms. Our task in this paper is to spell out some of the forms prices and full income take.

## 2. Stability of Tastes and "Addiction"

Tastes are frequently said to change as a result of consuming certain "addictive" goods. For example, smoking of cigarettes, drinking of alcohol, injection of heroin, or close contact with some persons over an appreciable period of time, often increases the desire (creates a craving) for these goods or persons, and thereby cause their consumption to grow over time. In utility language, their marginal utility is said to rise over time because tastes shift in their favor. This argument has been clearly stated by Alfred Marshall (1962, p. 94) when discussing the taste for "good" music:

> There is however an implicit condition in this law [of diminishing marginal utility] which should be made clear. It is that we do not suppose time to be allowed for any alteration in the character or tastes of the man himself. It is therefore no exception to the law that the more good music a man hears, the stronger is his taste for it likely to become . . .

We believe that the phenomenon Marshall is trying to explain, namely that exposure to good music increases the subsequent demand for good music (for some persons!), can be explained with some gain in insight by assuming constant tastes, whereas to assume a change in tastes has been an unilluminating "explanation." The essence of our explanation lies in the accumulation of what might be termed "consumption capital" by the

---

3. Full income is the maximum money income that a household could achieve by an appropriate allocation of its time and other resources.

consumer, and we distinguish "beneficial" addiction like Marshall's good music from "harmful" addiction like heroin.

Consider first beneficial addiction, and an unchanging utility function that depends on two produced commodities:

$$(2.4) \qquad\qquad U = U(M, Z)$$

where $M$ measures the amount of music "appreciation" produced and consumed, and $Z$ the production and consumption of other commodities. Music appreciation is produced by a function that depends on the time allocated to music $(t_m)$, and the training and other human capital conducive to music appreciation $(S_m)$ (other inputs are ignored):

$$(2.5) \qquad\qquad M = M_m(t_m, S_m)$$

We assume that

$$\frac{\partial M_m}{\partial t_m} > 0, \ \frac{\partial M_m}{\partial S_m} > 0$$

An increase in this music capital increases the productivity of time spent listening to or devoted in other ways to music.

In order to analyze the consequences for its consumption of "the more good music a man hears," the production and consumption of music appreciation has to be dated. The amount of appreciation produced at any moment $j$, $M_j$, would depend on the time allocated to music and the music human capital at $j$: $t_{m_j}$ and $S_{m_j}$, respectively. The latter in turn is produced partly through "on-the-job" training or "learning by doing" by accumulating the effects of earlier music appreciation:

$$(2.6) \qquad\qquad S_{m_j} = h(M_{j-1}, M_{j-2}, \ldots, E_j)$$

By definition, the addiction is beneficial if

$$\frac{\partial S_{m_j}}{\partial M_{j-v}} > 0, \text{ all } v \text{ in } (2.6)$$

The term $E_j$ measures the effect of education and other human capital on music appreciation skill, where

$$\frac{\partial S_{m_j}}{\partial E_j} > 0$$

and probably

$$\frac{\partial^2 S_{m_j}}{\partial M_{j-v} \partial E_j} > 0$$

We assume for simplicity a utility function that is a discounted sum of functions like the one in equation (2.4), where the $M$ and $Z$ commodities are dated, and the discount rate determined by time preference.[4] The optimal allocation of consumption is determined from the equality between the ratio of their marginal utilities and the ratio of their shadow prices:

(2.7) $$\frac{MU_{m_j}}{MU_{z_j}} = \frac{\partial U}{\partial M_j} \Big/ \frac{\partial U}{\partial Z_j} = \frac{\pi_{m_j}}{\pi_{z_j}}$$

The shadow price equals the marginal cost of adding a unit of commodity output. The marginal cost is complicated for music appreciation $M$ by the positive effect on subsequent music human capital of the production of music appreciation at any moment $j$. This effect on subsequent capital is an investment return from producing appreciation at $j$ that reduces the cost of production at $j$. It can be shown that the marginal cost at $j$ equals[5]

---

4. A consistent application of the assumption of stable preferences implies that the discount rate is zero; that is, the absence of time preference (see the brief discussion in Section 6).

5. The utility function

$$V = \sum_{j=1}^{n} a^j U(M_j, Z_j)$$

is maximized subject to the constraints

$$M_j = M(t_{m_j}, S_{m_j}); \; Z_j = Z(x_j, t_{z_j})$$

$$S_{m_j} = h(M_{j-1}, M_{j-2}, \ldots, E_j)$$

$$\sum \frac{p x_j}{(1+r)^j} = \sum \frac{w t_{w_j} + b_j}{(i+r)^j}$$

and $t_{w_j} + t_{m_j} + t_{x_j} = t$,

where $t_{w_j}$ is hours worked in the $j$th period, and $b_j$ is property income in that period. By substitution one derives the full wealth constraint:

$$\pi_{m_j} = \frac{w\,\partial t_{m_j}}{\partial M_j} - w \sum_{i=1}^{n-j} \frac{\partial M_{j+i}}{\partial S_{m_{j+i}}} \bigg/ \frac{\partial M_{j+i}}{\partial t_{m_{j+i}}}$$

(2.8)
$$\cdot \frac{dS_{m_{j+i}}}{dM_j} \cdot \frac{1}{(i+r)^i}$$

$$= \frac{w\,\partial t_{m_j}}{\partial M_j} - A_j = \frac{w}{MP_{t_{m_j}}} - A_j$$

where $w$ is the wage rate (assumed to be the same at all ages), $r$ the interest rate, $n$ the length of life, and $A_j$ the effect of addiction, measures the value of the saving in future time inputs from the effect of the production of $M$ in $j$ on subsequent music capital.

With no addiction, $A_j = 0$ and equation (2.8) reduces to the familiar marginal cost formula. Moreover, $A_j$ is positive as long as music is beneficially addictive, and tends to decline as $j$ increases, approaching zero as $j$ approaches $n$. The term $w/MP_{t_m}$ declines with age for a given time input as long as music capital grows with age. The term $A_j$ may not change so much with age at young ages because the percentage decline in the number of remaining years is small at these ages. Therefore, $\pi_m$ would tend to

---

$$\sum \frac{px_j + w(t_{m_j} + t_{z_j})}{(1+r)^j} = \sum \frac{wt + b_j}{(1+r)^j} = W$$

Maximization of $V$ with respect to $M_j$ and $Z_j$ subject to the production functions and the full wealth constraint gives the first-order conditions

$$a^j \frac{\partial U}{\partial Z_j} = \frac{\lambda}{(1+r)^j}\left(\frac{pdx_j}{dZ_j} + \frac{wdt_{z_j}}{dZ_j}\right) = \frac{\lambda}{(1+r)^j}\pi_{z_j}$$

$$a^j \frac{\partial U}{\partial M_j} = \frac{\lambda}{(1+r)^j}\cdot\left(\frac{w\,\partial t_{m_j}}{\partial M_j} + \sum_{i=1}^{n-j}\frac{wdt_{m_{j+i}}}{dM_j}\cdot\frac{1}{(1+r)^i}\right) = \frac{\lambda}{(1+r)^j}\pi_{m_j}$$

Since, however,

$$\frac{dM_{j+i}}{dM_j} = 0 = \frac{\partial M_{j+i}}{\partial S_{m_{j+i}}}\frac{dS_{m_{j+i}}}{dM_j} + \frac{\partial M_{j+i}}{\partial t_{m_{j+i}}}\frac{dt_{m_{j+i}}}{dM_j}$$

then

$$\frac{dt_{m_{j+1}}}{dM_j} = -\frac{\partial M_{j+i}}{\partial S_{m_{j+i}}}\bigg/\frac{\partial M_{j+i}}{\partial t_{m_{j+i}}}\cdot\frac{dS_{m_{j+i}}}{dM_j}$$

By substitution into the definition of $\pi_{m_j}$, equation (2.8) follows immediately.

decline with age at young ages because the effect on the marginal product of the time input would tend to dominate the effect on $A$. Although $\pi_m$ might not always decline at other ages, for the present we assume that $\pi_m$ declines continuously with age.

If $\pi_z$ does not depend on age, the relative price of music appreciation would decline with age; then by equation (2.7), the relative consumption of music appreciation would rise with age. On this interpretation, the (relative) consumption of music appreciation rises with exposure not because tastes shift in favor of music, but because its shadow price falls as skill and experience in the appreciation of music are acquired with exposure.

An alternative way to state the same analysis is that the marginal utility of time allocated to music is increased by an increase in the stock of music capital.[6] Then the consumption of music appreciation could be said to rise with exposure because the marginal utility of the time spent on music rose with exposure, even though tastes were unchanged.

The effect of exposure on the accumulation of music capital might well depend on the level of education and other human capital, as indicated by equation (2.6). This would explain why educated persons consume more "good" music (i.e., music that educated people like!) than other persons do.

Addiction lowers the price of music appreciation at younger ages without any comparable effect on the productivity of the time spent on music at these ages. Therefore, addiction would increase the time spent on music at younger ages: some of the time would be considered an investment that increases future music capital. Although the price of music tends to fall with age, and the consumption of music tends to rise, the time spent on music need not rise with age because the growth in music capital means that the consumption of music could rise even when the time spent fell with age. The time spent would be more likly to rise, the more elastic the demand curve for music appreciation. We can express this result in a form that will strike many readers as surprising; namely, that the time (or other inputs) spent on music appreciation is more likely to be addictive—that is, to rise with exposure to music—the more, not less, elastic is the demand curve for music appreciation.

---

6. The marginal utility of time allocated to music at $j$ includes the utility from the increase in the future stock of music capital that results from an increase in the time allocated at $j$. An argument similar to the one developed for the price of music appreciation shows that the marginal utility of time would tend to rise with age, at least at younger ages.

The stock of music capital might fall and the price of music appreciation rise at older ages because the incentive to invest in future capital would decline as the number of remaining years declined, whereas the investment required simply to maintain the capital stock intact would increase as the stock increased. If the price rose, the time spent on music would fall if the demand curve for music were elastic. Consequently, our analysis indicates that the observed addiction to music may be stronger at younger than at older ages.

These results for music also apply to other commodities that are beneficially addictive. Their prices fall at younger ages and their consumption rises because consumption capital is accumulated with exposure and age. The time and goods used to produce an addictive commodity need not rise with exposure, even though consumption of the commodity does; they are more likely to rise with exposure, the more elastic is the demand curve for the commodity. Even if they rose at younger ages, they might decline eventually as the stock of consumption capital fell at older ages.

Using the same arguments developed for beneficial addiction, we can show that all the results are reversed for harmful addiction,[7] which is defined by a negative sign of the derivatives in equation (2.6):

(2.9)
$$\frac{\partial S_j}{\partial H_{j-v}} < 0, \text{ all } v \text{ in } (2.6)$$

where $H$ is a harmfully addictive commodity. An increase in consumption at any age reduces the stock of consumption capital available subsequently, and this raises the shadow price at all ages.[8] The shadow price would rise with age and exposure, at least at younger ages, which would induce consumption to fall with age and exposure. The inputs of goods and time need not fall with exposure, however, because consumption capital falls with exposure; indeed, the inputs are likely to rise with exposure if the commodity's demand curve were inelastic.

To illustrate these conclusions, consider the commodity "euphoria" produced with input of heroin (or alcohol or amphetamines). An increase

---

7. In some ways, our analysis of beneficial and harmful addiction is a special case of the analysis of beneficial and detrimental joint production in Grossman (1971).

8. Instead of equation (2.8), one has

$$\pi_{h_j} = \frac{w}{MP_{t_j}} + A_j$$

where $A_j \geq 0$.

in the consumption of current euphoria raises the cost of producing euphoria in the future by reducing the future stock of "euphoric capital." The effect of exposure to euphoria on the cost of producing future euphoria reduces the consumption of euphoria as exposure continues. If the demand curve for euphoria were sufficiently inelastic, however, the use of heroin would grow with exposure at the same time that euphoria fell.

Note that the amount of heroin used at younger ages would be reduced because of the negative effect on later euphoric capital. Indeed, no heroin at all might be used only because the harmfully addictive effects are anticipated, and discourage any use. Note further that if heroin were used even though the subsequent adverse consequences were accurately anticipated, the utility of the user would be greater than it would be if he were prevented from using heroin. Of course, his utility would be still greater if technologies developed (methadone?) to reduce the harmfully addictive effects of euphoria.[9]

Most interestingly, note that the use of heroin would grow with exposure at the same time that the amount of euphoria fell, if the demand curve for euphoria and thus for heroin were sufficiently inelastic. That is, addiction to heroin—a growth in use with exposure—is the *result* of an inelastic demand for heroin, *not*, as commonly argued, the *cause* of an inelastic demand. In the same way, listening to music or playing tennis would be addictive if the demand curves for music or tennis appreciation were sufficiently elastic; the addiction again is the result, not the cause, of the particular elasticity. Put differently, if addiction were surmised (partly because the input of goods or time rose with age), but if it were not clear whether the addiction were harmful or beneficial, the elasticity of demand could be used to distinguish between them: a high elasticity suggests beneficial and a low elasticity suggests harmful addiction.[10]

---

9. That is, if new technology reduced and perhaps even changed the sign of the derivatives in equation (2.9). We should state explicitly, to avoid any misunderstanding, that "harmful" means only that the derivatives in (2.9) are negative, and not that the addiction harms others, nor, as we have just indicated, that it is unwise for addicts to consume such commodities.

10. The elasticity of demand can be estimated from the effects of changes in the prices of inputs. For example, if a commodity's production function were homogeneous of degree one, and if all its future as well as present input prices rose by the same known percentage, the elasticity of demand for the commodity could be estimated from the decline in the inputs. Therefore the distinction between beneficial and harmful addiction is operational: these independently estimated commodity elasticities could be used, as in the text, to determine whether an addiction was harmful or beneficial.

We do not have to assume that exposure to euphoria changes tastes in order to understand why the use of heroin grows with exposure, or why the amount used is insensitive to changes in its price. Even with constant tastes, the amount used would grow with exposure, and heroin is addictive precisely *because* of the insensitivity to price change.

An exogenous rise in the price of addictive goods or time, perhaps due to an excise tax, such as the tax on cigarettes and alcohol, or to restrictions on their sale, such as the imprisonment of dealers in heroin, would have a relatively small effect on their use by addicts if these are harmfully addictive goods, and a relatively large effect if they are beneficially addictive. That is, excise taxes and imprisonment mainly transfer resources away from addicts if the goods are harmfully addictive, and mainly reduce the consumption of addicts if the goods are beneficially addictive.

The extension of the capital concept to investment in the capacity to consume more efficiently has numerous other potential applications. For example, there is a fertile field in consumption capital for the application of the theory of division of labor among family members.

## 3. Stability of Tastes and Custom and Tradition

A "traditional" qualification to the scope of economic theory is the alleged powerful hold over human behavior of custom and tradition. An excellent statement in the context of the behavior of rulers is that of John Stuart Mill (1872, p. 484):

> It is not true that the actions even of average rulers are wholly, or anything approaching to wholly, determined by their personal interest, or even by their own opinion of their personal interest . . . I insist only on what is true of all rulers, viz., that the character and course of their actions is largely influenced (independently of personal calculations) by the habitual sentiments and feelings, the general modes of thinking and acting, which prevail throughout the community of which they are members; as well as by the feelings, habits, and modes of thought which characterize the particular class in that community to which they themselves belong . . . They are also much influenced by the maxims and traditions which have descended to them from other rulers, their predecessors; which maxims and traditions have been known to retain an ascendancy during long periods, even in opposition to the private interests of the rulers for the time being.

The specific political behavior that contradicts "personal interest" theories is not clear from Mill's statement, nor is it much clearer in similar statements by others applied to firms or households. Obviously, stable behavior by (say) households faced with stable prices and incomes—or more generally a stable environment—is no contradiction since stability then is implied as much by personal interest theories as by custom and tradition. On the other hand, stable behavior in the face of changing prices and incomes might contradict the approach taken in this essay that assumes utility maximizing with stable tastes.

Nevertheless, we believe that our approach better explains when behavior is stable than do approaches based on custom and tradition, and can at the same time explain how and when behavior does change. Mill's "habits and modes of thought," or his "maxims and traditions which have descended," in our analysis result from investment of time and other resources in the accumulation of knowledge about the environment, and of skills with which to cope with it.

The making of decisions is costly, and not simply because it is an activity which some people find unpleasant. In order to make a decision one requires information, and the information must be analyzed. The costs of searching for information and of applying the information to a new situation are such that habit is often a more efficient way to deal with moderate or temporary changes in the environment than would be a full, apparently utility-maximizing decision. This is precisely the avoidance of what J. M. Clark termed the irrational passion for dispassionate rationality.

A simple example of economizing on information by the habitual purchase from one source will illustrate the logic. A consumer buys one unit of commodity $S$ in each unit of time. He pays a price $p_t$ at a time $t$. The choices he faces are:

1. To search at the time of an act of purchase to obtain the lowest possible price $\hat{p}_t$ consistent with the cost of search. Then $\hat{p}_t$ is a function of the amount of search $s$ (assumed to be the same at each act of purchase):

(2.10) $$\hat{p}_t = f(s), \; f'(s) < 0$$

   where the total cost of $s$ is $C(s)$.

2. To search less frequently (but usually more intensively), relying between searches upon the outcome of the previous search in choosing a supplier. Then the price $p_t$ will be higher (relative to the

average market price), the longer the period since the previous search (at time $t_0$),

$$p_t = g(t - t_0), \, g' > 0$$

Ignoring interest, the latter method of purchase will have a total cost over period $T$ determined by

1. $K$ searches (all of equal intensity) at cost $KC(s)$.
2. Each search lasts for a period $T/K$, within which $r = T/K$ purchases are made, at cost $r\bar{p}$, where $\bar{p}$ is the average price. Assume that the results of search "depreciate" (prices appreciate) at rate $\delta$. A consumer minimizes his combined cost of the commodity and search over the total time period; the minimizing condition is[11]

(2.11)
$$r = \sqrt{\frac{2C}{\delta \hat{p}}}$$

In this simple model with $r$ purchases between successive searches, $r$ is larger the larger the amount spent on search per dollar spent on the commodity ($C/\hat{p}$), and the lower the rate of appreciation of prices ($\delta$). If

------

11. The price of the $i$th purchase within one of the $K$ search periods is $p_i = \hat{p}(1 + \delta)^{i-1}$. Hence

$$\bar{p} = \frac{1}{r} \sum_{i=1}^{r} \hat{p}(1 + \delta)^{i-1} = \hat{p} \frac{(1 + \delta)^r - 1}{r\delta}$$

The total cost to be minimized is

$$TC = Kr\bar{p} + KC(s) = K\hat{p} \frac{(1 + \delta)^r - 1}{\delta} + KC$$

By taking a second-order approximation to $(1 + \delta)^r$, we get

$$TC = T \left\{ \hat{p} \left[ 1 + \frac{(r - 1)\delta}{2} \right] + \frac{C}{r} \right\}$$

Minimizing with respect to $r$ gives

$$\frac{\partial TC}{\partial r} = 0 = T \left( \frac{\hat{p}\delta}{2} - \frac{C}{r^2} \right)$$

or

$$r = \sqrt{\frac{2C}{\delta \hat{p}}}$$

there were full search on each individual act of purchase, the total cost could not be less than the cost when the optimal frequency of search was chosen, and might be much greater.

When a temporary change takes place in the environment, perhaps in prices or income, it generally would not pay to disinvest the capital embodied in knowledge or skills, or to accumulate different types of capital. As a result, behavior will be relatively stable in the face of temporary changes.

A related situation arises when an unexpected change in the environment does not induce a major response immediately because time is required to accumulate the appropriate knowledge and skills. Therefore, stable preferences combined with investment in "specific" knowledge and skills can explain the small or "inelastic" responses that figure so prominently in short-run demand and supply curves.

A permanent change in the environment, perhaps due to economic development, usually causes a greater change in the behavior of young than of old persons. The common interpretation is that young persons are more readily seduced away from their customs and traditions by the glitter of the new (Western?) environment. On our interpretation, young and old persons respond differently, even if they have the same preferences and motivation. To change their behavior drastically, older persons have to either disinvest their capital that was attuned to the old environment, or invest in capital attuned to the new environment. Their incentive to do so may be quite weak, however, because relatively few years remain for them to collect the returns on new investments, and much human capital can only be disinvested slowly.

Young persons, on the other hand, are not so encumbered by accumulations of capital attuned to the old environment. Consequently, they need not have different preferences or motivation or be intrinsically more flexible in order to be more affected by a change in the environment: they simply have greater incentive to invest in knowledge and skills attuned to the new environment.

Note that this analysis is similar to that used in the previous section to explain addictive behavior: utility maximization with stable preferences, conditioned by the accumulation of specific knowledge and skills. One does not need one kind of theory to explain addictive behavior and another kind to explain habitual or customary behavior. The same theory based on stable preferences can explain both types of behavior, and can accommodate both habitual behavior and the departures therefrom.

## 4. Stability of Tastes and Advertising

Perhaps the most important class of cases in which "change of tastes" is invoked as an explanation for economic phenomena is that involving advertising. The advertiser "persuades" the consumer to prefer his product, and often a distinction is drawn between "persuasive" and "informative" advertising.[12] John Kenneth Galbraith (1958, pp. 155–156) is the most famous of the economists who argue that advertising molds consumer tastes:

> These [institutions of modern advertising and salesmanship] cannot be reconciled with the notion of independently determined desires for their central function is to create desires—to bring into being wants that previously did not exist. This is accomplished by the producer of the goods or at his behest.—Outlays for the manufacturing of a product are not more important in the strategy of modern business enterprise than outlays for the manufacturing of demand for the product.

We shall argue, in direct opposition to this view, that it is neither necessary nor useful to attribute to advertising the function of changing tastes.

A consumer may indirectly receive utility from a market good, yet the utility depends not only on the quantity of the good but also the consumer's knowledge of its true or alleged properties. If he does not know whether the berries are poisonous, they are not food; if he does not know that they contain vitamin C, they are not consumed to prevent scurvy. The quantity of information is a complex notion: its degree of accuracy, its multidimensional properties, its variable obsolescence with time are all qualities that make direct measurement of information extremely difficult.

How can this elusive variable be incorporated into the theory of demand while preserving the stability of tastes? Our approach is to continue to assume, as in the previous sections, that the ultimate objects of choice are commodities produced by each household with market goods, own time, *knowledge*, and perhaps other inputs. We now assume, in addition, that the knowledge, whether real or fancied, is produced by the advertising of producers and perhaps also the own search of households.

---

12. The distinction, if in fact one exists, between persuasive and informative advertising must be one of purpose or effect, not of content. A simple, accurately stated fact ("I offer you this genuine $1 bill for 10 cents") can be highly persuasive; the most bizarre claim ("If Napoleon could have bought our machine gun, he would have defeated Wellington") contains some information (machine guns were not available in 1814).

Our approach can be presented through a detailed analysis of the simple case where the output $x$ of a particular firm and its advertising $A$ are the inputs into a commodity produced and consumed by households; for a given household:

$$(2.12) \qquad\qquad Z = f(x, A, E, y)$$

where $\partial Z/\partial x > 0$, $\partial Z/\partial A > 0$, $E$ is the human capital of the household that affects these marginal products, and $y$ are other variables, possibly including advertising by other firms. Still more simply,

$$(2.13) \qquad\qquad Z = g(A, E, y)x$$

where $\partial g/\partial A = g' > 0$ and $\partial^2 g/\partial A^2 < 0$. With $A$, $E$, and $y$ held constant, the amount of the commodity produced and consumed by any household is assumed to be proportional to the amount of the firm's output used by that household.[13] If the advertising reaching any household were independent of its behavior, the shadow price of $Z$, the marginal cost of $x$, would simply be the expenditure on $x$ required to change $Z$ by one unit. From equation (2.13), that equals

$$(2.14) \qquad\qquad \pi_z = \frac{p_x}{g}$$

where $p_x$ is the price of $x$.

An increase in advertising may lower the commodity price to the household (by raising $g$), and thereby increase its demand for the commodity and change its demand for the firm's output, because the household is made to believe—correctly or incorrectly—that it gets a greater output of the commodity from a given input of the advertised product. Consequently, advertising affects consumption in this formulation not by changing tastes, but by changing prices. That is, a movement along a stable demand curve for commodities is seen as generating the apparently unstable demand curves of market goods and other inputs.

More than a simple change in language is involved: our formulation has quite different implications from the conventional ones. To develop these implications, consider a firm that is determining its optimal advertising along with its optimal output. We assume initially that the commodity indirectly produced by this firm (equation 2.12) is a perfect substitute to consumers for commodities indirectly produced by many other firms.

---

13. Stated differently, $Z$ is homogeneous of the first degree in $x$ alone.

Therefore, the firm is perfectly competitive in the commodity market and could (indirectly) sell an unlimited amount of this commodity at a fixed commodity price. Observe that a firm can have many perfect substitutes in the commodity market even though few other firms produce the same physical product. For example, a firm may be the sole designer of jewelry that contributes to the social prestige of consumers, and yet compete fully with many other products that also contribute to prestige: large automobiles, expensive furs, fashionable clothing, elaborate parties, a respected occupation, etc.

If the level of advertising were fixed, there would be a one-to-one correspondence between the price of the commodity and the price of the firm's output (see equation 2.14). If $\pi_z$ were given by the competitive market, $p_x$ would then also be given, and the firm would find its optimal output in the conventional way by equating marginal cost to the given product price. There is no longer such a one-to-one correspondence between $\pi_z$ and $p_x$, however, when the level of advertising is also a variable, and even a firm faced with a fixed commodity price in a prefectly competitive commodity market could sell its product at different prices by varying the level of advertising. Since an increase in advertising would increase the commodity output that consumers receive from a given amount of this firm's product, the price of its product would then be increased relative to the fixed commodity price.

The optimal advertising, product price, and output of the firm can be found by maximizing its income

$$(2.15) \qquad\qquad I = p_x X - TC(X) - Ap_a$$

where $X$ is the firm's total output, $TC$ its costs of production other than advertising, and $p_a$ the (constant) cost of a unit of advertising. By substituting from equation (2.14), $I$ can be written as

$$(2.15') \qquad\qquad I = \pi_z^0 g(A)X - TC(X) - Ap_a$$

where $\pi_z^0$ is the given market commodity price, the advertising-effectiveness function ($g$) is assumed to be the same for all consumers,[14] and the

_____

14. Therefore,

$$p_x X = \pi_z^0 g \sum_{i=1}^{n} x_i$$

where $n$ is the number of households.

variables $E$ and $y$ in $g$ are suppressed. The first-order maximum conditions with respect to $X$ and $A$ are

(2.16)
$$p_x = \pi_z^0 g = MC(X)$$

(2.17)
$$\frac{\partial p_x}{\partial A} X = \pi_z^0 X g' = p_a$$

Equation (2.16) is the usual equality between price and marginal cost for a competitive firm, which continues to hold when advertising exists and is a decision variable. Not surprisingly, equation (2.17) says that marginal revenue and marginal cost of advertising are equal, where marginal revenue is determined by the level of output and the increase in product price "induced" by an increase in advertising. Although the commodity price is fixed, an increase in advertising increases the firm's product price by an amount that is proportional to the increased capacity (measured by $g'$) of its product to contribute (at least in the minds of consumers) to commodity output.

In the conventional analysis, firms in perfectly competitive markets gain nothing from advertising and thus have no incentive to advertise because they are assumed to be unable to differentiate their products to consumers who have perfect knowledge. In our analysis, on the other hand, consumers have imperfect information, including misinformation, and a skilled advertiser might well be able to differentiate his product from other apparently similar products. Put differently, advertisers could increase the value of their output to consumers without increasing to the same extent the value of the output even of perfect competitors in the *commodity* market. To simplify, we assume that the value of competitors' output is unaffected, in the sense that the commodity price (more generally, the commodity demand curve) to any firm is not affected by its advertising. Note that when firms in perfectly competitive commodity markets differentiate their products by advertising, they still preserve the perfect competition in these markets. Note moreover, that if different firms were producing the same physical product in the same competitive commodity market, and had the same marginal cost and advertising-effectiveness functions, they would produce the same output, charge the same product price, and advertise at the same rate. If, however, either their marginal costs or advertising-effectiveness differed, they would charge different product prices, advertise at different rates, and yet still be perfect competitors (although not of one another)!

Not only can firms in perfectly competitive commodity markets—that is, firms faced with infinitely elastic commodity demand curves—have an incentive to advertise, but the incentive may actually be greater, the more competitive the commodity market is. Let us consider the case of a finite commodity demand elasticity.

The necessary conditions to maximize income given by equation (2.15′), if $\pi_z$ varies as a function of $Z$, are

$$(2.18) \qquad \frac{\partial I}{\partial X} = \pi_z g + X \frac{\partial \pi_z}{\partial Z} \frac{\partial Z}{\partial X} g - MC(X) = 0,$$

or since $Z = gX$, and $\partial Z/\partial X = g$,

$$(2.18') \qquad \pi_z g \left( 1 + \frac{1}{\epsilon_{\pi_z}} \right) = p_x \left( 1 + \frac{1}{\epsilon_{\pi_z}} \right) = MC(X)$$

where $\epsilon_{\pi_z}$ is the elasticity of the firm's commodity demand curve. Also

$$(2.19) \qquad \frac{\partial I}{\partial A} = X \frac{\partial p_x}{\partial A} - p_a = \pi_z \frac{\partial Z}{\partial A} + \frac{\partial \pi_z}{\partial Z} \cdot \frac{\partial Z}{\partial A} \cdot Z - p_a = 0$$

or

$$(2.19') \qquad X \frac{\partial p_x}{\partial A} = \pi_z g' X \left( 1 + \frac{1}{\epsilon_{\pi_z}} \right) = p_a$$

Equation (2.18′) is simply the usual maximizing condition for a monopolist that continues to hold when there is advertising.[15] Equation (2.19′) clearly shows that, given $\pi_z G' X$, the marginal revenue from additional advertising is greater, the greater is the elasticity of the commodity demand curve; therefore, the optimal level of advertising would be positively related to the commodity elasticity.

This important result can be made intuitive by considering Figure 2.1. The curve $DD$ gives the firm's commodity demand curve, where $\pi_z$ is measured along the vertical and commodity output $Z$ along the horizontal axis. The firm's production of $X$ is held fixed so that $Z$ varies only because of variations in the level of advertising. At point $e^0$, the level of advertising is $A_0$, the product price is $p_x^0$, and commodity output and price are $Z_0$ and $\pi_z^0$, respectively. An increase in advertising to $A_1$ would increase $Z$ to $Z_1$

---

15. If the level of advertising is held constant, $Z$ is proportional to $X$, so

$$\epsilon_{\pi_z} = \frac{dZ}{Z} \bigg/ \frac{d\pi_z}{\pi_z} = \epsilon_{p_x} = \frac{dX}{X} \bigg/ \frac{dp_x}{p_x}$$

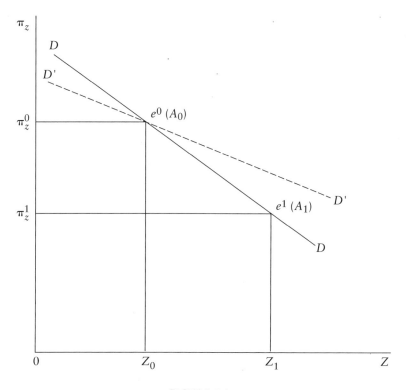

FIGURE 2.1

(the increase in $Z$ is determined by the given $g'$ function). The decline in $\pi_z$ induced by the increase in $Z$ would be negatively related to the elasticity of the commodity demand curve: it would be less, for example, if the demand curve were $D'D'$ rather than $DD$. Since the increase in $p_x$ is negatively related to the decline in $\pi_z$,[16] the increase in $p_x$, and thus the marginal

---

16. Since $\pi_z g = p_x$,

$$\frac{\partial p_x}{\partial A} = \pi_z g' + g \frac{\partial \pi_z}{\partial A} > 0$$

The first term on the right is positive and the second term is negative. If $g$, $g'$, and $\pi_z$ are given, $\partial p_x/\partial A$ is linearly and negatively related to $\partial \pi_z/\partial A$.

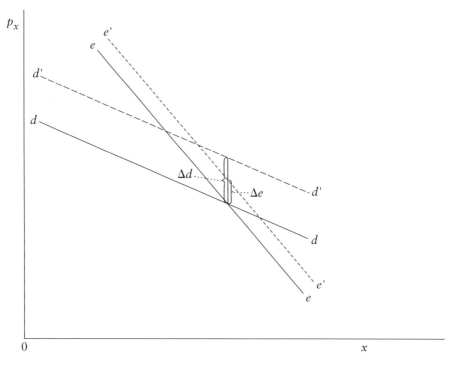

FIGURE 2.2

revenue from the increase in $A$, is directly related to the elasticity of the commodity demand curve.[17]

The same result is illustrated with a more conventional demand in Figure 2.2: the firm's product output and price are shown along the horizontal and vertical axes. The demand curve for its product with a given level of advertising is given by $dd$. We proved earlier (fn. 15) that with advertising constant, the elasticity of the product demand curve is the same as the elas-

---

17. Recall again our assumption, however, that even firms in perfectly competitive markets can fully differentiate their products. If the capacity of a firm to differentiate itself were inversely related to the elasticity of its commodity demand curve, that is, to the amount of competition in the commodity market, the increase in its product price generated by its advertising might not be directly related to the elasticity of its commodity demand curve.

ticity of its commodity demand curve. An increase in advertising "shifts" the product demand curve upward to $d'd'$, and the marginal revenue from additional advertising is directly related to the size of the shift; that is, to the increase in product price for any given product output. Our basic result is that the shift is itself directly related to the elasticity of the demand curve. For example, with the same increase in advertising, the shift is larger from $dd$ to $d'd'$ than from $ee$ to $e'e'$ because $dd$ is more elastic than $ee$.

This role of information in consumer demand is capable of extension in various directions. For example, the demand for knowledge is affected by the formal education of a person, so systematic variations of demand for advertisements with formal education can be explored. The stock of information possessed by the individual is a function of his age, period of residence in a community, and other variables, so systematic patterns of purchase of heavily and lightly advertised goods are implied by the theory.

## 5. Fashions and Fads

The existence of fashions and fads (short episodes or cycles in the consumption habits of people) seems an especially striking contradiction of our thesis of the stability of tastes. We find fashions in dress, food, automobiles, furniture, books, and even scientific doctrines.[18] Some are modest in amplitude, or few in their followers, but others are of violent amplitude: who now buys an ouija board, or a bustle? The rise and fall of fashions is often attributed to the fickleness of people's tastes. Herbert Blumer (1968, p. 344), the distinguished sociologist, gave a characteristic expression of this view:

> Tastes are themselves a product of experience, they usually develop from an initial state of vagueness to a state of refinement and stability, but once formed they may decay and disintegrate . . .
>
> The fashion process involves both a formation and an expression of collective taste in the given area of fashion. The taste is initially a loose fusion of vague inclinations and dissatisfactions that are aroused by new experience in the field of fashion and in the larger surrounding world. In this initial state, collective taste is amorphous, inarticulate, and awaiting specific direction. Through

---

18. "Fashion" indeed, does not necessarily refer only to the shorter-term preferences. Adam Smith says that the influence of fashion "over dress and furniture is not more absolute than over architecture, poetry, and music" (1976, p. 321).

models and proposals, fashion innovators sketch possible lines along which the incipient taste may gain objective expression and take definite form.

The obvious method of reconciling fashion with our thesis is to resort again to the now familiar argument that people consume commodities, and only indirectly do they consume market goods, so fashions in market goods are compatible with stability in the utility function of commodities. The task here, as elsewhere, is to show that this formulation helps to illuminate our understanding of the phenomena under discussion; we have some tentative comments in this direction.

The commodity apparently produced by fashion goods is social distinction: the demonstration of alert leadership, or at least not lethargy, in recognizing and adopting that which will in due time be widely approved. This commodity—it might be termed *style*—sounds somewhat circular, because new things appear to be chosen simply because they are new. Such circularity is no more peculiar than that which is literally displayed in a race—the runners obviously do not run around a track in order to reach a new destination. Moreover, it is a commendation of a style good that it be superior to previous goods, and style will not be sought intentionally through less functional goods. Indeed, if the stylish soon becomes inferior to the unstylish, it would lose its attractiveness.

Style, moreover, is not achieved simply by change: the newness must be of a special sort that requires a subtle prediction of what will be approved novelty, and a trained person can make better predictions than an untrained person. Style is social rivalry, and it is, like all rivalry, both an incentive to individuality and a source of conformity.

The areas in which the rivalry of fashion takes place are characterized by public exposure and reasonably short life. An unexposed good (automobile pistons) cannot be judged as to its fashionableness, and fashions in a good whose efficient life is long would be expensive. Hence fashion generally concentrates on the cheaper classes of garments and reading matter, and there is more fashion in furniture than in housing.

Fashion can be pursued with the purse or with the expenditure of time. A person may be well-read (i.e., have read the recent books generally believed to be important), but if his time is valuable in the market place, it is much more likely that his spouse will be the well-read member of the family. (So the ratio of the literacy of wife to that of husband is positively related to the husband's earning power, and inversely related to her earning power.)

The demand for fashion can be formalized by assuming that the distinction available to any person depends on his social environment, and his own efforts: he can be fashionable, give to approved charities, choose prestigious occupations, and do other things that affect his distinction. Following recent work on social interactions, we can write the social distinction of the $i$th person as

$$(2.20) \qquad\qquad\qquad R_i = D_i + h_i$$

where $D_i$ is the contribution to his distinction of his social environment, and $h_i$ is his own contribution. Each person maximizes a utility function of $R$ and other commodities subject to a budget constraint that depends on his own income and the exogenously given social environment.[19] A number of general results have been developed with this approach (see Chapter 8), and a few are mentioned here to indicate that the demand for fashion (and other determinants of social distinction) can be systematically analyzed without assuming that tastes shift.

An increase in $i$'s own income, prices held constant, would increase his demand for social distinction and other commodities. If his social environment were unchanged, the whole increase in his distinction would be produced by an increase in his own contributions to fashion and other distinction-producing goods. Therefore, even an average income elasticity of demand for distinction would imply a high income elasticity of demand for fashion (and these other distinction-producing) goods, which is consistent with the common judgment that fashion is a luxury good.[20]

If other persons increase their contributions to their own distinction, this may lower $i$'s distinction by reducing his social environment. For distinction is scarce and is to a large extent simply redistributed among persons: an increase in one person's distinction generally requires a reduction in that of other persons. This is why people are often "forced" to conform to new fashions. When some gain distinction by paying attention to (say) new fashions, they lower the social environment of others. The latter

---

19. The budget constraint for $i$ can be written as

$$\prod\nolimits_{R_i} R + \prod\nolimits_z Z = I_i + \prod\nolimits_{R_i} D_i = S_i$$

where $Z$ are other commodities, $\prod_{R_i}$ is his marginal cost of changing $R$, $I_i$ is his own full income, and $S_i$ is his "social income."

20. Marshall believed that the desire for distinction was the most powerful of passions and a major source of the demand for luxury expenditures (see Marshall, 1962, pp. 87–88, 106).

are induced to increase their own efforts to achieve distinction, including a demand for these new fashions, because an exogenous decline in their social environment induces them to increase their own contributions to their distinction.

Therefore, an increase in all incomes induces an even greater increase in $i$'s contribution to his distinction than does an increase in his own income alone. For an increase in the income of others lowers $i$'s social environment because they spend more on their own distinction; the reduction in his environment induces a further increase in $i$'s contribution to his distinction. Consequently, we expect wealthy countries like the United States to pay more attention to fashion than poor countries like India, even if tastes were the same in wealthy and poor countries.

## 6. Conclusion

We have surveyed four classes of phenomena widely believed to be inconsistent with the stability of tastes: addiction, habitual behavior, advertising, and fashions, and in each case offered an alternative explanation. That alternative explanation did not simply reconcile the phenomena in question with the stability of tastes, but also sought to show that the hypothesis of stable tastes yielded more useful predictions about observable behavior.

Of course, this short list of categories is far from comprehensive: for example, we have not entered into the literature of risk aversion and risk preference, one of the richest sources of *ad hoc* assumptions concerning tastes. Nor have we considered the extensive literature on time preference, which often alleges that people "systematically undervalue . . . future wants."[21] The taste for consumption in, say, 2001 is alleged to continue to shift upward as 2001 gets closer to the present. In spite of the importance frequently attached to time preference, we do not know of any significant behavior that has been illuminated by this assumption. Indeed, given additional space, we would argue that the assumption of time pref-

---

21. This quote is taken from the following longer passage in Böhm-Bawerk (1959, p. 268): "We must now consider a *second* phenomenon of human experience—one that is heavily fraught with consequence. That is the fact that we feel less concerned about future sensations of joy and sorrow simply because they do lie in the future, and the lessening of our concern is in proportion to the remoteness of that future. Consequently we accord to goods which are intended to serve future ends a value which falls short of the true intensity of their future marginal utility. *We systematically undervalue our future wants and also the means which serve to satisfy them.*"

erence impedes the explanation of life cycle variations in the allocations of resources, the secular growth in real incomes, and other phenomena.

Moreover, we have not considered systematic differences in tastes by wealth or other classifications. We also claim, however, that no significant behavior has been illuminated by assumptions of differences in tastes. Instead, they, along with assumptions of unstable tastes, have been a convenient crutch to lean on when the analysis has bogged down. They give the appearance of considered judgment, yet really have only been *ad hoc* arguments that disguise analytical failures.

We have partly translated "unstable tastes" into variables in the household production functions for commodities. The great advantage, however, of relying only on changes in the arguments entering household production functions is that *all* changes in behavior are explained by changes in prices and incomes, precisely the variables that organize and give power to economic analysis. Addiction, advertising, etc. affect not tastes with the endless degrees of freedom they provide, but prices and incomes, and are subject therefore to the constraints imposed by the theorem on negatively inclined demand curves, and other results. Needless to say, we would welcome explanations of why some people become addicted to alcohol and others to Mozart, whether the explanation was a development of our approach or a contribution from some other behavioral discipline.

As we remarked at the outset, no conceivable expenditure of effort on our part could begin to exhaust the possible tests of the hypothesis of stable and uniform preferences. Our task has been oddly two-sided. Our hypothesis is trivial, for it merely asserts that we should apply standard economic logic as extensively as possible. But the self-same hypothesis is also a demanding challenge, for it urges us not to abandon opaque and complicated problems with the easy suggestion that the further explanation will perhaps someday be produced by one of our sister behavioral sciences.

# A Theory of
# Rational Addiction

# 3

> Use doth breed a habit.
> —Shakespeare, *Two Gentlemen of Verona*

## 1. Introduction

Rational consumers maximize utility from stable preferences as they try to anticipate the future consequences of their choices. Addictions would seem to be the antithesis of rational behavior. Does an alcoholic or heroin user maximize or weigh the future? Surely his preferences shift rapidly over time as his mood changes? Yet, as the title of our paper indicates, we claim that addictions, even strong ones, are usually rational in the sense of involving forward-looking maximization with stable preferences. Our claim is even stronger: a rational framework permits new insights into addictive behavior.

People get addicted not only to alcohol, cocaine, and cigarettes but also to work, eating, music, television, their standard of living, other people, religion, and many other activities. Therefore, much behavior would be excluded from the rational choice framework if addictions have to be explained in another way. Fortunately, a separate theory is not necessary since rational choice theory can explain a wide variety of addictive behavior.

Sections 2 and 3 develop our model of rational addiction. They set out first-order conditions for utility maximization and consider dynamic aspects of addictive consumption. They derive conditions that determine whether steady-state consumption levels are unstable or stable. Unstable steady states are crucial to the understanding of rational addiction.

By Gary S. Becker and Kevin M. Murphy; originally published in *Journal of Political Economy,* 96, no. 4 (1988): 675–700. ©1988 by The University of Chicago. All rights reserved.

Sections 4 and 5 consider in detail the variables highlighted by the previous sections that determine whether a person becomes addicted to a particular good. These sections also derive the effects on the long-run demand for addictive goods of permanent changes in income and in the current and future cost of addictive goods.

Section 6 shows that consumption of addictive goods responds less to temporary changes in prices than to permanent changes. In addition, the effects on future consumption of changes in current prices become weaker over time when steady-state consumption is stable, but they get stronger when the steady state is unstable. This section also shows how divorce, unemployment, and similar tension-raising events affect the demand for addictive goods.

Section 7 indicates why strong rational addictions must terminate abruptly, that is, must require going "cold turkey." Rational binges are also considered.

Our analysis builds on the model of rational addiction introduced by Stigler and Becker (Chapter 2) and developed much further by Iannaccone (1984, 1986). He also relates the analysis of addiction to the literature on habit persistence, especially to the work by Pollak (1970, 1976), Ryder and Heal (1973), Boyer (1978, 1983), and Spinnewyn (1981). We appear to be the first to stress the importance for addictions of unstable steady-state consumption levels, to derive explicit long- and short-run demand functions for addictive goods, to show why addictions lead to abrupt withdrawals and binges, and to relate even temporary stressful events to permanent addictions.


## 2. The Model

Utility of an individual at any moment depends on the consumption of two goods, $c$ and $y$. These goods are distinguished by assuming that current utility also depends on a measure of past consumption of $c$ but not of $y$, as in

(3.1) $$u(t) = u[y(t), c(t), S(t)]$$

For most of the discussion we assume that $u$ is a strongly concave function of $y$, $c$, and $S$. Past consumption of $c$ affects current utility through a process of "learning by doing," as summarized by the stock of "consumption capital" ($S$). Although more general formulations can be readily handled, a simple investment function is adopted for the present:

(3.2)                          $$\dot{S}(t) = c(t) - \delta S(t) - h[D(t)]$$

where $\dot{S}$ is the rate of change over time in $S$, $c$ is gross investment in "learning," the instantaneous depreciation rate $\delta$ measures the exogenous rate of disappearance of the physical and mental effects of past consumption of $c$, and $D(t)$ represents expenditures on endogenous depreciation or appreciation.

   With a length of life equal to $T$ and a constant rate of time preference, $\sigma$, the utility function would be

(3.3)                          $$U(0) = \int_0^T e^{-\sigma t} u[y(t), c(t), S(t)] dt$$

Utility is separable over time in $y$, $c$, and $S$ but not in $y$ and $c$ alone because their marginal utilities depend on past values of $c$, as measured by $S$.

   A rational person maximizes utility subject to a constraint on his expenditures. If $A_0$ is the initial value of assets, if the rate of interest $(r)$ is constant over time, if earnings at time $t$ are a concave function of the stock of consumption capital at $t$, $w(S)$, and if capital markets are perfect, then the budget equation would be

(3.4)  $$\int_0^T e^{-rt}[y(t) + p_c(t)c(t) + p_d(t)D(t)]dt \leq A_0 + \int_0^T e^{-rt}w(S(t))dt$$

where the numeraire $(y)$ has a constant price over time. A person maximizes his utility in equation (3.3) subject to this budget constraint and to the investment equation (3.2). The value (in utility terms) of the optimal solution, $V(A_0, S_0, w, p)$, gives the maximum obtainable utility from initial assets $A_0$, initial stock of capital $S_0$, the earnings function $w(S)$, and a price structure $p(t)$. Since $u(\cdot)$ and $w(S)$ are concave functions, $V(A_0, S_0, p)$ is concave in $A_0$ and $S_0$. If $\mu = \partial V / \partial A_0$, then by concavity $d\mu/dA_0 \leq 0$.

   The optimal paths of $y(t)$ and $c(t)$ are determined by the first-order conditions. If we let

(3.5)       $$a(t) = \int_t^T e^{-(\sigma+\delta)(\tau-t)}u_s d\tau + \mu \int_t^T e^{-(r+\delta)(\tau-t)}w_s d\tau$$

then

$$u_y(t) = \mu e^{(\sigma - r)t}$$

(3.6)

$$h_d(t)a(t) = \mu p_d(t)e^{(\sigma - r)t}$$

$$u_c(t) = \mu p_c(t)e^{(\sigma - r)t} - a(t) = \prod_c(t)$$

The expression $a(t)$ represents the discounted utility and monetary cost or benefit of additional consumption of $c$ through the effect on future stocks. It measures the shadow price of an additional unit of stock. A rational person recognizes that consumption of a harmful good ($u_s, w_s < 0$) has adverse effects on future utility and earnings, while consumption of a beneficial good ($u_s, w_s > 0$) has positive effects on future utility and earnings. The shadow, or full, price of $c(t)$, $\prod_c(t)$, equals the sum of its market price and the money value of the future cost or benefit of consumption (see also Chapter 2, eq. 2.8). The stock component of the full price is itself endogenously determined by the optimal path, and yet it can also be said to help determine the optimal path by affecting the cost of $c$.

Clearly, if future consumption is held fixed, the absolute value of $a(t)$ is smaller when the depreciation rate on past consumption ($\delta$) and the rate of preference for the present ($\sigma$) are greater. This suggests that consumption of a harmful $c$ is larger, and consumption of a beneficial $c$ is smaller, when $\delta$ and $\sigma$ are greater. We will see that $\delta$ and $\sigma$ are also important in determining whether $c$ is addictive.

It is clear from the second first-order condition that the optimal expenditure on endogenous depreciation ($D$) to reduce the stock of capital is larger, or the optimal expenditure on endogenous appreciation to increase the stock is smaller, when the marginal value of the stock, $a(t)$, is smaller. This value falls as the stock increases since the value function is concave in $S$. Therefore, individuals will take steps to depreciate the stock more rapidly when it is larger.

## 3. Dynamics

The first-order conditions (3.5) determine the initial consumption level of $c$, $c_0$, as a function of the initial stock of consumption capital, $S_0$, prices $p(t)$, and the marginal utility of wealth $\mu$. To simplify the discussion of dynamics, we first assume an infinite life ($T = \infty$), a rate of time preference equal to the rate of interest ($\sigma = r$), and no endogenous depreciation ($D(t) = 0$). Since $\mu$ remains constant over time, the relations between $c_0$ and $S_0$ for given $\mu$ and $p$ also give the relation over time between $c$ and $S$ for these values of $\mu$ and $p$.

To analyze the dynamic behavior of $c$ and $S$ near a steady state, we can either take linear approximations to the first-order conditions or assume quadratic utility and earnings functions that have linear first-order conditions. (Related dynamics were developed by Ryder and Heal, 1973, and Boyer, 1983). If the utility function $u$ is quadratic in $c$, $y$, and $S$, if earnings are quadratic in $S$, and if $p_c(t) = p_c$ for all $t$, then the value function is also quadratic. By optimizing $y$ out with its first-order condition, we obtain a function that is quadratic only in $c(t)$ and $S(t)$:

$$F(t) = \alpha_c c(T) + \alpha_s S(t) + \frac{\alpha_{cc}}{2}[c(t)]^2 + \frac{\alpha_{ss}}{2}[S(t)]^2$$

(3.7)

$$+ \alpha_{cs} c(t) S(t) - \mu p_c c(t)$$

where the coefficients $\alpha_s$ and $\alpha_{ss}$ depend on the coefficients of both the utility and earnings functions. We know that $\alpha_{ss} < 0$ and $\alpha_{cc} < 0$ by concavity of the $u$ and $w$ functions. Then the optimization problem involves only $c(t)$ and $S(t)$:

(3.8) $$V(A_0, S_0, p_c) = k + \max_{c,S} \int_0^\infty e^{-\sigma t} F[S(t), c(t)] dt$$

where $k$ is a constant that depends on $A_0, \mu, \sigma$, and the coefficients for $y$ in the quadratic utility function. The maximization occurs subject to equation (3.2) with $h = 0$ and to the transversality condition

(3.9) $$\lim_{t \to \infty} e^{-\sigma t}[S(t)]^2 = 0$$

Equation (3.8) is a straightforward maximization problem in the calculus of variations, where $F$ is a function only of $S$ and $\dot{S}$ through the linear relation between $c$, $S$, and $\dot{S}$ in equation (3.2). The Euler equation can be expressed as

(3.10) $$\ddot{S} - \sigma \dot{S} - BS = \frac{(\sigma + \delta)\alpha_c + \alpha_s}{\alpha_{cc}} - \frac{(\sigma + \delta)p_c \mu}{\alpha_{cc}}$$

with

(3.11) $$B = \delta(\sigma + \delta) + \frac{\alpha_{ss}}{\alpha_{cc}} + (\sigma + 2\delta)\frac{\alpha_{cs}}{\alpha_{cc}}$$

This is a second-order linear differential equation in $S(t)$, with two roots given by

(3.12)
$$\lambda = \frac{\sigma \pm \sqrt{\sigma^2 + 4B}}{2}$$

The term under the radical is positive because essentially it is a quadratic form in $\sigma + 2\delta$ and 2:

(3.13) $\qquad \sigma^2 + 4B = \dfrac{1}{\alpha_{cc}}[(\sigma + 2\delta)^2\alpha_{cc} + 4\alpha_{ss} + 4(\sigma + 2\delta)\alpha_{cs}] > 0$

and the Hessian of the concave function $F$ is negative definite. Hence both roots of (3.12) are real. Moreover, the larger root exceeds $\sigma/2$ and can be ignored with an infinite horizon; otherwise, $[c(t)]^2$ would eventually grow at a faster rate than $\sigma$, which would violate the transversality condition in equation (3.8).

The optimal path of the capital stock is determined from the initial condition and the smaller root alone:

(3.14) $\qquad S(t) = de^{\lambda_1 t} + S^*$   with $\lambda_1 = \dfrac{\sigma - \sqrt{\sigma^2 + 4B}}{2}, d = S_0 - S^*$

If the steady state, $S^*$, is stable, $S$ grows over time to $S^*$ if $S_0 < S^*$ and declines over time to $S^*$ if $S_0 > S^*$. Equation (3.14) shows that $S^*$ is stable if and only if $B > 0$ because then $\lambda_1 < 0$.

Equation (3.14) also implies that

(3.15)
$$c(t) = (\delta + \lambda_1)S(t) - \lambda_1 S^*$$

The slope between $c$ and $S$ increases as $\lambda_1$ increases, and it reaches a maximum value when $\lambda_1 = \sigma/2$, that is, when $\sigma^2 + 4B = 0$. Given the definition of $\lambda_1$ in equation (3.14) and of $B$ in equation (3.11), equation (3.15) implies that $c$ and $S$ are positively related ($\lambda_1 > -\delta$), negatively related ($\lambda_1 < -\delta$), or unrelated ($\lambda_1 = -\delta$) as

(3.16)
$$(\sigma + 2\delta)\alpha_{cs} \gtreqless -\alpha_{ss} > 0$$

Since "unrelated" means that past consumption of $c$ has no effect on its present consumption, behavior would then be the same as when preferences are additively separable over time in $c$ and $y$, even though the utility function is nonseparable in $S$ and $c$. Whether behavior is effectively separable over time depends not only on the current-period utility and

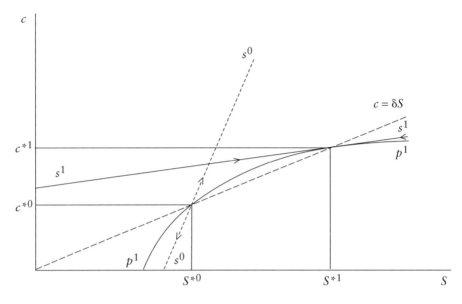

FIGURE 3.1

earning functions but also on time preference and the rate of depreciation of past consumption.

The line $s^1s^1$ in Figure 3.1 has a stable steady state at $\delta S^{*1} = c^{*1}$, whereas the line $s^0s^0$ has an unstable steady state at $\delta S^{*0} = c^{*0}$. The arrows indicate that deviations from $S^{*1}$ cause a return to $S^{*1}$ along the linear path $s^1s^1$. Deviations from $S^{*0}$ cause further deviations in the same direction along the linear path $s^0s^0$.

## 4. Adjacent Complementarity and Addiction

If the marginal utility of $c$ in the $F$ function is greater when the stock of consumption capital ($S$) is greater ($\alpha_{cs} > 0$), the marginal utility of $c$ would rise over time if $S$ rose over time. Consumption of $c$, however, might still fall over time because the full price of $c$ ($\prod_c$ in eq. 3.6) also rises over time since $\alpha_{ss} < 0$. The rise in full price would be larger when the function $F$ is more concave in $S$ ($\alpha_{ss}$ is larger in absolute value for a given value of $\alpha_{cs}$), when the future is less heavily discounted ($\sigma$ is smaller), and when depreciation of past consumption ($\delta$) is less rapid. The increase over time in the marginal utility of $c$ would exceed the increase in full price if and only if the left-hand side of equation (3.16) exceeds the right-hand side. There is said to be "adjacent complementarity" when this inequality holds (the concepts of adjacent and distant complementarity were introduced by Ryder and Heal, 1973).

The basic definition of addiction at the foundation of our analysis is that a person is potentially addicted to $c$ if an increase in his current consumption of $c$ increases his future consumption of $c$. This occurs if and only if his behavior displays adjacent complementarity. This definition has the plausible implication that someone is addicted to a good only when past consumption of the good raises the marginal utility of present consumption ($\alpha_{cs} > 0$). However, such an effect on the marginal utility is necessary but is by no means sufficient even for potential addiction since potential addiction also depends on the other variables in equation (3.16).

The relation between addiction and adjacent complementarity was first recognized by Boyer (1983) and Iannaccone (1986). Boyer considers discrete time and the special case in which (in our notation) $S_t = c_{t-1}$. The distinction between adjacent complementarity and the effect of $S$ on the marginal utility of $c$ is not interesting analytically in that case because the sign of $\alpha_{cs}$ is then the sole determinant of whether past and present consumption are complements or substitutes.

Experimental and other studies of harmful addictions have usually found reinforcement and tolerance (Donegan et al., 1983). Reinforcement means that greater current consumption of a good raises its future consumption. Reinforcement is closely related to the concept of adjacent complementarity. Tolerance means that given levels of consumption are less satisfying when past consumption has been greater. Rational harmful addictions (but not beneficial addictions) do imply a form of tolerance because higher past consumption of harmful goods lowers the present utility from the same consumption level.

According to our definition of addiction, a good may be addictive to some persons but not to others, and a person may be addicted to some goods but not to other goods. Addictions involve an *interaction* between persons and goods. For example, liquor, jogging, cigarettes, gambling, and religion are addictive to some people but not to others. The importance of the individual is clearest in the role of time preference in determining whether there is adjacent complementarity. Our analysis implies the common view that present-oriented individuals are potentially more addicted to harmful goods than future-oriented individuals. The reason for this is that an increase in past consumption leads to a smaller rise in full price when the future is more heavily discounted.

The rate of depreciation of past consumption ($\delta$), complementarity between present and past consumption ($\alpha_{cs}$), and the effect of changes in the stock of consumption capital on earnings depend on the individual as well as on the good. For example, drunkenness is much more harmful to productivity in some jobs than in other jobs.

Whether a potentially addictive person does become addicted depends on his initial stock of consumption capital and the location of his demand curve. For example, the curves that relate $c$ and $S$ in Figure 3.1 display adjacent complementarity, yet the person with these relations would ultimately abstain from consuming $c$ if $S_0 < S^{*0}$ and $s^0 s^0$ is relevant. We postpone until Section 6 a discussion of the determination of the initial stock of consumption capital and the location of demand functions.

The smaller root ($\lambda_1$) in (3.12) is larger in algebraic value when the degree of adjacent complementarity increases because of increases in $\sigma$, $\delta$, or $\alpha_{cs}$. This root along with the larger root would be positive if adjacent complementarity is sufficiently strong to make $B < 0$. The steady state is then unstable: consumption grows over time if initial consumption exceeds the steady-state level, and it falls to zero if initial consumption is below that level.

Unstable steady states are not an analytical nuisance to be eliminated by appropriate assumptions, for they are crucial to the understanding of rational addictive behavior. The reason is that an increase in the degree of potential addiction (i.e., an increase in the degree of adjacent complementarity) raises the likelihood that the steady state is unstable. Moreover, there must be adjacent complementarity in the vicinity of an unstable steady state because the curve that relates $c$ and $S$ must cut the positively sloped steady-state line from below at unstable points; see point ($c^{*0}$, $S^{*0}$) in Figure 3.1. Unstable steady states are needed to explain rational "pathological" addictions, in which a person's consumption of a good continues to increase over time even though he fully anticipates the future and his rate of time preference is no smaller than the rate of interest. However, they are also important in explaining "normal" addictions that may involve rapid increases in consumption only for a while.

Unstable steady states also lead to another key feature of addictions: multiple steady states. Quadratic utility and earnings functions cannot explain multiple steady states because they imply the linear relation between $c$ and $S$ in equation (3.16). However, if a quadratic function were only a local approximation to the true function near a steady state and if the true function, say, had a cubic term in $S^3$ with a negative coefficient added to a quadratic function, the first-order conditions in equation (3.6) would then generally imply two interior steady states, one stable and one unstable. The negative coefficient for $S^3$ means that the degree of adjacent complementarity declines as $S$ increases (see curve $p^1p^1$ in Fig. 3.1) so that the level of $c$ is smaller at the unstable steady state $(c^{*0}, S^{*0})$ than at the stable steady state $(c^{*1}, S^{*1})$.

With two steady states, relatively few persons consistently consume small quantities of addictive goods. Consumption diverges from the unstable state toward zero or toward the sizable steady-state level. Therefore, goods that are highly addictive to most people tend to have a bimodal distribution of consumption, with one mode located near abstention. Cigarettes and cocaine consumption are good examples of such bimodality. The distribution of alcohol consumption is more continuous presumably because alcoholic beverages are not addictive for many people.

This paper relies on a weak concept of rationality that does not rule out strong discounts of future events. The consumers in our model become more and more myopic as time preference for the present ($\sigma$) gets larger. The definition of $a(t)$ in equation (3.5) shows that the present value of the cost of an increase in the current consumption goes to zero as $\sigma$ goes to infinity (if the interest rate equals $\sigma$). It is then "rational" to ignore the future effects of a change in current consumption.

The definition of adjacent complementarity in equation (3.16) makes clear that time preference for the present is not necessary for addiction. However, fully myopic consumers ($\sigma = \infty$) do have the potential to become addicted whenever an increase in past consumption raises the marginal utility of current consumption ($\alpha_{cs} > 0$). Although fully myopic behavior is formally consistent with our definition of rational behavior, should someone who entirely or largely neglects future consequences of his actions be called rational? Some economists and philosophers even suggest that rationality excludes *all* time preference.

Fortunately, we can reinterpret $\sigma$ so that it may be positive even when individuals have neutral time preferences. If lives are finite, the inverse of the number of years of life remaining is an approximation to the rate of "time preference" for people who do not discount the future. Then old people are rationally "myopic" because they have few years of life remaining. Other things the same, therefore, older persons are less concerned about the future consequences of current consumption, and hence they are more likely to become addicted. Of course, other things are not usually the same: older people are less healthy and subject to different life cycle events than younger people. Moreover, people who manage to become old are less likely to be strongly addicted to harmful goods.

To simplify the discussion, we have assumed that $\sigma = r$, but the analysis also has novel implications about the consequences of changes in $\sigma$ relative to $r$. When utility functions are separable over time, an increase in preference for the present compared with the interest rate raises current consumption and reduces future consumption. This intuitive conclusion may not apply with addictive goods because the full cost of an addictive good depends on the degree of time preference. Indeed, if the degree of addiction is sufficiently strong, a higher $\sigma$ is likely to *raise* the growth over time in consumption of the addictive good (see the fuller discussion in Becker and Murphy, 1986, sec. 8). This steepening of the consumption profile over time as time preference increases is contrary to the intuition built up from prolonged consideration of separable utility functions, but it is not contrary to any significant empirical evidence.

We follow the argument in Chapter 2 in distinguishing harmful from beneficial addictions by whether consumption capital has negative or positive effects on utility and earnings. Since the definitions of adjacent complementarity and addiction do not depend on first derivatives of the utility and earnings functions, they apply to both harmful and beneficial addictions. For example, increases in $\sigma$ and $\delta$ raise the degree of adjacent complementarity, and hence they raise the extent of potential addiction to both beneficial and harmful goods.

The stock component of full price—the term $a(t)$ in equation (3.5)—does depend on the signs of $u_s$ and $w_s$: a future cost is added to the current market price of harmful addictive goods, whereas a future benefit is subtracted from the current price of beneficial goods. Therefore, an increase in the rate of preference for the present and in the depreciation rate on consumption capital raises the demand for harmful goods but lowers the demand for beneficial goods. As a result, drug addicts and alcoholics tend to be present-oriented, while religious individuals and joggers tend to be future-oriented.

## 5. Permanent Changes in Price

A permanent decline in the price of $c$, $p_c$, that is compensated to maintain the marginal utility of wealth ($\mu$) constant would raise $c(t)$ because the value function is concave. Moreover,

$$(3.17) \qquad \frac{\partial}{\partial t}\left[\frac{\partial c(t)}{\partial p_c}\right] = \frac{\partial \dot{c}}{\partial p_c} = \frac{\partial}{\partial p_c}\left(\frac{dc}{dS}\dot{S}\right) = \frac{dc}{dS}\frac{\partial \dot{S}}{\partial p_c} + \dot{S}\frac{\partial}{\partial p_c}\left(\frac{dc}{dS}\right)$$

The second term on the far right-hand side is zero in the vicinity of a steady state because $\dot{S}$ equals zero at the steady state. The sign of the first term is the opposite of the sign of $dc/dS$ because $p_c$ has a negative effect on $c(t)$ and hence on $\dot{S}$. By definition, the sign of $dc/dS$ is positive with adjacent complementarity, zero with independence, and negative with adjacent substitution.

Therefore, the effect of a compensated change in $p_c$ on $c$ grows over time when present and past consumption are adjacent complements; that is, the effect grows over time for addictive goods. A permanent change in the price of an addictive good may have only a small initial effect on demand, but the effect grows over time until a new steady state is reached (assuming that consumption eventually approaches a stable state).

Indeed, if the utility function is quadratic, the long-run effect on consumption of a permanent change in price tends to be larger for addictive goods. To show this, differentiate the first-order conditions in equations (3.6) with a quadratic utility function to get the change in consumption between stable steady states:

$$(3.18) \qquad \frac{dc^*}{dp_c} = \frac{\mu}{\alpha_{cc}}\frac{\delta(\sigma+\delta)}{B} < 0$$

The denominator is negative near stable steady states because $\alpha_{cc} < 0$ and $B > 0$ (see eq. 3.14). Since greater addiction lowers $B$, greater addiction raises the long-run effect on consumption of a change in own price.

Long-run elasticities would be proportional to the slopes in equation (3.18) if initial steady-state consumption were independent of $B$. Changes in $B$ need not affect the initial steady-state consumption because steady-state consumption is determined by first derivatives of the utility and wage functions that do not affect $B$.

The full effect of a finite change in price on the aggregate consumption of addictive goods could be much greater than the effect in equation (3.18) because of unstable steady states. In Figure 3.2, all households with initial consumption capital between $S^{*2}$ and $S^{*1}$ would be to the left of the unstable state when $p_c = p^1$ and the relevant curve is $p^1p^1$, but they would be to the right of the unstable state when $p_c = p^2$ and the relevant curve is $p^2p^2$. Hence a reduction in price from $p^1$ to $p^2$ greatly raises the long-run demand for $c$ by these households.

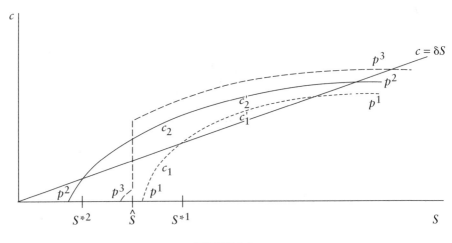

FIGURE 3.2

Smoking and drinking are the only harmful addictions that have been extensively studied empirically. Mullahy (1985, chap. 2) reviews many estimates of the demand for cigarettes and shows that they are mainly distributed between .4 and .5. Estimates that implement our model of addiction imply long-run price elasticities for cigarettes of about .6 (see Chapter 4). This is not small compared to elasticities estimated for other goods. Price elasticities for alcoholic beverages appear to be higher, especially for liquor (see the studies reviewed in Cook and Tauchen, 1982).

The aggregate demand for drinking and smoking could be quite responsive to price, and yet the most addicted might have modest responses. Fortunately, Cook and Tauchen consider the effect of the cost of liquor on heavy drinking as well as on the aggregate amount of drinking. They measure heavy drinking by the death rate from cirrhosis of the liver (heavy drinking is a major cause of death from this disease). They conclude that even small changes in state excise taxes on liquor have a large effect on death rates from this disease. This suggests either that heavy drinkers greatly reduce their consumption when liquor becomes more expensive or that the number of individuals who become heavy drinkers is sensitive to the price of alcohol.

Heroin, cocaine, gambling, and other harmfully addictive goods are often illegal; beneficially addictive goods, such as particular religions or types of music, are also sometimes banned. Banned goods become more expensive when the ban is supported by punishments to consumers and producers. Our analysis implies that the long-run demand for illegal heroin and other illegal addictive drugs tends to be much reduced by severe punishments that greatly raise their cost. However, the demand for banned addictive goods may not respond much to a temporary rise in price due to a temporary burst of active law enforcement or during the first year after a permanent ban is imposed.

The full price of addictive goods to rational consumers includes the money value of changes in future utility and earnings induced by changes in current consumption. The information that began to become available in the late 1950s on the relation between smoking and health provides an excellent experiment on whether persons addicted to smoking consider delayed harmful consequences or whether, instead, they are myopic. Ippolito, Murphy, and Sant (1979) estimate that 11 years after the first Surgeon General's report on smoking in 1964, per capita consumption of cigarettes and of tar and nicotine had been reduced by 34 percent and 45 percent, respectively. This evidence blatantly contradicts the view that the majority of smokers were myopic and would not respond to information about future consequences because they discounted the future heavily.

Of course, persons who continued to smoke, and those who began to smoke after the new information became available, might be more myopic than quitters and persons who did not begin to smoke. One explanation for the much stronger negative relation between smoking and education in the 1970s and 1980s than prior to the Surgeon General's report is that more educated people tend to have lower rates of preference for the present. Presumably, this is partly why they accept the delayed benefits of higher education. Farrell and Fuchs (1982) do show that the negative association between education and smoking is not fully explained by any effects of education on the propensity to smoke.

The behavior of teenagers is persuasive evidence of forward-looking behavior by smokers. Teenagers are often said to be among the most impatient (see the questionnaire evidence in Davids and Falkoff, 1975). If so, their propensity to smoke should be hardly affected by health consequences delayed for 20 or more years, although parental disapproval may have a big effect. Yet smoking rates of males between ages 21 and 24 declined by over one-third from 1964 to 1975 (see Harris, 1980).

The long-run change in the consumption of addictive goods due to a change in wealth also exceeds the short-run change because the stock of consumption capital would change over time until a new steady state is reached (Spinnewyn, 1981, p. 101, has a similar result for wealth effects). By differentiating the first-order conditions in equation (3.6) with respect to $\mu$, the marginal utility of wealth, we get the response of steady-state consumption to a change in wealth (if the utility function is quadratic):

$$(3.19) \qquad \frac{dc^*}{d\mu} = \frac{\delta}{\alpha_{cc}B}\left[(\sigma + \delta)p_c - \frac{d\alpha_s}{d\mu}\right]$$

Since $\mu$ and wealth are negatively related, $c$ is a superior or inferior good as $dc^*/d\mu \lessgtr 0$. If wealth rises because of an increase in earnings, the term $d\alpha_s/d\mu$ is likely to be positive for harmfully addictive goods because the negative effect on earnings of increased consumption is likely to be greater when earnings are greater $(d\mu w_s/d\mu > 0)$. For example, heavy drinking on the job reduces the productivity of an airline pilot or doctor more than that of a janitor or busboy. Equation (3.19) shows that $c$ would be an inferior good if the negative effect on earnings were sufficiently large. Therefore, the spread of information about the health hazards of smoking should have reduced the income elasticity of smoking, and it could have made smoking an inferior good. This elasticity apparently did decline after the 1960s to a negligible level (see Schneider, Klein, and Murphy, 1981). Since women earn less than men, this may help explain why smoking by women has grown relative to smoking by men during the past 25 years.

## 6. Temporary Changes in Price and Life Cycle Events

If utility and earnings functions are quadratic, the demand for $c$ at each moment in time can be explicitly related to the initial $S$ and to past and future prices of $c$ (see eq. 3.A2 in Appendix 3A). Both past and future prices affect current consumption, but the effects are not symmetrical. Changes in past prices affect current consumption by changing the current stock of consumption capital, whereas changes in future prices affect current consumption by changing current full prices through the effects on future stocks and future consumption.

The effect on consumption of a differential change in price over a small interval divided by the length of this interval has a nonzero limit as the length of the interval goes to zero. Equation (3.A2) implies that these limits are

$$(3.20) \qquad \frac{dc(t)}{dp(\tau)} = \frac{(\delta + \lambda_1)e^{-\lambda_2\tau}}{\alpha_{cc}(\lambda_2 - \lambda_1)}[(\delta + \lambda_2)e^{\lambda_2 t} - (\delta + \lambda_1)e^{\lambda_1 t}] \quad \text{for } \tau > t$$

$$(3.21) \quad \frac{dc(t)}{dp(\tau)} = \frac{(\delta + \lambda_1)e^{\lambda_1 t}}{\alpha_{cc}(\lambda_2 - \lambda_1)}[(\delta + \lambda_2)e^{-\lambda_1 \tau} - (\delta + \lambda_1)e^{-\lambda_2 \tau}] \quad \text{for } t > \tau$$

where changes in price are compensated to hold the marginal utility of wealth constant, and $\lambda_2$ and $\lambda_1$ are the larger and smaller roots of equation (3.12).

The important implication of these equations is that the signs of both cross-price derivatives depend only on the sign of $\delta + \lambda_1$. Section 3 shows that this term is positive with adjacent complementarity and negative with adjacent substitution. Since the terms in brackets are always positive and $\alpha_{cc}$ is negative, $dc(t)/dp(\tau)$ will be negative if and only if $\delta + \lambda_1$ is positive. Hence, adjacent complementarity is a necessary and sufficient condition for negative compensated cross-price effects.

A negative cross derivative when marginal utility of income is held constant is a common definition of complementarity in consumption theory. Therefore, adjacent complementarity is a necessary and sufficient condition for present and future consumption, and for present and past consumption, to be complements. This conclusion strongly qualifies the claim by Ryder and Heal that adjacent "complementarity . . . is different from complementarity in the Slutsky sense" (1973, p. 4). Since our definition of potential addiction is linked to adjacent complementarity, a good is addictive if and only if consumption of the good at different moments in time are complements. Moreover, the degree of addiction is stronger when the complementarity in consumption is greater.

The link between addiction and complementarity implies that an anticipated increase in future prices of addictive goods lowers current consumption. These negative effects of anticipated future price changes on the present consumption of addictive goods are a major way to distinguish rational addiction or rational habit formation from myopic behavior (myopic behavior is assumed, e.g., by Pollak, 1970, 1976; von Weizsäcker, 1971; and Phlips, 1974).

The longer that future price changes are anticipated, the bigger is their effect on the current consumption of addictive goods. In equation (3.20), where $\tau > t$, an increase in $\tau$ (with $\tau - t$ held constant) increases the absolute value of $dc(t)/dp(\tau)$ if $\lambda_1 + \delta > 0$. The reason is that the longer a future price rise of an addictive good is anticipated, the greater is the reduction in past consumption of the good. Therefore, the smaller would be the stock of capital carried into the present period. We are not merely restating the familiar result that elasticities of demand are greater when price changes are anticipated since the elasticity for goods with adjacent substitution ($\lambda_1 + \delta < 0$) is smaller when future price changes have been anticipated for a longer period of time.

Equation (3.21) shows that recent past prices have larger effects on current consumption than more distant past prices when steady states are stable. However, with an unstable steady state, changes in consumption at one point in time lead to larger and larger changes in future consumption since consumption capital continues to grow.

The permanent changes in stationary price considered in Section 5 can be said to combine changes in price during the present period with equal changes in price during all future periods. Since a (compensated) future price increase of an addictive good reduces its current consumption, an increase only in its current price has a smaller effect on current consumption than a permanent increase in its price.

The complementarity between present and future consumption is larger for more addictive goods. Therefore, permanent changes in prices of addictive goods might have large effects on their current consumption. Although our analysis implies that rational addicts respond more to price in the long run than in the short run, they may also respond a lot in the short run.

The beginning and resumption of harmful addictions, such as smoking, heavy drinking, gambling, cocaine use, and overeating, and of beneficial addictions, such as religiosity and jogging, are often traceable to the anxiety, tension, and insecurity produced by adolescence, marital breakup, job loss, and other events (see the many studies reviewed in Peele, 1985, chap. 5). This suggests that consumption of many harmfully addictive goods is stimulated by divorce, unemployment, death of a loved one, and other stressful events. If these events lower utility while raising the marginal utility of addictive goods, then changes in life cycle events have the same effect on consumption as changes in prices (see Appendix 3A). For example, a compensated increase in stress during a future finite time interval raises future $c$'s and future $S$'s. The same reasoning used to show that declines in future prices raise present consumption of addictive goods shows that anticipated future stress raises the current consumption of addictive goods if it raises future consumption.

Therefore, even persons with the same utility function and the same wealth who face the same prices may have different degrees of addiction if they have different experiences. However, to avoid the unattractive implication of equation (3.2) that all persons who never consumed an addictive good—such as teenagers who never smoked—would have a zero initial stock of consumption capital, we assume that some events directly affect the stock of consumption capital. If $Z(t)$ is the rate of such events at time $t$, the stock adjustment equation would be changed to

$$(3.22) \qquad \dot{S} = c(t) + Z(t) - \delta S(t)$$

Even if $c$ had not been consumed in the past, $S$ would vary across individuals because of different experiences ($Z$). Appendix 3A analyzes the effects of past and future $Z$'s on the current consumption of $c$.

Temporary events can permanently "hook" rational persons to addictive goods. For example, a person may become permanently addicted to heroin or liquor as a result of peer pressure while a teenager or of extraordinary stress while fighting in Vietnam. If adolescence or a temporary assignment in Vietnam raises demand for $c$ in Figure 3.2 from $c_1$ to $c_2$, he would temporarily move along the path $p^2 p^2$ from $c_2$ to $c_2'$. At that point—when the stress ceases—he abruptly returns to the path $p^1 p^1$ at $c_1'$. (Note that his consumption during the stressful events is affected by how temporary they are.) In this example, he accumulates sufficient capital while under stress to remain hooked afterward. Starting at $c_1$, he would have eventually abstained if he had never been subject to such stress, but instead he ends up with a sizable steady-state consumption. Although most Vietnam veterans did end their addiction to drugs after returning to the United States, many did not, and others shifted from dependence on drugs to dependence on alcohol (see Robins et al., 1980).

Some critics claim that the model in Chapter 2—presumably also the model in this paper—is unsatisfactory because it implies that addicts are "happy," whereas real-life addicts are often discontented and depressed (see, e.g., Winston, 1980). Although our model does assume that addicts are rational and maximize utility, they would not be happy if their addiction results from anxiety-raising events, such as a death or divorce, that lower their utility. Therefore, our model recognizes that people often become addicted precisely because they are unhappy. However, they would be even more unhappy if they were prevented from consuming the addictive goods.

It might seem that only language distinguishes our approach to the effects of events on addictions from approaches based on changes in preferences. But more than language is involved. In many of these other approaches, different preferences or personalities fight for control over behavior (see Yaari, 1977; Elster, 1979; Winston, 1980; Schelling, 1984a). For example, the nonaddictive personality makes commitments when in control of behavior that try to reduce the power of the addictive personality when it is in control. The nonaddictive personality might join Alcoholics Anonymous, enroll in a course to end smoking, and so forth (see the many examples in Schelling, 1984a). By contrast, in our model present and future consumption of addictive goods are complements, and a person becomes more addicted at present when he expects events to raise his future consumption. That is, in our model, both present and future behavior are part of a consistent maximizing plan.

## 7. Cold Turkey and Binges

Our theory of rational addiction can explain why many severe addictions are stopped only with "cold turkey," that is, with abrupt cessation of consumption. Indeed, it implies that strong addictions end *only* with cold turkey. A rational person decides to end his addiction if events lower either his demand for the addictive good sufficiently or his stock of consumption capital sufficiently. His consumption declines over time more rapidly when a change in current consumption has a larger effect on future consumption. The effect on future consumption is larger when the degree of complementarity and the degree of addiction are stronger. Therefore, rational persons end stronger addictions more rapidly than weaker ones.

If the degree of complementarity and potential addiction became sufficiently strong, the utility function in equation (3.1) would no longer be concave. Appendix 3B shows that the relation between present consumption of an addictive good ($c$) and its past consumption ($S$) can then become discontinuous at a point ($\hat{S}$) (see Fig. 3.2), such that $c > \delta\hat{S}$ when $S > \hat{S}$ and $c < \delta\hat{S}$ when $S < \hat{S}$. Although $\hat{S}$ is not a steady-state stock, it plays a role similar to that of an unstable steady-state stock when the utility function is concave. If $S$ is even slightly less than $\hat{S}$, consumption falls along $p^3$ to zero over time. Similarly, if $S$ is even slightly above $\hat{S}$, consumption rises over time along $p^3$, perhaps to a stable level. However, a decline in $S$ from just above to just below $\hat{S}$ causes an infinite rate of fall in $c$ because the relation between $c$ and $S$ is discontinuous at $\hat{S}$. Indeed, with a sufficiently large discontinuity, an addict who quits would use cold turkey; that is, he would immediately stop consuming once he decides to stop.

The explanation of this discontinuity is straightforward. If $S$ is even slightly bigger than $\hat{S}$, the optimal consumption plan calls for high $c$ in the future because the good is highly addictive. Strong complementarity between present and future consumption then requires a high level of current $c$. If $S$ is even slightly below $\hat{S}$, future $c$ will be very low because the addiction ends quickly and strong complementarity then requires a low level of current $c$.

Clearly, then, quitting by cold turkey is not inconsistent with our theory of rational addiction. Indeed, our theory even *requires* strong addictions to terminate with cold turkey. Moreover, when complementarity is sufficiently strong to result in a nonconcave utility function, we generate sharp swings in consumption in response to small changes in the environment when individuals either are beginning or are terminating their addiction.

The short-run loss in utility from stopping consumption gets bigger as an addiction gets stronger. Yet we have shown that rational persons use cold turkey to end a strong addiction even though the short-run "pain" is considerable. Their behavior is rational because they exchange a large short-term loss in utility for an even larger long-term gain. Weak wills and limited self-control are not needed to understand why addictions to smoking, heroin, and liquor can end only when the consumption stops abruptly.

A rational addict might postpone terminating his addiction as he looks for ways to reduce the sizable short-run loss in utility from stopping abruptly. He may first try to stop smoking by attending a smoking clinic but may conclude that this is not a good way for him. He may try to substitute gum chewing and jogging for smoking. These too may fail. Eventually, he may hit on a successful method that reduces the short-term loss from stopping. Nothing about rationality rules out such experiments and failures. Indeed, rationality implies that failures will be common with uncertainty about the method best suited to each person and with a substantial short-run loss in utility from stopping.

The claims of some heavy drinkers and smokers that they want to but cannot end their addictions seem to us no different from the claims of single persons that they want to but are unable to marry or from the claims of disorganized persons that they want to become better organized. What these claims mean is that a person will make certain changes—for example, marry or stop smoking—when he finds a way to raise long-term benefits sufficiently above the short-term costs of adjustment.

"Binges" are common in alcoholism, overeating, and certain other addictions. We define a binge as a cycle over time in the consumption of a good. Binging may seem to be the prototype of irrational behavior, yet a small extension of our model makes binging consistent with rationality.

Consider overeating. Weight rises and health falls as eating increases. We assume that two stocks of consumption capital determine current eating: call one stock weight and the other "eating capital." Our analysis so far, in effect, has absorbed weight and eating capital into a single stock ($S$). We readily generate binges if the two stocks have different depreciation rates and different degrees of complementarity and substitutability with consumption.

To get cycles of overeating and dieting, one stock (say eating capital) must be complementary with eating and have the higher depreciation rate, while the other stock (weight) must be substitutable (see eq. 3.C8 in Appendix 3C). Assume that a person with low weight and eating capital became addicted to eating. As eating rose over time, eating capital would rise more rapidly than weight because it has the higher depreciation rate.

Ultimately, eating would level off and begin to fall because weight continues to increase. Lower food consumption then depreciates the stock of eating capital relative to weight, and the reduced level of eating capital keeps eating down even after weight begins to fall. Eating picks up again only when weight reaches a sufficiently low level. The increase in eating then raises eating capital, and the cycle begins again. These cycles can be either damped or explosive (or constant) depending on whether the steady state is stable or unstable.

Although, as is usual in such problems, two capital stocks are needed to get cycles (Ryder and Heal, 1973, also get cycles in consumption with two capital stocks), these stocks in our analysis have a plausible interpretation in terms of differences in rates of depreciation and degrees of complementarity and substitutability. In our analysis, binges do not reflect inconsistent behavior that results from the struggle among different personalities for control. Rather, they are the outcome of consistent maximization over time that recognizes the effects of increased current eating on both future weight and the desire to eat more in the future.

## 8. Summary and Conclusions

In our theory of rational addiction, "rational" means that individuals maximize utility consistently over time, and a good is potentially addictive if increases in past consumption raise current consumption. We show that steady-state consumption of addictive goods is unstable when the degree of addiction is strong, that is, when the complementarity between past and current consumption is strong. Unstable steady states are a major tool in our analysis of addictive behavior. Consumption rises over time when above unstable steady-state levels, and it falls over time, perhaps until abstention, when below unstable steady states.

Addictions require interaction between a person and a good. Obviously, cigarettes and heroin are more addictive than sweaters and sherbet. Yet not all smokers and heroin users become addicted. We show that, other things the same, individuals who discount the future heavily are more likely to become addicted. The level of incomes, temporary stressful events that stimulate the demand for addictive goods, and the level and path of prices also affect the likelihood of becoming addicted.

Permanent changes in prices of addictive goods may have a modest short-run effect on the consumption of addictive goods. This could be the source of a general perception that addicts do not respond much to changes in price. However, we show that the long-run demand for addictive goods tends to be more elastic than the demand for nonaddictive goods.

Anticipated future increases in price reduce current consumption of addictive goods because their consumption at different moments of time are complements. This implies that temporary changes in the price of an addictive good have smaller effects on current consumption than (compensated) permanent changes.

Strong addictions to smoking, drinking, and drug use are usually broken only by going cold turkey, that is, by abrupt withdrawal. The need for cold turkey may suggest a weak will or other forms of less-than-rational behavior. Yet we show that cold turkey is consistent with rational behavior. Indeed, rational persons end strong addictions only with rapid and sometimes discontinuous reductions in consumption.

Addiction is a major challenge to the theory of rational behavior. Not only cigarettes, alcoholic beverages, and cocaine are obviously addictive, but many other goods and activities have addictive aspects. We do not claim that all the idiosyncratic behavior associated with particular kinds of addictions are consistent with rationality. However, a theory of rational addiction does explain well-known features of addictions and appears to have a richer set of additional implications about addictive behavior than other approaches. This is the challenge posed by our model of rational addiction.

## Appendix 3A

If the utility function is quadratic, if the events $Z(t)$ affect the stock of consumption capital (see eq. 3.22), and if the events $E(t)$ affect the utility function, then the capital stock is a solution to the differential equation

$$\ddot{S}(t) - \sigma \dot{S}(t) - B S(t) = h(t) = a + \frac{\dot{p}(t)}{\alpha_{cc}} - \frac{\sigma + \delta}{\alpha_{cc}} p(t)$$

(3.A1)
$$- \frac{\alpha_{ec}}{\alpha_{cc}} \dot{E}(t) + (\sigma + \delta) \frac{\alpha_{ec}}{\alpha_{cc}} E(t)$$

$$+ \dot{Z}(t) - \left(\sigma + \delta + \frac{\alpha_{cs}}{\alpha_{cc}}\right) Z(t)$$

where $\mu p(t)$ has been replaced by $p(t)$ to save on notation, $\alpha_{ec}$ is the coefficient of $E(t)c(t)$, $a = (\delta + \sigma)(\alpha_c/\alpha_{cc}) + (\alpha_s/\alpha_{cc})$, and $B$ is given by equation (3.11). With the relation between $S$ and $c$ in equation (3.22), the solution to this equation for $c(t)$ that satisfies the initial condition $S(0) = S^0$ and the transversality condition in equation (3.8) is

$$c(t) = -\delta \frac{a}{B} + (\delta + \lambda_1)\left(S^0 + \frac{a}{B}\right) e^{\lambda_1 t} - \frac{(\delta + \lambda_1)^2 e^{\lambda_1 t}}{\alpha_{cc}(\lambda_2 - \lambda_1)} \int_0^\infty e^{-\lambda_2 \tau} p(\tau) d\tau$$

$$+ \frac{(\delta + \lambda_1)(\delta + \lambda_2)}{\alpha_{cc}(\lambda_2 - \lambda_1)} \int_0^t e^{\lambda_1(t-\tau)} p(\tau) d\tau$$

$$+ \frac{(\delta + \lambda_1)(\delta + \lambda_2)}{\alpha_{cc}(\lambda_2 - \lambda_1)} \int_t^\infty e^{\lambda_2(t-\tau)} p(\tau) d\tau$$

(3.A2)
$$+ \frac{p(t)}{\alpha_{cc}} - \frac{(\delta + \lambda_1)[\delta + \lambda_2 + (\alpha_{cs}/\alpha_{cc})]}{\lambda_2 - \lambda_1} e^{\lambda_1 t} \int_0^t e^{-\lambda_1 \tau} Z(\tau) d\tau$$

$$+ \frac{(\delta + \lambda_2)[\delta + \lambda_1 + (\alpha_{cs}/\alpha_{cc})]}{\lambda_2 - \lambda_1} e^{\lambda_2 t} \int_t^\infty e^{\lambda_2 \tau} Z(\tau) d\tau$$

$$- \frac{(\delta + \lambda_1)[\delta + \lambda_1 + (\alpha_{cs}/\alpha_{cc})]}{\lambda_2 - \lambda_1} e^{\lambda_1 t} \int_0^\infty e^{-\lambda_2 \tau} Z(\tau) d\tau$$

+ terms for $E(t)$ that equal $-\alpha_{ec}$ times the corresponding terms for $p(t)$.

The definitions of $\lambda_1$ and $\lambda_2$ in equation (3.12) together with some simple calculations show that

(3.A3)        $\delta + \lambda_1 + \dfrac{\alpha_{cs}}{\alpha_{cc}} < 0, \ \delta + \lambda_2 + \dfrac{\alpha_{cs}}{\alpha_{cc}} > \delta + \dfrac{\sigma}{2} + \dfrac{\alpha_{cs}}{\alpha_{cc}} > 0$

Equation (3.A2) implies the derivatives in equations (3.20) and (3.21) of $c(t)$ with respect to $p(\tau)$, $\tau >$ or $< t$. Essentially identical derivatives of $c(t)$ with respect to $E(\tau)$ hold, so that if $\alpha_{ec} > 0$,

(3.A4)
$$\frac{\partial c(t)}{\partial p(\tau)} \lesseqgtr 0 \text{ and } \left.\frac{\partial c(t)}{\partial E(\tau)}\right|_{\tau < t} \gtreqless 0 \text{ as } \delta + \lambda_1 \gtreqless 0$$

which is the condition for adjacent complementarity; similarly when $\tau > t$.

We also have

(3.A5)
$$\left.\frac{\partial c(t)}{\partial Z(\tau)}\right|_{\tau < t} = \frac{\delta + \lambda_1}{\lambda_2 - \lambda_1} e^{\lambda_1 t} \left[ \left(\delta + \lambda_2 + \frac{\alpha_{cs}}{\alpha_{cc}}\right) e^{-\lambda_1 \tau} - \left(\delta + \lambda_1 + \frac{\alpha_{cs}}{\alpha_{cc}}\right) e^{-\lambda_2 \tau} \right]$$

$$\gtreqless 0 \text{ as } \delta + \lambda_1 \gtreqless 0$$

via equation (3.A3). However,

(3.A6)
$$\left.\frac{\partial c(t)}{\partial Z(\tau)}\right|_{\tau > t} = \left(\delta + \lambda_1 + \frac{\alpha_{cs}}{\alpha_{cc}}\right) e^{-\lambda_2 \tau} [(\delta + \lambda_2) e^{\lambda_2 t} - (\delta + \lambda_1) e^{\lambda_1 t}] < 0$$

Therefore, future events that raise the stock have a negative effect on current consumption independent of whether there is adjacent complementarity.

## Appendix 3B

If the degree of adjacent complementarity is sufficiently strong that the utility function is no longer concave in $c(t)$ and $S(t)$, the two roots in equation (3.12) will be complex, and the form of the optimal consumption path will change significantly. We consider the case in which the utility function is still concave in $c(t)$ and $S(t)$ separately, but it is not jointly concave in $c(t)$ and $S(t)$:

(3.B1)
$$\alpha_{cc} < 0, \alpha_{ss} < 0, \alpha_{cc}\alpha_{ss} < \alpha_{cs}^2$$

These assumptions indicate that a high degree of complementarity between past and current consumption—that is, between $c(t)$ and $S(t)$—is what creates some convexity in the utility function, not a lack of concavity in either $c(t)$ or $S(t)$ alone. In regions in which $4B < -\sigma^2$, both roots of the characteristic equation $\lambda^2 - \sigma\lambda - B$ will be complex (see eq. 3.13).

If the roots are complex, the unstable steady state is replaced by a discontinuity in the optimal consumption function that relates consumption

$c$ to the current stock $S$. However, as long as the utility function satisfies $\alpha_{cc} < 0$, then this discontinuity will always be of a particular form: $c(S) < \delta S$ to the left of a critical stock value $\hat{S}$ ($\hat{S}$ is not the same stock that satisfies the steady-state equation), and $c(S) > \delta\hat{S}$ to the right of $\hat{S}$.

If $\hat{S}$ is above a lower steady state at abstinence, the critical stock can generate the phenomenon of quitting cold turkey. That is, consumption could fall considerably in response to even a small rise in price or a "small" event.

A simple example may be the best way to illustrate this result. Unfortunately, quadratic utility functions that satisfy the inequalities in equation (3.B1) have unbounded utility if the horizon is infinite. However, consider the following modified quadratic utility function:

$$(3.B2) \qquad u(c(t),\ S(t)) = -\infty \quad \text{for } c(t) < 0 \text{ or } c(t) > \hat{C}$$

so that consumption is restricted to the interval $[0,\ \hat{C}]$, and

$$u(c(t),\ S(t)) = \alpha_c c(t) + \alpha_s S(t) + \alpha_{cs} c(t) S(t) + \tfrac{1}{2}\alpha_{cc} c(t)^2 \quad \text{for } 0 < c(t) < \hat{C}$$

Although we assume $\alpha_{ss} = 0$ to simplify the calculations, the basic results require only that $\alpha_{cs}^2 > \alpha_{cc}\alpha_{ss}$, and $4B < \sigma^2$.

The first-order conditions are

$$c(t) = 0 \qquad \text{then } (\alpha_c - \mu) + \alpha_{cs} S(t) + \alpha_{cc} c(t) + q(t) \leq 0$$

$$(3.B3) \quad 0 < c(t) < \hat{C} \quad \text{then } (\alpha_c - \mu) + \alpha_{cs} S(t) + \alpha_{cc} c(t) + q(t) = 0$$

$$c(t) = \hat{C} \qquad \text{then } (\alpha_c - \mu) + \alpha_{cs} S(t) + \alpha_{cc} c(t) + q(t) \geq 0$$

The term $\mu$ is the product of the marginal utility of income and the constant price of $c$, and $q(t)$ is the shadow price of the stock.

Define $S_\ell > 0$ to be the highest stock such that $c(t) = 0$ satisfies the Euler condition for a locally optimal solution. Clearly, $S_\ell$ must satisfy

$$(3.B4) \quad (\alpha_c - \mu) + \alpha_{cs} S_\ell + \frac{\alpha_s}{\sigma + \delta} = 0 \text{ or } S_\ell = \frac{-\{(\alpha_c - \mu) + [\alpha_s/(\sigma + \delta)]\}}{\alpha_{cs}}$$

We assume that $S_\ell$ is strictly positive; that is, we assume that the cost of increasing from a zero stock exceeds the benefits. Similarly, define the smallest stock, $S_h$, such that $c(t) = \hat{C}$ satisfies the Euler equation (and transversality condition). This stock is defined by

(3.B5)
$$S_h = S_\ell - \hat{C}\left(\frac{\alpha_{cc}}{\alpha_{cs}} + \frac{1}{\sigma + \delta}\right)$$

Finally, the stock, $S^*$, that satisfies the steady-state equation is

(3.B6)
$$(\alpha_c - \mu) + \alpha_{cs}S^* + \alpha_{cc}\delta S^* + \frac{\alpha_s + \alpha_{cs}\delta S^*}{\sigma + \delta} = 0$$

If $\alpha_{cs}/(\sigma + \delta) = -\alpha_{cc}$, then $S_\ell = S_h = S^*$. In this case, $c(t) = 0$, $c(t) = \hat{C}$, and $c(t) = \delta S^*$ are all solutions to the Euler equation. However, the convexity induced by the strong complementarity between $c$ and $S$ implies that lifetime utility will be maximized by choosing either $c(t) = 0$ or $c(t) = \hat{C}$ when the initial stock is $S^*$.

### Appendix 3C

We assume a quadratic utility function in $c$, $y$, and two stocks, $S_1$ and $S_2$, where $S_1$ and $S_2$ do not interact ($\alpha_{12} = 0$). While the steady-state results are similar for the two-stock and one-stock models, the dynamics are quite different. To simplify notation, we transform the definitions of the stocks and consumption so that the steady-state values of $c$ and $S$ are zero. The solution to this standard control problem is of the form

(3.C1)
$$S_1(t) = \phi_{11}e^{\lambda_1 t} + \phi_{12}e^{\lambda_2 t}$$

$$S_2(t) = \phi_{21}e^{\lambda_1 t} + \phi_{22}e^{\lambda_2 t}$$

The restriction that both stocks accumulate by the same consumption process implies that

(3.C2)
$$\phi_{11}(\lambda_1 + \delta_1) = \phi_{21}(\lambda_1 + \delta_2), \quad \phi_{12}(\lambda_2 + \delta_1) = \phi_{22}(\lambda_2 + \delta_2)$$

The characteristic equation for these roots requires

(3.C3)
$$\alpha_{cc}\phi_{1j}(\lambda_j + \delta_1) + \phi_{1j}\alpha_{c1} + \phi_{2j}\alpha_{c2} + \frac{\phi_{1j}\alpha_{11} + \phi_{1j}\alpha_{c1}(\lambda_j + \delta_1)}{\sigma + \delta_1 - \lambda_j}$$

$$+ \frac{\phi_{2j}\alpha_{22} + \phi_{2j}\alpha_{c2}(\lambda_j + \delta_1)}{\sigma + \delta_2 - \lambda_j} = 0, \quad j = 1, 2$$

If (3.C2) is used to substitute $\phi_{11}(\lambda_j + \delta_1)/(\lambda_j + \delta_2)$ for $\phi_{21}$ in equation (3.C3), then the characteristic equation becomes

$$(\lambda + \delta_1)(\lambda + \delta_2)(\sigma + \delta_1 - \lambda)(\sigma + \delta_2 - \lambda)$$

(3.C4)

$$- (\lambda + \delta_2)(\sigma + \delta_2 - \lambda)A_1 - (\lambda + \delta_1)(\sigma + \delta_1 - \lambda)A_2 = 0$$

where

(3.C5)
$$A_j = \frac{-1}{\alpha_{cc}}[(\sigma + 2\delta_j)\alpha_{cj} + \alpha_{jj}], \quad j = 1, 2$$

measures the degree of substitution or complementarity.

Multiplying out and collecting terms yields a polynomial for the roots, $\lambda$:

$$\lambda^4 - 2\sigma\lambda^3 + (\sigma^2 - \gamma_1 - \gamma_2 + A_1 + A_2)\lambda^2$$

(3.C6)

$$+ \sigma(\gamma_1 + \gamma_2 - A_1 - A_2)\lambda + (\gamma_1\gamma_2 - \gamma_1 A_2 - \gamma_2 A_1) = 0$$

with $\gamma_j = \delta_j(\delta_j + \sigma)$, $j = 1, 2$, and where $\gamma_1\gamma_2 - \gamma_1 A_2 - \gamma_2 A_1 > 0$ is a necessary condition for the steady state to be stable.

The roots will be complex if

(3.C7)
$$(\gamma_1 - \gamma_2)^2 + 2(\gamma_1 - \gamma_2)(A_2 - A_1) + (A_1 + A_2)^2 < 0$$

Equation (3.C6) implies that a necessary and sufficient condition for complex roots is that

(3.C8)
$$[(\gamma_1 - \gamma_2) + (A_2 - A_1)]^2 + 4A_1 A_2 < 0$$

Equations (3.C7) and (3.C8) together show that complex roots require the stock with the higher depreciation rate to have adjacent complementarity and the other stock to have adjacent substitution.

# Rational Addiction and the Effect of Price on Consumption

# 4

Legalization of such substances as marijuana, heroin, and cocaine surely will reduce the prices of these harmful addictive drugs. By the law of the downward-sloping demand function, their consumption will rise. But by how much? According to conventional wisdom, the consumption of these illegal addictive substances is not responsive to price.

However, conventional wisdom is contradicted by the theoretical model of rational addiction presented in Chapter 3. This analysis implies that addictive substances are likely to be quite responsive to price. In this paper, after a brief review of the model of rational addiction and the empirical evidence in support of it, we use the theory and evidence to draw highly tentative inferences concerning the effects of legalization of currently banned substances on consumption in the aggregate and for selected groups in the population.

Addictive behavior is usually assumed to involve both "reinforcement" and "tolerance." Reinforcement means that greater past consumption of addictive goods, such as drugs or cigarettes, increases the desire for present consumption. But tolerance cautions that the utility from a given amount of consumption is lower when past consumption is greater.

These aspects of addictive behavior imply several restrictions on the instantaneous utility function

$$(4.1) \qquad U(t) = u[c(t), S(t), y(t)]$$

where $U(t)$ is utility at $t$, $c(t)$ is consumption of the addictive good, $y(t)$

By Gary S. Becker, Michael Grossman, and Kevin M. Murphy; originally published in *American Economic Review*, 81, no. 2 (1991): 237–241.

is a nonaddictive good, and $S(t)$ is the stock of "addictive capital" that depends on past consumption of $c$ and on life cycle events. Tolerance is defined by $\partial u / \partial S = u_s < 0$, which means that addictions are harmful in the sense that greater past consumption of addictive goods lowers current utility. Stated differently, higher $c(t)$ lowers future utility by raising future values of $S$.

Reinforcement $(dc/dS > 0)$ requires that an increase in past use raises the marginal utility of current consumption: $(\partial^2 u / \partial c \partial S = u_{cs} > 0)$. This is a sufficient condition for myopic utility maximizers who do not consider the future consequences of their current behavior. But rational utility maximizers also consider the future harmful consequences of their current behavior. Reinforcement for them requires that the positive effect of an increase in $S(t)$ on the marginal utility of $c(t)$ exceeds the negative effect of higher $S(t)$ on the future harm from greater $c(t)$.

A necessary and sufficient condition for reinforcement near a steady state (where $c = \delta S$) is

(4.2) $$(\sigma + 2\delta) u_{cs} > -u_{ss}$$

where $u_{cs}$ and $u_{ss}$ are local approximations near the steady state, $\sigma$ is the rate of time preference, and $\delta$ is the rate of depreciation on addictive capital. Reinforcement is stronger, the bigger the left-hand side is relative to the right-hand side. Clearly, $u_{cs} > 0$ is necessary if $u$ is concave in $S(u_{ss} < 0)$; that is, if tolerance increases as $S$ increases.

It is not surprising that addiction is more likely for people who discount the future heavily (a higher $\sigma$) since they pay less attention to the adverse consequences. Addiction to a good is also stronger when the effects of past consumption depreciate more rapidly ($\delta$ is larger), for then current consumption has smaller negative effects on future utility. The harmful effects of smoking, drinking, and much drug use do generally disappear within a few years after a person stops the addiction unless vital organs, such as the liver, get irreversibly damaged.

Reinforcement as summarized in equation (4.2) has the important implication that the amounts of an addictive good consumed at different times are complements. Therefore, an increase in either past or expected future prices decreases current consumption. The relation between these effects of past and future prices depends on both time preference and the depreciation rate.

Figure 4.1 illustrates several implications of our approach to addiction, where $S(t)$ is measured along the horizontal axis and $c(t)$ along the vertical

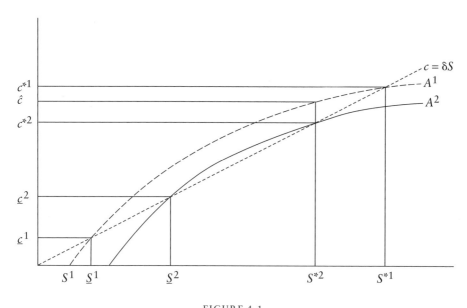

FIGURE 4.1

one. The line $c = \delta S$ gives all possible steady states where $c$ and $S$ are constant over time. The positively sloped curves $A^1$ give the relation between $c$ and $S$ for an addicted consumer who has a particular utility function, faces given prices of $c$ and $y$, and has a given wealth. The initial stock ($S^0$) depends on past consumption and past life cycle experience. Both $c$ and $S$ grow over time when $S^0$ is in the interval where $A^1$ is above the steady-state line, and both fall over time when $S^0$ is in the intervals where $A^1$ is below the steady-state line.

Figure 4.1 shows clearly why the degree of addiction is very sensitive to the initial level of addictive capital. If $S^0$ is below $\underline{S}^1$ in the figure, a rational consumer eventually lays off the addictive good. But if $S_0$ is above $\underline{S}^1$, even a rational consumer becomes addicted, and ends up consuming large quantities of the addictive good.

The curve $A^1$ intersects the steady-state line at two points: $\underline{c}^1 = \delta \underline{S}^1$, and $c^{*1} = \delta S^{*1}$. Other relevant points are where $c = 0$ and $S \leq S^1$. The second point and third set of points are locally stable. If initially $c = 0$, $S \leq S^1$, and a divorce or other events raise the stock of addictive capital to a level below $\underline{S}^1$, $c$ may become positive, but eventually the consumer again refrains from consuming $c$. Similarly, if initially $c = c^{*1} = \delta S^{*1}$, $c$ falls at first if say finding a good job lowers $S$ from $S^{*1}$ to a level $> \underline{S}^1$. But $c$ then begins to rise over time and returns toward $c^{*1}$. The other steady state, $\underline{c}^1 = \delta \underline{S}^1$, is locally and globally unstable: even small changes in $S$ cause cumulative movements toward $c = 0$ or $c = c^{*1}$.

Unstable steady states are an important part of the analysis of rational addictions, for they explain why the same person is sometimes heavily addicted to cigarettes, drugs, or other goods, and yet at other times lays off completely. Suppose the consumer starts out at $c^{*1} = \delta S^{*1}$, and experiences favorable events that lower his stock of addictive capital below $\underline{S}^1$, the unstable steady state with $A^1$. The consumer goes from being strongly addicted to eventually giving up $c$ entirely. If $A^1$ is very steep when $S$ is below the unstable steady state (if reinforcement is powerful in this interval), consumers would quit their addiction "cold turkey" (see the more extended analysis in Chapter 3, Section 7).

To analyze rational addicts' responses to changes in the cost of addictive goods, suppose they are at $c^{*2} = \delta S^{*2}$ along $A^2$, and that a fall in the price of $c$ raises the demand curve for $c$ from $A^2$ to $A^1$. Consumption increases at first from $c^{*2}$ to $\hat{c}$, and then $c$ grows further over time since $\hat{c}$ is above the steady-state line. Consumption grows toward the new stable steady state at $c^{*1} = \delta S^{*1}$. This shows that long-run responses to price changes exceed short-run responses because initial increases in consumption of addictive goods cause a subsequent growth in the stocks of addictive capital, which then stimulates further growth in consumption.

Since the degree of addiction is stronger when $A$ is steeper, and since long-run responses to price changes are also greater when $A$ is steeper, strong addictions do not imply weak price elasticities. Indeed, if anything, rational addicts respond more to price changes in the long run than do nonaddicts.[1] The short-run change is smaller than the long-run change because the stock of addictive capital is fixed. Even in the short run, however, rational addicts respond to the anticipated growth in future consumption since future and current consumption of addictive goods are complements

---

1. The long-run response between stable steady states to a permanent change in $p_c$ is $dc^*/dp_c = \mu/\alpha_{cc}B'$, where $\mu$ is the marginal utility of wealth. The term $B'$ measures the degree of addiction, where $B'$ ranges between 1 (no addiction) and 0 for an addictive good that has a stable steady state. (See Chapter 3, eq. 3.18, for discussion.)

for them. But the *ratio* of short- to long-run responses does decline as the degree of addiction increases.[2]

The presence of unstable steady states for highly addictive goods means that the full effect of a price change on consumption could be much greater for these goods than the change between stable steady states given in footnote 1. Households with initial consumption capital between $\underline{S}^2$ and $\underline{S}^1$ in Figure 4.1 would be to the left of the unstable steady state at $\underline{S}^2$ when price equals $p^2$, but they would be to the right of the unstable steady state at $\underline{S}^1$ when price equals $p^1$. A reduction in price from $p^2$ to $p^1$ greatly raises the long-run demand by these households because they move from low initial consumption to a stable steady state with a high level of consumption.

The total cost of addictive goods to consumers equals the sum of the good's price and the money value of any future adverse effects, such as the negative effects on earnings and health of smoking, heavy drinking, or dependence on crack. Either a higher price of the good (due perhaps to a larger tax) or a higher future cost (due perhaps to greater information about health hazards) reduces consumption in both the short and long run.

It is intuitively plausible that as price becomes a bigger share of total cost, long-run changes in demand induced by a given percentage change in the money price get larger *relative* to the long-run changes induced by an equal percentage change in future costs (see Becker, Grossman, and Murphy, 1991, fn. 3). Money price tends to be relatively more important to poorer and younger consumers, partly because they generally place a smaller monetary value on health and other harmful future effects.

Poorer and younger persons also appear to discount the future more heavily (this is suggested by the theoretical analysis in Becker and Mulligan, 1995). It can be shown that addicts with higher discount rates respond more to changes in money prices of addictive goods, whereas addicts with lower rates of discount respond more to changes in the harmful future consequences.[3]

---

2. One can show that a rational addict's short-run response to a permanent change in $p_c$ equals $dc_s/dp_c = -(\lambda/\delta)(dc^*/dp_c)$, where $-\delta \leq \lambda \leq 0$, and $\lambda$ is larger when the degree of addiction is stronger (see Chapter 3, Section 3). Therefore, the ratio of the short- to long-term response gets smaller as the degree of addiction (measured by $\lambda$) is larger. But one can also show that $dc_s/dp_c$ itself gets larger as the degree of addiction increases.

3. If $u$ is concave, $-\delta^2 u_{cc} - u_{ss} > 2\delta u_{cs}$. This implies that either or both of the following inequalities hold: $-u_{ss}/\delta^2 > u_{cs}/\delta$, and $-u_{cc} > u_{cs}/\delta$. We assume both hold. The second inequality states that an increase in $c$ between steady states reduces the

These implications of rational addiction can be tested with evidence on the demand for cigarettes, heavy consumption of alcohol, and gambling. In an earlier paper (Becker, Grossman, and Murphy, 1990), we fit models of rational addiction to cigarettes to a time-series of state cross sections for the period 1955–85. We find a sizable long-run price elasticity of demand ranging between −.7 and −.8, while the elasticity of consumption with respect to price in the first year after a permanent price change (the short-run price elasticity) is about −.4. Smoking in different years appear to be complements: cigarette consumption in any year is lower when both future prices and past prices are higher.

Frank Chaloupka (1991) analyzes cigarette smoking over time by a panel of individuals. He finds similar short- and long-run price elasticities to those we estimate, and that future as well as past increases in cigarette prices reduce current smoking. He also finds that smoking by the less educated responds much more to changes in cigarette prices than does smoking by the more educated; a similar result has been obtained by Joy Townsend (1987) with British data. Eugene Lewit et al. (1981) and Lewit and Douglas Coate (1982) report that youths respond more than adults to changes in cigarette prices. By contrast, the information that began to emerge in the early 1960s about the harmful long-run effects of smoking has had a much greater effect on smoking by the rich and more educated than by the poor and less educated (see Philip Farrell and Victor Fuchs, 1982, for the United States; Townsend for Britain).

Philip Cook and George Tauchen (1982) examine variations in death rates from cirrhosis of the liver (a standard measure of heavy alcohol use), as well as variations in per capita consumption of distilled spirits in a time-series of state cross sections for 1962–77. They find that state excise taxes on distilled spirits have a negative and statistically significant effect on the cirrhosis death rate. Moreover, a small increase in prices in a state's excise tax lowers death rates by a larger percentage than it lowers per capita consumption.

Pamela Mobilia (1990) applies the rational addiction framework to

---

marginal utility of $c$ by more than the increase in $S$ raises it. The first inequality assumes that the increase in $S$ has a larger effect on its marginal utility than does the increase in $c$.

The absolute value of the long-run change in $c$ induced by a change in $p_c$ is raised by an increase in $\sigma$ if $-u_{ss} > \delta u_{cs}$. Similarly, the absolute value of the long-run change in $c$ with respect to a change in future costs is reduced by an increase in $\sigma$ if $-u_{cc}\delta > u_{cs}$. (For more details, see Becker, Grossman, and Murphy, 1991, fn. 4.)

the demand for gambling at horse racing tracks. Her data consist of a U.S. time-series of racing track cross sections for the period 1950–86 (tracks over time are the units of observation). She measures consumption by the real amount bet per person attending (handle per attendant), and price by the takeout rate (the fraction of the total amount bet that is retained by the track). Her findings are similar to those in the rational addictive studies of cigarettes. The long-run price elasticity of demand for gambling equals −.7 and is more than twice as large as the short-run elasticity of −.3. Moreover, an increase in the current takeout rate lowers handle per attendant in both past and future years.

The evidence from smoking, heavy drinking, and gambling rather strongly supports our model of rational addiction. In particular, long-run price elasticities are sizable and much bigger than short-run elasticities, higher future as well as past prices reduce current consumption, lower-income persons respond more to changes in prices of addictive goods than do higher-income persons, whereas the latter respond more to changes in future harmful effects, and younger persons respond more to price changes than older persons. It seems reasonable to us that what holds for smoking, heavy drinking, and gambling tends to hold also for drug use, although direct evidence is not yet available, and many experts on drugs would be skeptical. Lacking the evidence, we simply indicate what to expect from various kinds of price changes if responses of drug addicts are similar to those of persons addicted to other goods.

To fix ideas, consider a large permanent reduction in the price of drugs (perhaps due to partial or complete legalization) combined with much greater efforts to educate the population about the harm from drug use. Our analysis predicts that much lower prices could significantly expand use even in the short run, and it would surely stimulate much greater addiction in the long run. Note, however, that the elasticity of response to large price changes would be less than that to modest changes if the elasticity is smaller at lower prices.

The effects of a fall in drug prices on demand would be countered by the education program. But since drug use by the poor would be more sensitive to the price fall than to greater information about harmful longer-run effects, drug addiction among the poor is likely to become more important relative to addiction among the middle classes and rich. For similar reasons, addiction among the young may rise more than that among other segments of the population.

A misleading impression about the reaction to permanent price changes may have been created by the effects of temporary police crackdowns on drugs, or temporary federal "wars" on drugs. Since temporary policies raise current but not future prices (they would even lower future prices if drug inventories are built up during a crackdown period), there is no complementary fall in current use from a fall in future use. Consequently, even if drug addicts are rational, a temporary war that greatly raised street prices of drugs may well have only a small effect on drug use, whereas a permanent war could have much bigger effects, even in the short run.

Clearly, we have not provided enough evidence to evaluate whether or not the use of heroin, cocaine, and other drugs should be legalized. A cost-benefit analysis of many effects is needed to decide between a regime in which drugs are legal and one in which they are not. What this paper shows is that the permanent reduction in price caused by legalization is likely to have a substantial positive effect on use, particularly among the poor and young.

# An Empirical Analysis of Cigarette Addiction

5

In Chapter 3, a theoretical model was developed in which utility-maximizing consumers may become "addicted" to the consumption of a product, and the key empirical predictions were outlined. In this framework consumers are rational or farsighted in the sense that they anticipate the expected future consequences of their current actions. This chapter uses that framework to analyze empirically the demand for cigarettes. The data consist of per capita cigarette sales (in packs) annually by state for the period 1955–1985. The empirical results indicate that smoking is addictive.

The "rational addiction" model follows Harl E. Ryder, Jr., and Geoffrey M. Heal (1973), George J. Stigler and Becker (Chapter 2), Marcel Boyer (1978, 1983), Frans Spinnewyn (1981), and Laurence R. Iannaccone (1986) by considering the interaction of past and current consumption in a model with utility-maximizing consumers. The main feature of these models is that past consumption of some goods influences their current consumption by affecting the marginal utility of current and future consumption. Greater past consumption of harmfully addictive goods such as cigarettes stimulates current consumption by increasing the marginal utility of current consumption more than the present value of the marginal harm from future consumption. Therefore, past consumption is reinforcing for addictive goods.

This chapter tests the model of rational addiction by considering the response of cigarette consumption to a change in cigarette prices. We examine whether lower past and future prices for cigarettes raise current

By Gary S. Becker, Michael Grossman, and Kevin M. Murphy; originally published in *American Economic Review,* 84, no. 3 (1994): 396–418.

cigarette consumption. The empirical results tend to support the implication of addictive behavior that cross price effects are negative and that
long-run responses exceed short-run responses.

We find that a 10-percent permanent increase in the price of cigarettes
reduces current consumption by 4 percent in the short run and by 7.5
percent in the long run. In contrast, a 10-percent increase in price for only
one period decreases consumption by only 3 percent. In addition, a one-
period price increase of 10 percent decreases consumption in the previous
period by approximately 0.6 percent and decreases consumption in the
subsequent period by 1.5 percent. These estimates illustrate the importance
of the intertemporal linkages in cigarette demand implied by addictive
behavior. We are not able to test other implications of the model developed
in Chapter 3, such as abrupt quitting behavior by cold turkey.

In myopic models of addictive behavior, past consumption stimulates
current consumption, but individuals ignore the future when making consumption decisions. We show that these models imply that past prices have
negative effects on current consumption, but that they imply that there is
no effect of anticipated future prices on current consumption. Since rational models always exhibit the symmetry of (compensated) cross price effects implied by optimizing behavior, testing for the effects of future prices
on current consumption distinguishes rational models of addiction from
myopic models. The results strongly reject myopic behavior, while they
tend to support the model of rational addiction. However, some results
cannot readily be explained by rational addiction.

The cigarette industry raised the price of cigarettes in 1982 as well as
in 1983 when the federal excise tax on cigarettes increased. The industry
also raised cigarette prices throughout the 1980s presumably in anticipa-
tion of a continuing fall in smoking. Such pricing is inconsistent with perfect competition, but it is consistent with monopoly power in the cigarette
industry if cigarette smoking is addictive. Since other evidence also suggests that the industry has monopoly power, this pricing policy is further
testimony to the effect of addictive behavior on aggregate cigarette consumption, because a monopolist will take account of the effect of current
price on the demand for future consumption.

Our results are relevant to government regulation of the cigarette industry. Since the first Surgeon General's Report on Smoking and Health in
1964, the federal government and state governments have carried out policies to increase public knowledge about the harmful effects of smoking, to
restrict advertising by cigarette manufacturers, and to create no-smoking
areas in public places and in the workplace. These policies will induce mo-

nopolistic producers to raise current prices because the decline in future demand that they cause reduces the gains from maintaining a lower price to stimulate future consumption. This indirect effect of the antismoking campaign in the form of higher prices has not been taken into account in evaluations of the campaign (e.g., Kenneth E. Warner, 1986).

Our results also are relevant in estimating the potential revenue yield of an increase in the federal excise tax rate on cigarettes to help finance national health-care reform or to reduce the federal deficit. Given the addictive nature of smoking, consumption of cigarettes is positively related to past consumption. For example, a price hike in 1993 due to an increase in the federal excise tax rate would reduce consumption in 1993, which would cause consumption in 1994 and in all future years to fall. Since we find that the long-run price elasticity is almost twice as large as the short-run price elasticity, the long-run increase in tax revenue would be considerably smaller than the short-run increase.

## 1. The Basic Model

Most empirical analyses of consumption deal with single-period models or assume time-separable utility. By definition, single-period models cannot deal with the dynamics of consumption behavior, and the usual two-stage budgeting property of time-separable models precludes any dynamics other than those arising from dynamic wealth changes and aggregate consumption effects. Since addictions imply linkages in consumption of the same good over time, it is essential to relax the additive-separability assumption in order to model consumption of addictive goods.

The simplest way to relax the separability assumption is to allow utility in each period to depend on consumption in that period and consumption in the previous period. In particular, following Boyer (1978, 1983), we consider a model with two goods and current-period utility in period $t$ given by a concave utility function

(5.1) $$U(Y_t, C_t, C_{t-1}, e_t)$$

Here $C_t$ is the quantity of cigarettes consumed in period $t$, $C_{t-1}$ is the quantity of cigarettes consumed in period $t-1$, $Y_t$ is the consumption of a composite commodity in period $t$, and $e_t$ reflects the impact of unmeasured life-cycle variables on utility. Individuals are assumed to be infinite-lived and to maximize the sum of lifetime utility discounted at the rate $r$.

If the composite commodity, $Y$, is taken as numeraire, if the rate of interest is equal to the rate of time preference, and if the price of cigarettes in period $t$ is denoted by $P_t$, then the consumer's problem is

(5.2) $$\max \sum_{t=1}^{\infty} \beta^{t-1} U(C_t, C_{t-1}, Y_t, e_t)$$

such that $C_0 = C^0$ and

$$\sum_{t=1}^{\infty} \beta^{t-1}(Y_t + P_t C_t) = A^0$$

where $\beta = 1/(1+r)$. We ignore any effect of $C$ on earnings, and hence on the present value of wealth ($A^0$), and we also ignore any effect of $C$ on the length of life and all other types of uncertainty. The initial condition for the consumer in period 1, $C^0$, measures the level of cigarette consumption in the period prior to that under consideration.

The associated first-order conditions are

(5.3a) $$U_y(C_t, C_{t-1}, Y_t, e_t) = \lambda$$

(5.3b) $$U_1(C_t, C_{t-1}, Y_t, e_t) + \beta U_2(C_{t+1}, C_t, Y_{t+1}, e_{t+1}) = \lambda P_t$$

Equation (5.3a) is the usual condition that the marginal utility of other consumption in each period, $U_y$, equals the marginal utility of wealth, $\lambda$. Equation (5.3b) implies that the marginal utility of current cigarette consumption, $U_1$, plus the discounted marginal effect on next period's utility of today's consumption, $U_2$, equals the current price multiplied by the marginal utility of wealth. In the case of a harmfully addictive good such as cigarettes, $U_2$ is negative, although the model that we develop simply assumes that this term is not zero. That is, the predictions contained in this section also are valid in the case of beneficial addiction ($U_2 > 0$).

Since with perfect certainty the marginal utility of wealth, $\lambda$, is constant over time, variations in the price of cigarettes over time trace out marginal utility of wealth-constant demand curves for $Y$ and $C$. In the time-separable case, these demand curves depend only on the current price ($P_t$) and the marginal utility of wealth, but with nonseparable utility, they depend on prices in all periods through the effects of past and future prices on past and future consumption.

To illustrate, consider a utility function that is quadratic in $Y_t$, $C_t$, and $e_t$. By solving the first-order condition for $Y_t$ and substituting the result into the first-order condition for $C_t$, we get a linear difference equation that determines current cigarette consumption as a function of past and future cigarette consumption, the current price of cigarettes, $P_t$, and the shift variables $e_t$ and $e_{t+1}$:

(5.4)
$$C_t = \theta C_{t-1} + \beta\theta C_{t+1} + \theta_1 P_t + \theta_2 e_t + \theta_3 e_{t+1}$$

where

$$\theta_1 = \frac{u_{yy}\lambda}{(u_{11}u_{yy} - u_{1y}^2) + \beta(u_{22}u_{yy} - u_{2y}^2)} < 0$$

$$\theta_2 = \frac{-(u_{yy}u_{1e} - u_{1y}u_{ey})}{(u_{11}u_{yy} - u_{1y}^2) + \beta(u_{22}u_{yy} - u_{2y}^2)}$$

$$\theta_3 = \frac{-\beta(u_{yy}u_{2e} - u_{2y}u_{2e})}{(u_{11}u_{yy} - u_{1y}^2) + \beta(u_{22}u_{yy} - u_{2y}^2)}$$

where lowercase letters denote the coefficients of the quadratic utility function, and the intercept is suppressed.

Since $\theta_1$ is negative by concavity of $U$, equation (5.4) implies that increases in the current price decrease current consumption, $C_t$, when the marginal utility of wealth, past consumption, and future consumption are fixed.[1] The effects of changes in future or past consumption on current consumption depend only on the sign of the term $\theta$. When $\theta$ is positive, forces that increase past or future consumption, such as lower past or future cigarette prices, also increase current consumption. In contrast, when $\theta$ is negative, greater past or future consumption decreases current consumption. Hence current and past consumption are complements if and only if

(5.5)
$$\theta = \frac{-(u_{12}u_{yy} - u_{1y}u_{2y})}{(u_{11}u_{yy} - u_{1y}^2) + \beta(u_{22}u_{yy} - u_{2y}^2)} > 0$$

Since past consumption reinforces current consumption when behavior is addictive, we say that a good is addictive if and only if an increase in past consumption leads to an increase in current consumption holding current prices, $e_t, e_{t+1}$, and the marginal utility of wealth fixed. A good is more addictive when the reinforcement from past consumption is greater.

---

1. Price effects that do not hold past and future consumption constant are considered later in the chapter.

This definition means that a good is addictive if $\theta > 0$, and the degree of addiction is greater when $\theta$ is larger.

Equation (5.4) is the basis of the empirical analysis in this paper. Cigarette consumption in period $t$ is a function of cigarette consumption in periods $t - 1$ and $t + 1$, the current price of cigarettes ($P_t$), and the unobservables $e_t$ and $e_{t+1}$. Ordinary-least-squares estimation of equation (5.4) would lead to inconsistent estimates of the parameters of interest. The unobserved errors, $e_t$, that affect utility in each period are likely to be serially correlated; even if these variables are uncorrelated, the same error $e_t$ directly affects consumption at all dates through the optimizing behavior implied by equation (5.4). Positive serial correlation in the unobserved effects incorrectly implies that past and future consumption positively affect current consumption, even when the true value of $\theta$ is zero.

Fortunately, the specification in equation (5.4) suggests a way to solve this endogeneity problem, since it implies that current consumption is independent of past and future prices when $C_{t-1}$ and $C_{t+1}$ are held fixed. That is, any effect of past or future prices must come through their effects on $C_{t-1}$ or $C_{t+1}$. Provided that the unobservables are uncorrelated with prices in these periods, past and future prices are logical instruments for $C_{t-1}$ and $C_{t+1}$, since past prices directly affect past consumption, and future prices directly affect future consumption. Therefore, our empirical strategy is to estimate $\theta$ and $\theta_1$, the main parameters of equation (5.4), by using past and future price variables as instruments for past and future consumption.

These estimates can be used to derive short- and long-run demand elasticities for cigarettes and to derive cross price elasticities between cigarette consumption levels at different points in time that test how important addiction is to aggregate cigarette consumption. It is intuitively clear from equation (5.4) that a fall in the current price of cigarettes, $P_t$, increases current consumption, $C_t$, which will increase cigarette consumption at time $t + 1$ when $\theta$ is positive. Similarly, if this fall in $P_t$ is anticipated in period $t - 1$, the rise in $C_t$ also stimulates a rise in consumption at time $t - 1$. In addition, a permanent fall in price has a larger effect on current consumption than does a temporary fall in price, since a permanent fall in price combines a fall in the current price with a fall in all future prices.

These and other results can be seen more formally by solving the second-order difference equation in (5.4). The solution and the various price effects in the model are contained in Appendix 5A. The solution results in an equation in which consumption in period $t$ depends on prices in all periods. This equation determines the sign of the effects of changes in the price of cigarettes in period $\tau$ on cigarette consumption in period $t$.

These effects are temporary in nature since prices in other periods are held constant. The temporary own or current price effect must be negative. The sign of the cross price effect depends entirely on the sign of the coefficient of past consumption ($\theta$) in equation (5.4). The goods in any two consecutive periods are complements (i.e., negative cross price effects) if and only if $\theta$ is positive.

Since an increase in past consumption increases current consumption if a good is addictive, fully anticipated price effects must exceed completely unanticipated price effects in absolute value. The latter describes a price change in period $t$ that is not anticipated until that period, so that past consumption is not affected. The former describes a price change in period $t$ that is anticipated as of the planning date, so that past consumption is affected.

In addition to the own price effects, cross price effects, and the difference between anticipated and unanticipated price effects, there are important differences between long- and short-run responses to permanent price changes in the context of addiction. The short-run price effect describes the response to a change in price in period $t$ and all future periods that is not anticipated until period $t$. The long-run price effect pertains to a price change in *all* periods. Since $C_{t-1}$ remains the same if a price change is not anticipated until period $t$, the long-run price effect must exceed the short-run price effect. In addition, the long-run price effect must exceed the fully anticipated temporary own price effect.

The differences between long-run and short-run, temporary and permanent, and anticipated and unanticipated price changes are greater when there is a greater degree of addiction or complementarity (i.e., when $\theta$ is larger). The cross price effects, and hence the differences between these various elasticities, are small when $\theta$ is close to zero. The simplicity of a time-separable model then would make it superior to the addiction model. However, if $\theta$ is quite different from zero, a time-separable model is likely to give highly misleading predictions about both the short-run and long-run response of consumption to changes in prices.

## 2. A Myopic Model of Addiction

While the model presented in Chapter 3 shows that addictive behavior can be successfully modeled in a rational-choice framework, many previous researchers have considered nonrational or myopic models of addiction and habit formation (see e.g., Robert A. Pollak, 1970, 1976; Menahem E. Yaari, 1977). We cannot hope to develop an empirical framework that encompasses the structures used in all nonrational models, but this section presents a myopic model related to those suggested in the literature. Even this sample model highlights an important empirical distinction between myopic and nonmyopic models.

To maintain as much similarity to the previous model as possible, we use the same utility function and the same assumptions about the goods $Y$ and $C$. The key distinction is that myopic individuals fail to consider the impact of current consumption on future utility and future consumption. Analytically, this corresponds to individuals using a first-order condition that does not contain the future effect $\beta U_2$.

Differences between myopic and rational behavior are highlighted by solving the myopic first-order condition for $C_t$ to get the myopic equivalent of equation (5.4). The major difference between equation (5.4) and the myopic equation is that the latter is entirely backward-looking. Current consumption depends only on current price, lagged consumption, the marginal utility of wealth, and current events. Current consumption is independent of both future consumption, $C_{t+1}$, and future events, $e_{t+1}$. Because of these distinctions, myopic models and rational models have different implications about responses to future changes. In particular, rational addicts increase their current consumption when future prices are expected to fall, but myopic addicts do not.

Empirically, the difference between the two equations provides a clear test between rational and myopic addiction. Myopic behavior implies that the coefficient on instrumented future consumption should be zero, while the rational model implies that it should have the same sign as the coefficient on lagged consumption (the sizes differ only by the discount factor). Future price (and consumption) changes have no impact on the current consumption of a myopic addict, but they have significant effects on the current consumption of a rational addict.

## 3. Data and Empirical Implementation

The data consist of a time series of state cross sections covering the period from 1955 through 1985. We assume that per capita cigarette consumption in these data reflects the behavior of a representative consumer. To be sure, we cannot study the decision to start or quit smoking, given the aggregate nature of the data. But the treatment of unstable steady states in Chapter 3 indicates that the same forces that govern consumption of an addictive good, given participation, also govern these decisions. For example, the quit probability in period $t$ is positively related to current price and negatively related to consumption in periods $t - 1$ and $t + 1$. However, it depends on where a person starts from and the magnitude of these changes in price and consumption.

Table 5.1 contains definitions, means, and standard deviations of the primary variables on the data set (see Appendix 5B for a detailed discussion of the data). All prices, taxes, and income measures were deflated to 1967 dollars with the consumer price index for all goods. State- and year-specific cigarette prices were obtained from the Tobacco Tax Council (1986). The consumption data were taken from the same source and pertain to per capita tax-paid cigarette sales (in packs). A number of studies have used these data to estimate cigarette demand functions. The most recent one, which contains a review of past research, is by Badi H. Baltagi and Dan Levin (1986). None of them contains the refined measures of

*Table 5.1*   Definitions, Means, and Standard Deviations (SD) of Variables

| Variable | Definition (mean, SD) |
| --- | --- |
| $C_t$ | Per capita cigarette consumption in packs in fiscal year $t$, as derived from state tax-paid sales (mean = 126.171, SD = 31.794) |
| $P_t$ | Average retail cigarette price per pack in January of fiscal year $t$ in 1967 cents (mean = 29.812, SD = 3.184) |
| income | Per capita income on a fiscal-year basis, in hundreds of 1967 dollars (mean = 31.439, SD = 8.092) |
| $\ell$dtax | Index which measures the incentives to smuggle cigarettes long distance from Kentucky, Virginia, or North Carolina. The index is positively related to the difference between the state's excise tax and the excise taxes of the exporting states (mean = 0.160, SD = 15.572) |
| sdtexp | Index which measures short-distance (export) smuggling incentives. The index is a weighted average of differences between the exporting state's excise tax and excise taxes of neighboring states, with weights based on border populations (mean = −0.828, SD = 1.847) |
| sdtimp | Index which measures short-distance (import) smuggling incentives in a state. Similar to sdtexp (mean = 0.494, SD = 0.792) |
| tax | Sum of state and local excise taxes on cigarettes in 1967 cents per pack (mean = 6.582, SD = 2.651) |

incentives for short- and long-distance smuggling of cigarettes across state lines that we employ (see below) or considers how addiction affects the estimates.

Cigarette sales are reported on the basis of a fiscal year running from July 1 through June 30. Therefore, real per capita income also is on a fiscal-year basis, and the retail price of a pack of cigarettes pertains to January of the year at issue. The price is given as a weighted-average price per pack, using national weights for type of cigarette (regular, king, 100-mm) and type of transaction (carton, single pack, machine). It is inclusive of federal, state, and municipal excise taxes and state sales taxes imposed on cigarettes.

There are 1,581 potential observations in the data set (50 states and the District of Columbia times 31 years). Missing sales and price data in nine states in certain years reduce the actual number of observations to 1,517. There are no gaps in the state-specific price and sales series. That is, if one of these variables is reported in year $t$, it is reported in all future years. Note that states are deleted *only* in years for which data are missing.

The existence of state excise taxes on cigarettes provides much of the empirical leverage required to estimate the parameters of cigarette demand. Cigarette tax rates vary greatly across states at a point in time and within a given state over time. For example, for the period of our sample, the average tax level (in 1967 dollars) is 6.4 cents per pack, or about 21 percent of the average retail price of 30 cents. The range of tax rates also is substantial. A rate one standard deviation above the mean is 6 cents higher than a rate one standard deviation below the mean. This difference is 20 percent of the average retail price. The variation in retail prices due to differences in taxes across states and over time within a state helps identify the impact of price changes on consumption.

The state and time-series data have several pitfalls. In particular, the diffusion of new information about the health hazards of smoking may have greatly affected smoking over the period of our sample. To incorporate such effects, we use time-specific dummy variables. Unfortunately, the coefficients of these time variables also contain the responses in aggregate consumption to national changes in the price of cigarettes.

In addition, states differ in demographic composition, income, and other variables that are correlated with smoking. Our estimates of price effects would be biased if these differences are also correlated with tax or price differentials across states. To mitigate this bias, we estimate all specifications with real per capita income and fixed state effects (dichotomous variables for each state except one).

The measure of cigarette smoking refers to per capita sales within states, which can differ from per capita consumption within states. When adjacent states have significantly different tax policies, there is an obvious incentive to smuggle cigarettes across states. We constructed three measures that attempt to correct for both short-distance and long-distance smuggling. The short-distance smuggling variables use tax differentials between surrounding states together with information on the proportion of individuals living within 20 miles of neighboring states that have lower cigarette tax rates (for imports) or higher tax rates (for exports). The long-distance smuggling measure uses the difference between a state's tax and the tax in each of the states of Kentucky, North Carolina, and Virginia. These three states account for almost all of the cigarettes produced in the United States, based on value added and had the three lowest excise tax rates in the country starting in fiscal 1967.

The demand function developed in Section 1 of this chapter is one that holds the marginal utility of wealth constant. In a model with perfect foresight, the marginal utility of wealth is fixed over time but varies among individuals and therefore among states. Thus, the state dummies capture this variation. The coefficients of the time dummies reflect in part the effects of unanticipated growth in wealth, which cause the marginal utility of wealth to change over time. We assume that deviations in real per capita income around state- and time-specific means follow a random walk, or more generally a first-order autoregressive process. In these cases unanticipated state-specific changes in real wealth over time, or deviations in real wealth from state- and time-specific means, are determined fully by deviations in real per capita income from state- and time-specific means. Put differently, with the state and time dummies held constant, the coefficient of real per capita income reflects forces associated with state-specific changes in the marginal utility of wealth over time.[2]

---

2. The coefficient of current price $(\theta_1)$ in equation (5.4) depends on the parameters of the utility function, the discount factor, and the marginal utility of wealth. Strictly speaking, price should be interacted with any variable that determines the marginal utility of wealth. Such an equation is not tractable from the standpoint of estimation due to its large set of regressors and potential for creating severe problems of multicollinearity. Our procedure, which captures variations in the marginal utility of wealth but not interactions between the determinants of this variable and price, may be viewed as a linear approximation to the true model. Essentially, we estimate the price coefficient associated with the marginal utility of wealth evaluated at its mean value. Technically, if the marginal utility of $C_t$ does not depend on $Y_t$, the only coefficient in equation (5.4) that depends on the marginal utility of wealth is the coefficient

## 4. Empirical Results

Our estimation strategy is to begin with the myopic model. We then test the myopic model by testing whether future prices are significant predictors of current consumption as they would be in the rational-addiction model, but not under the myopic framework. Since consumers base their current consumption decisions on expected future price under the rational-addiction framework, the actual future price suffers from the classical errors-in-variable problem in which the measurement error is uncorrelated with expected future price and all other variables in the equation. Under the null hypothesis of the myopic framework, our coefficient estimate is still unbiased and represents a valid test of the myopic model.

The first three columns of Table 5.2 contain two-stage least-squares (2SLS) estimates of myopic models of addiction, while the last column contains an ordinary least-squares (OLS) estimate. Past consumption is treated as an endogenous variable in the first three columns because of the high likelihood that the unobserved variables that affect current utility ($e_t$) are serially correlated.[3] The instruments used in column (i) consist of past price ($P_{t-1}$) plus the other explanatory variables in the model. Column (ii) adds the current and one-period lag values of the state cigarette tax to the instruments, and column (iii) further adds two additional lags of the price and tax variables. State excise taxes are used as instruments in

---

of current price. That coefficient equals $\lambda\alpha$, where $\alpha$ equals $1/(u_{11} + \beta u_{22})$. Suppressing subscripts and variables other than current price and the constant, this equation can be written as

$$C = \theta_0 + \alpha\lambda P$$

As an identity,

$$\lambda P = \overline{\lambda}\,\overline{P} + v\overline{\lambda} + w\overline{P} + vw$$

where a bar over a variable denotes a mean, $v$ equals the deviation of $P$ from its mean, and $w$ equals the deviation of $\lambda$ from its mean. If $vw$ approaches zero,

$$C = \theta_0 + \alpha\overline{\lambda}\,\overline{P} + \alpha\overline{\lambda}P + \alpha\overline{P}\lambda$$

3. In the rational-addiction model, $C_{t-1}$ depends on $e_t$ through the optimizing behavior implied by the first-order conditions. Therefore, past consumption must be treated as an endogenous variable in estimating this model even if $e_t$ is not serially correlated.

*Table 5.2*   Estimates of Myopic Models of Addiction, Dependent
Variable $= C_t$ (Asymptotic $t$ Statistics in Parentheses)

| Independent variable | 2SLS | | | OLS |
|---|---|---|---|---|
| | (i) | (ii) | (iii) | (iv) |
| $C_{t-1}$ | 0.478 | 0.502 | 0.602 | 0.755 |
| | (12.07) | (14.68) | (21.43) | (64.84) |
| $P_t$ | −1.603 | −1.538 | −1.269 | −0.860 |
| | (10.12) | (10.48) | (9.74) | (8.33) |
| $Y_t$ | 0.942 | 0.903 | 0.741 | 0.493 |
| | (7.61) | (7.71) | (6.96) | (5.44) |
| $\ell$ dtax | −0.240 | −0.233 | 0.212 | −0.160 |
| | (7.33) | (7.40) | (7.22) | (6.17) |
| sdtimp | −1.541 | −1.514 | −1.372 | −1.228 |
| | (5.04) | (5.09) | (4.97) | (4.84) |
| sdtexp | −3.659 | −3.544 | −3.059 | −2.328 |
| | (13.24) | (13.88) | (13.71) | (13.15) |
| $R^2$: | 0.969 | 0.970 | 0.976 | 0.979 |
| Wu $F$ ratio: | 84.76 | 94.42 | 41.61 | — |
| $N$: | 1,415 | 1,415 | 1,371 | 1,415 |

*Notes:* Intercepts are not shown. Regressors include state and year dummy variables. Columns (i)–(iii) give two-stage least squares (2SLS) estimates with $C_{t-1}$ treated as endogenous. Column (iv) gives an ordinary least-squares (OLS) estimate. The instruments in column (i) consist of the one-period lag of price plus the other explanatory variables in the model. Column (ii) adds the current and one-period lag values of the state cigarette tax to the instruments, and column (iii) further adds two additional lags of the price and tax variables. The Wu $F$ ratios pertain to tests of the hypothesis that the OLS models corresponding to the first three columns are consistent. They all are significant at the 1-percent level.

some of the models for reasons indicated below.[4] The table also contains $F$ ratios resulting from De-Min Wu's (1973) test of the hypothesis that OLS estimates are consistent. Since this hypothesis always is rejected, we stress the 2SLS results.

---

4. Since the regressions in Table 5.2 are reestimated after adding future price, models (i) and (ii) contain 1,415 (1,517−102) observations. Fewer than 51 observations are lost when the second lag of price is introduced, due to the pattern of missing price data. In particular, seven states have missing cigarette sales but known prices in certain years.

According to the parameter estimates of the myopic model presented in Table 5.2, cigarette smoking is inversely related to current price and positively related to income.[5] The highly significant effects of the smuggling variables ($\ell$dtax, sdimp, sdexp) indicate the importance of interstate smuggling of cigarettes. The positive and significant past-consumption coefficient is consistent with the hypothesis that cigarette smoking is an addictive behavior. The parameter estimates in the table are quite stable across the three alternative sets of instruments for past consumption.

When the one-period lead of price is added to the 2SLS models in Table 5.2, its coefficient is negative and significant at all conventional levels. The absolute $t$ ratio associated with the coefficient of this variable is 5.06 in model (i), 5.54 in model (ii), and 6.45 in model (iii). These results suggest that decisions about current consumption depend on future price. They are inconsistent with a myopic model of addiction, but consistent with a rational model of this behavior in which a reduction in expected future price raises expected future consumption, which in turn raises current consumption. While these tests soundly reject the myopic model, they do not provide definitive evidence in support of the rational-addiction model outlined above because they do not impose the constraint that the future-price effect works solely through future consumption. Nevertheless, they

---

5. The residuals from several of the models in Table 5.2 were examined for autocorrelation. The algorithm assumed a common time-series error structure among states, and no autocorrelations for lag lengths greater than 10. The first ten autocorrelation coefficients were obtained and were used to compute a variance-covariance matrix of regression coefficients (var) of the form

$$\text{var} = (\hat{Z}'\hat{Z})^{-1}\hat{Z}'V\hat{Z}(\hat{Z}'\hat{Z})^{-1}$$

where $V$ is the variance-covariance matrix of the disturbance term and

$$\hat{Z} = \begin{bmatrix} \hat{Y}X_1 \end{bmatrix}$$

The last equation specifies a matrix of the predicted values of the endogenous variables ($\hat{Y}$) and exogenous variables ($X_1$) in the structural demand function for current consumption. Standard errors of regression coefficients based on this algorithm (available from the authors upon request) were very similar to those that did not correct for autocorrelation. In most cases the corrected standard error was *smaller* than the corresponding uncorrected standard error. The same comment applies to the estimates in Tables 5.3 and 5.5. The regression residuals also were examined for cross-sectional heteroscedasticity due to averaging over an unequal number of people in each state. This analysis suggested that there were no efficiency gains to weighting by the square root of the state population.

suggest that consumers do consider future prices in their current consumption decisions and hence that it is worth trying to obtain structural estimates of rational-addiction demand functions.

Two strategies can be pursued in fitting the rational-addiction model. One is to use the actual future price as an instrument for future consumption. The problem with this strategy is that the forecast error in future price creates a downward bias in the coefficient of future consumption. The second strategy is to restrict the set of instruments to lagged values of prices and taxes. This is a common general strategy in estimating the effects of expected future variables.

There are two problems with the second strategy. First, consumers have a good deal of information concerning the state-specific future price of cigarettes, because this price depends to a large extent on the future state excise tax rate on cigarettes. Excise tax hikes are announced in advance and receive a good deal of publicity as a result of delays in the legislative process. Moreover, most states raise their excise tax rates in response to revenue shortfalls (see, e.g., Eugene E. Lewit, 1982). Hence, it is plausible that tax hikes are anticipated even before the corresponding bills are introduced in state legislatures. Phrased differently, if consumers have information concerning future prices and taxes, then one is losing valuable information by discarding these variables as instruments.

Second, past prices and taxes simply are not good predictors of the future price. Consider a regression of the future price on all the exogenous variables in the demand function, the one-period lag of the price, the one-period lag of the tax, and the current tax. At the 1-percent level, the last three variables are not significant as a set in the regression ($F = 3.0$, compared to a critical $F$ ratio of 3.8). Addition of a second lag of the price and the tax does not improve matters because the $F$ statistic falls to 2.0, compared to a critical $F$ of 3.0. Even these computed $F$ ratios are, however, biased upward because the real issue is whether past prices and taxes are significant predictors of future price net of their contribution to the prediction of past consumption. When predicted past consumption is added to the regressions just described, the $F$ statistics fall to 0.1 and 1.5, respectively.

Charles R. Nelson and Richard Startz (1990) have shown that the use of a poor instrument (an instrument that explains little of the variation in an endogenous right-hand-side variable) can produce a large bias in the estimated coefficient of the endogenous variable relative to its standard error. They state (p. S139), "In the context of estimating stochastic Euler equations, we would particularly caution against the use of lagged changes in consumption or lagged stock returns as instruments for current values."

In our case, this implies even more caution against the use of past prices as instruments for future consumption. Therefore, our preferred estimation strategy uses future price directly as a predictor of future consumption; but we present results both for this strategy and for the one that restricts the instruments to past prices and taxes.

Table 5.3 tests the rational-addiction model directly by estimating equation (5.4) with past and future consumption treated as endogenous

*Table 5.3*   Estimates of Rational Models of Addiction, Dependent Variable $= C_t$ (Asymptotic $t$ Statistics in Parentheses)

| Independent variable | 2SLS | | | | OLS |
|---|---|---|---|---|---|
| | (i) | (ii) | (iii) | (iv) | (v) |
| $C_{t-1}$ | 0.418 | 0.373 | 0.443 | 0.481 | 0.485 |
| | (8.88) | (9.18) | (11.72) | (14.58) | (36.92) |
| $C_{t+1}$ | 0.135 | 0.236 | 0.169 | 0.228 | 0.423 |
| | (2.45) | (5.04) | (3.79) | (5.87) | (28.61) |
| $P_t$ | −1.388 | −1.230 | −1.227 | −0.971 | −0.412 |
| | (8.94) | (9.11) | (9.11) | (8.36) | (4.98) |
| $Y_t$ | 0.837 | 0.761 | 0.746 | 0.608 | 0.302 |
| | (7.34) | (7.44) | (7.31) | (6.72) | (4.21) |
| $\ell$ dtax | −0.188 | −0.150 | −0.164 | −0.127 | −0.022 |
| | (5.42) | (4.82) | (5.30) | (4.50) | (1.05) |
| sdtimp | −1.358 | −1.222 | −1.266 | −1.090 | −0.748 |
| | (4.82) | (4.70) | (4.88) | (4.63) | (3.73) |
| sdtexp | −3.218 | −2.892 | −2.914 | −2.401 | −1.347 |
| | (11.37) | (11.84) | (11.96) | (11.58) | (9.39) |
| $R^2$: | 0.975 | 0.978 | 0.978 | 0.983 | 0.987 |
| Wu $F$ ratio: | 87.15 | 85.13 | 82.63 | 46.62 | — |
| $N$: | 1,415 | 1,415 | 1,415 | 1,371 | 1,415 |

*Notes:* Intercepts are not shown. Regressors include state and year dummy variables. Columns (i)–(iv) give two-stage least-squares (2SLS) estimates with $C_{t-1}$ and $C_{t+1}$ treated as endogenous. Column (v) gives an ordinary least-squares (OLS) estimate. The instruments in column (i) consist of the one-period lag and lead of price plus the other explanatory variables in the model. Column (ii) adds the current and one-period lag values of the state cigarette tax to the instruments; column (iii) further adds the one-period lead of the tax; and column (iv) further adds two additional lags of the price and tax variables. The Wu $F$ ratios pertain to tests of the hypothesis that the OLS models corresponding to the first four columns are consistent. They all are significant at the 1-percent level.

variables and with future prices included in the set of instruments. The instruments used in column (i) consist of past and future prices ($P_{t-1}$ and $P_{t+1}$, respectively) plus the other explanatory variables in the model. Column (ii) adds the current and one-period lag values of the state cigarette tax to the instruments, column (iii) further adds the one-period lead value of the tax, and column (iv) further adds two additional lags of the price and tax variables. As indicated above, state excise taxes are used as instruments in some of the models because consumers may have more knowledge about taxes, especially future taxes, than about future prices.[6] Column (v) presents an OLS estimate of the rational-addiction model. As in Table 5.2, the Wu test rejects the hypothesis that OLS coefficients are consistent.

The estimated effects of past and future consumption on current consumption are significantly positive in the four 2SLS models in Table 5.3, and the estimated price effects are significantly negative in all cases. The positive and significant past consumption coefficient is consistent with the hypothesis that cigarette smoking is an addictive behavior. The positive and significant future consumption coefficient (though downward-biased) is consistent with the hypothesis of rational addiction and inconsistent with the hypothesis of myopic addiction.

Table 5.4 uses the 2SLS estimates from Table 5.3 to compute the elasticity of cigarette consumption with respect to various price changes defined in Section 1 and Appendix 5A at the sample means of price and consumption. Estimates of the long-run response to a permanent change in price in the first row range from $-0.73$ to $-0.79$ (average equals $-0.75$) and are at the high end of those in the literature that omit past and future consumption from the demand function. More important are the significant cross price effects. A 10-percent unanticipated reduction in current price leads to an increase of between 1.4 percent and 1.6 percent in next period's consumption (see row 5, which assumes that the price change is not anticipated until the current period) and to a 0.5–0.8-percent increase in the previous period's consumption (see row 4, which assumes that the price change is not anticipated until the previous period).

These estimates imply that a 10-percent decline in cigarette prices causes a short-run increase in cigarette consumption of 4 percent (see row 6), which is only about 50 percent of the estimated long-run response of

---

6. Inclusion of the future price as well as the future tax allows for the possibility that consumers have additional information about the price exclusive of tax or about the relationship between the price inclusive of tax and the tax.

*Table 5.4*   Price Elasticities for Two-Stage Least-Squares Models
(Approximate *t* Statistics in Parentheses)

| Elasticity | (i) | (ii) | (iii) | (iv) |
|---|---|---|---|---|
| Long-run | −0.734 | −0.743 | −0.747 | −0.788 |
|  | (13.06) | (12.43) | (12.43) | (10.67) |
| Own price: |  |  |  |  |
|   Anticipated | −0.373 | −0.361 | −0.346 | −0.306 |
|  | (10.73) | (11.13) | (10.86) | (9.87) |
|   Unanticipated | −0.349 | −0.322 | −0.316 | −0.262 |
|  | (9.97) | (10.09) | (10.10) | (9.20) |
| Future price, | −0.050 | −0.084 | −0.058 | −0.068 |
|   unanticipated | (2.37) | (4.90) | (3.70) | (5.14) |
| Past price, | −0.155 | −0.133 | −0.152 | −0.144 |
|   unanticipated | (8.99) | (8.01) | (9.80) | (9.43) |
| Short-run | −0.407 | −0.436 | −0.387 | −0.355 |
|  | (9.34) | (9.51) | (9.69) | (8.80) |

7.5 percent. Finally, a 10-percent temporary increase in the current price of cigarettes would decrease current consumption by 3.5 percent if it is anticipated (see row 2) and by 3 percent if it is unanticipated (see row 3). Each of these responses is less than half of the long-run response of approximately 7.5 percent.

Clearly, the estimates indicate that cigarettes are addictive, that past and future changes significantly impact current consumption. This evidence is inconsistent with the hypothesis that cigarette consumers are myopic. Still, the estimates are not fully consistent with rational addiction, because the point estimates of the discount factor ($\beta$) are implausibly low: the ratio of the estimated coefficient of future consumption to the estimated coefficient of past consumption in the 2SLS models in Table 5.3 ranges from 0.31 to 0.64. These discount factors correspond to interest rates ranging from 56.3 percent to 222.6 percent. However, as we already indicated, uncertainty about future prices could account for the implausibly high interest rates implied by our estimates.

Although the OLS coefficients in column (v) of Table 5.3 are not consistent, they provide further support for the hypotheses that smoking is addictive (the coefficient of past consumption is positive and significant) and that consumers are rational (the coefficient of future consumption is positive, significant, and smaller than the coefficient of past consumption).

The long-run price elasticity in the OLS model is −1.06, and the short-run elasticity is −0.34. The implied discount factor of 0.87 (interest rate of 14.9 percent) is quite reasonable. We return to the issue of inferring the discount factor from the estimates at the end of this section.

Table 5.5 contains estimates of rational-addiction demand functions that exclude the one-period lead value of price and the one-period lead value of the excise tax from the set of instruments. Model (i) in Table 5.5 employs the exogenous variables in the demand function and the first and second lag of price as instruments. Like the first model in Table 5.3,

*Table 5.5*  Two-Stage Least-Squares Estimates of Rational-Addiction Models, Future Price and Tax Excluded from Set of Instruments, Dependent Variable = $C_t$ (Asymptotic $t$ Statistics in Parentheses)

| Independent variable | Model | | |
|---|---|---|---|
| | (i) | (ii) | (iv) |
| $C_{t-1}$ | −0.235 | 0.139 | 0.109 |
| | (1.03) | (2.25) | (1.69) |
| $C_{t+1}$ | 1.601 | 0.737 | 0.887 |
| | (3.75) | (6.62) | (8.55) |
| $P_t$ | 0.865 | −0.472 | −0.164 |
| | (1.39) | (2.33) | (0.89) |
| $Y_t$ | −0.217 | 0.397 | 0.258 |
| | (−0.67) | (3.19) | (2.14) |
| $\ell$ dtax | 0.393 | 0.038 | 0.115 |
| | (2.30) | (0.77) | (2.39) |
| sdtimp | 0.630 | −0.559 | −0.297 |
| | (0.86) | (1.94) | (0.98) |
| sdtexp | 1.571 | 1.325 | −0.631 |
| | (1.20) | (3.33) | (1.75) |
| $R^2$: | 0.926 | 0.979 | 0.976 |
| Wu $F$ ratio: | 39.35 | 51.85 | 42.36 |
| $N$: | 1,371 | 1,415 | 1,371 |

*Notes:* Intercepts are not shown. Regressors include state and year dummy variables. $C_{t-1}$ and $C_{t+1}$ are treated as endogenous. The instruments in model (i) consist of the first and second lag of price plus the other explanatory variables in the model. Model (ii) adds the current and one-period lag values of the state cigarette tax to the instruments and deletes the second lag of price, and model (iv) further adds two additional lags of the price and tax variables. The Wu $F$ ratios pertain to tests of the hypothesis that the OLS estimates corresponding to the first three columns are consistent. They all are significant at the 1-percent level.

it is exactly identified. The last two models in Table 5.5 correspond to models (ii) and (iv) in Table 5.3 after future variables are deleted from the instruments. The last model in Table 5.5 is labeled model (iv) because it corresponds to model (iv) in Table 5.3.[7] As in Table 5.3, the Wu test rejects the hypothesis that OLS yields consistent estimates.[8]

The coefficients in Table 5.5 are very different from those in Table 5.3. The current-price and lagged-consumption coefficients fall dramatically, and the future-consumption coefficients rise dramatically (as Nelson and Startz, 1990, would predict) when future variables are not used as instruments. The estimates in Table 5.5 still offer some support for the rational-addiction model, because the coefficient of future consumption is positive and significant. But the point estimates of the discount factor now are too high rather than too low: 5.30 in model (ii) and 8.14 in model (iv).[9] These discount factors correspond to negative interest rates of $-81$ percent and $-88$ percent, respectively.

The results in Table 5.5 are less supportive of the rational and myopic addiction models than are the results in Table 5.3. First, the implied discount factors in Table 5.5 are less plausible than those in Table 5.3. Second, the price coefficient in the first model in Table 5.5 is positive, and the corresponding coefficient in the third model, while negative, is not significant. Third, the estimate of the degree of addiction ($\theta$), which is given by the coefficient of past consumption, in the second model in Table 5.5, is approximately one-third as large as the estimates of this parameter in Table 5.3. As a result, the short-run price elasticity of $-0.76$ in the second model in Table 5.5 is only 15-percent smaller than the long-run price elasticity of $-0.90$, while the short-run price elasticity is 50-percent smaller than the long-run price elasticity in all the models in Table 5.3. Finally, the estimates in Table 5.3 are much more stable across alternative sets of instruments than those in Table 5.5.

One way to choose between the estimates in Tables 5.3 and 5.5 is to perform Hausman tests (Jerry A. Hausman, 1978) of the hypothesis that future prices and taxes are legitimate estimates. Under the null hypothesis of perfect foresight (no measurement error in future prices), the estimates

---

7. Models (ii) and (iii) in Table 5.3 are the same when future variables are deleted from the instruments.

8. An OLS demand function is not presented in Table 5.5 because it is identical to the one in Table 5.3.

9. We do not compute the discount factor in model (i) because the coefficient of past consumption has the wrong sign.

in both tables are consistent, but those in Table 5.3 are more efficient. Under the alternative hypothesis of measurement error in future prices, only the estimates in Table 5.5 are consistent. Therefore, Hausman's procedure amounts to a Wald test of the hypothesis that the coefficients in the second model in Table 5.5 are the same as the coefficients in the second or third model in Table 5.3, and that the coefficients in the third model in Table 5.5 are the same as those in the corresponding model in Table 5.3.

The computed $\chi^2$ statistics associated with these three tests are 24.4, 48.9, and 56.2, respectively. The first test has one degree of freedom since one instrument is excluded when future price is deleted. The second and third tests have two degrees of freedom since two instruments are excluded when the future price and the future tax are deleted. At the 1-percent level, the critical value of $\chi^2$ is 6.6 in the first test and 9.2 in the second and third tests. Since the computed $\chi^2$ always greatly exceeds the critical value, the hypothesis that future values are legitimate instruments is rejected by this test given the maintained hypothesis that the past variables themselves are excluded from the demand equation.

However, before too much weight is placed on this rejection, one should recall the problems associated with the estimates in Table 5.5 that are not taken into account by the Hausman test. In particular, by limiting the set of instruments to poor predictors of future price and, therefore, to poor predictors of future consumption, it becomes difficult to sort out the past and future consumption effects. This is reflected in part by the dramatic increase in the standard errors of the past- and future-consumption coefficients, suggesting that the degree of multicollinearity rises when the future price and tax are not employed as instruments.

Therefore, it is useful to look at other ways to choose between the estimates in Tables 5.3 and 5.5. One way is to examine what happens if the true structural demand function was slightly different. Suppose that the second lag of consumption belongs in the true model with a coefficient of 0.1 or 0.2. When the first model in Table 5.3 is reestimated with either of these constraints imposed, the coefficient of future consumption remains unchanged at 0.14.[10] When the first model in Table 5.5 is reestimated with a constraint of 0.1 on the second lag of consumption, the coefficient of future consumption falls from 1.60 to 1.26. This coefficient drops even further to 0.88 when a constraint of 0.2 is used.

---

10. The coefficient in Table 5.3 is 0.135. The same coefficient is 0.139 in a model that omits the second lag of consumption but is estimated on the reduced sample that results when the constraint is imposed.

Similar results emerge with model (iv) in Tables 5.3 and 5.5. Since these models are overidentified, they can be estimated by including the second lag of consumption as an endogenous right-hand-side variable with no constraint imposed on its coefficient. When model (iv) in Table 5.3 is fit in this fashion, the coefficient of future consumption falls slightly from 0.23 to 0.20. With an imposed constraint of 0.1, this coefficient equals 0.22, and with a constraint of 0.2, it equals 0.21. The same exercises applied to model (iv) in Table 5.5 result in future consumption coefficients of 0.72, 0.80, and 0.72, respectively. These values should be compared to the coefficient of 0.89 in the table.

Although we have only considered the effect on the future-consumption coefficient, the results are similar when variations in the current-price coefficient are examined. In each case, models that use future prices and future taxes as instruments are much less sensitive to changes in the specification of the structural demand function than those that exclude these instruments. This is not surprising since the future-price variable provides variation that is correlated with future consumption and not highly correlated with potentially omitted past price and consumption variables.

A final way to choose between the estimates in Tables 5.3 and 5.5 is to simulate the impact of overstating the covariance between expected future price and expected future consumption. Consider the exactly identified model estimated in the first column in Table 5.3. Let $c$ be current consumption, $f$ be expected future consumption, $\ell$ be the first lag of consumption, $p$ be expected future price, $z$ be past price, and $\sigma_{ij}$ be the covariance between any two of these variables net of all other variables in the demand function (current price, income, the three smuggling measures, and the state and time dummies).[11] If $f$ and $p$ were observed, the two-stage least-squares coefficients of future consumption ($\theta_f$) and past consumption ($\theta_\ell$) would be

$$(5.6) \qquad \theta_f = (\sigma_{cp}\sigma_{\ell z} - \sigma_{\ell p}\sigma_{cz})/(\sigma_{fp}\sigma_{\ell z} - \sigma_{\ell p}\sigma_{fz})$$

$$(5.7) \qquad \theta_\ell = (\sigma_{cz}\sigma_{fp} - \sigma_{fz}\sigma_{cp})/(\sigma_{fp}\sigma_{\ell z} - \sigma_{\ell p}\sigma_{fz})$$

Let $\pi$ be actual future price and let $a$ be actual future consumption. Note that $\pi = p + u$ and $a = f + \varepsilon$, where the forecast error in future consumption ($\varepsilon$) is negatively related to the forecast error in future price ($u$). Since

---

11. That is, $c$, $f$, $\ell$, $p$, and $z$ are residuals from, for example, a regression of actual current consumption on the exogenous variables in the demand function.

$u$ is uncorrelated with current or past variables, the only covariance that is affected when $\pi$ replaces $p$ and $a$ replaces $f$ is that between $\pi$ and $a$. In particular,

(5.8) $$\sigma_{fp} = k\sigma_{a\pi} \quad k = [1 - (\sigma_{\varepsilon u}/\sigma_{a\pi})]$$

Presumably, $k$ is less than 1. Therefore, if $\sigma_{a\pi}$ rather than $\sigma_{fp}$ is used in equations (5.10) and (5.11), the coefficient of future consumption and the ratio of the coefficient of future consumption to the coefficient of past consumption are understated.

Table 5.6 presents estimates of $\theta_f$, $\theta_\ell$, and the ratio of the long-run price elasticity to the short-run price elasticity for alternative assumed values of $k$. As long as $k$ is at least as large as 0.75 (the forecast error covariance is no larger than 25 percent of the total covariance), the true estimates are similar to those in the first column of the Table 5.3. These latter estimates assume that $k = 1$, or that the forecast error covariance is zero. Not surprisingly, if one attempts to reconcile the large divergence between the estimates in Tables 5.3 and 5.5 based only on imperfect information concerning future prices, it is necessary to assume that the forecast error covariance is extremely (and in our view unreasonably) large. We have already pointed out a better way to reconcile these estimates. This is to use the empirical fact that past prices and taxes are poor predictors of future prices and relatively good predictors of potentially omitted past effects. This makes these variables poor predictors of future consumption.

*Table 5.6*  Future Consumption Coefficient ($\theta_f$), Past Consumption Coefficient ($\theta_\ell$), and Ratio of Long-Run to Short-Run Price Elasticity, Corrected for Forecast Error

| $k$ | $\theta_f$ | $\theta_\ell$ | Ratio of long-run to short-run price elasticity |
|---|---|---|---|
| 1.000 | 0.135 | 0.418 | 1.803 |
| 0.750 | 0.179 | 0.399 | 1.762 |
| 0.500 | 0.268 | 0.360 | 1.676 |
| 0.400 | 0.336 | 0.330 | 1.608 |
| 0.333 | 0.407 | 0.299 | 1.535 |

*Notes:* In the first column, $k$ is the ratio of the partial covariance between expected future consumption and expected future price to the partial covariance between actual future consumption and actual future price, with current price, income, the three smuggling measures, and the state and time dummies held constant.

The conclusions to be drawn from these tests of the estimates in Tables 5.3 and 5.5 depend on one's priors. If one believes that the structural demand function is correctly specified, and that the errors in forecasting future cigarette prices are enormous, then the estimates in Table 5.5 are preferable. However, if one believes that the structural demand function is misspecified—if only slightly—and that consumers do have relevant information to forecast future cigarette prices, then the estimates in Table 5.3 are clearly preferable. For the reasons already given, we prefer the second interpretation, which is supportive of the rational-addiction model. It should be noted that none of the models in either table supports the myopic-addiction model. In fact the results in Table 5.5 reject the rational model because they imply that consumers put *too much* weight on future consumption.

Even if the rational-addiction model is accepted, it is not possible to infer the discount rate reliably from these cigarette data. One approach is simply to impose the discount factor a priori. We do this in Table 5.7, by imposing six alternative discount factors ranging from 0.70 to 0.95 (interest rates ranging from 5.3 percent to 42.9 percent) in estimating models (ii) and (iv). That is, we constrain the coefficient of future consumption to equal $\beta$ multiplied by the estimated coefficient of past consumption. We impose this constraint both in the specifications that include the future price and the future tax as instruments, and in the specifications that exclude these variables as instruments.

The table presents price coefficients, past-consumption coefficients, long-run price elasticities, and short-run price elasticities that emerge from the restricted estimates. The marginal significance level of the restriction, based on a Lagrange multiplier (LM) test, also is indicated. Regardless of the discount factor imposed, the long-run price elasticities are very similar to each other and to those in Table 5.4. The same comment applies to the short-run price elasticities. Moreover, the specifications that employ the future price and the future tax as instruments yield elasticities that are almost identical to those that exclude these two instruments.[12]

---

12. When future variables are used as instruments, the restriction is not significant (the imposed discount factor is valid) at the 1-percent level in eight out of 12 cases, and it is not significant at the 5-percent level in seven out of 12 cases. On the other hand, when future variables are not used as instruments, the restriction is significant in every case at any conventional level of confidence. These results are to be expected since the estimates in Table 5.5 imply discount factors that exceed 1.

Discount factors of 0.85 and 0.90 are very similar to the discount factor of 0.87 implied by the OLS regression in Table 5.5. Yet the application of the Wu test to the constrained estimates in Table 5.7 that impose these discount factors rejects the hypothesis that OLS is consistent. When the imposed discount factor is 0.85, the $F$ ratios in panel A are 167.5 in model (ii) and 77.8 in model (iv). The corresponding $F$ ratios in panel B are 72.3 and 27.7. When the imposed discount factor in 0.90, the $F$ ratios in panel A are 167.5 in model (ii) and 78.0 in model (iv). The corresponding $F$ ratios in panel B are 68.0 and 25.2. All are significant at the 1-percent level. The eight models in Table 5.7 with discount factors of 0.85 and 0.90 imply an average long-run price elasticity of $-0.78$ and an average short-run price elasticity of $-0.44$. We are more confident in these estimates than in the long-run elasticity of $-1.06$ and the short-run elasticity of $-0.34$ associated with the OLS regression in Table 5.3.

The results in Tables 5.3, 5.5, and 5.7 suggest that the data are not rich enough to pin down the discount factor with precision. This is not surprising. Estimates of consumer discount factors from studies of aggregate consumption, the consumption of specific goods, or the consumption of leisure over time vary considerably. Some of these estimates imply extremely high interest rates, while others imply very low and even negative interest rates (e.g., Lars Peter Hansen and Kenneth J. Singleton, 1983; N. Gregory Mankiw et al., 1985; V. Joseph Hotz et al., 1988; Olympia Bover, 1991; Larry G. Epstein and Stanley E. Zin, 1991). Nevertheless, it is reassuring that our estimates of the basic parameters of the model are not sensitive to the choice of alternative discount factors. Moreover, in the specifications with the future price and tax as instruments, we cannot reject the hypothesis (at the 1-percent level) that the discount factor is as high as 0.90 or 0.95 in two of four cases. Finally, when we compensate for the narrow set of instruments that results from the deletion of future variables by imposing a discount factor, the estimates of short-run and long-run price elasticities are not sensitive to the instruments used to obtain them.

Frank Chaloupka (1991) provides further evidence in support of a model of cigarette addiction in a micro data set: the second National Health and Nutrition Examination Survey. Using measures of cigarette consumption in three adjacent periods, he fits demand functions similar to those in Table 5.3. He finds a short-run price elasticity ($-0.20$) that is less than half of the long-run price elasticity of $-0.45$. His significant future-consumption coefficient is further evidence against myopic addiction.

Table 5.7 Current Price Coefficients, Lagged Consumption Coefficients, Long-Run Price Elasticities, and Short-Run Price Elasticities in Restricted Models

| | | Panel A: Future price or future price and future tax included as instruments | | | | | Panel B: No future variables included as instruments | | | | |
|---|---|---|---|---|---|---|---|---|---|---|---|
| $\beta$ | Model | Marginal significance level of restriction | $P_t$ | $C_{t-1}$ | Long-run price elasticity | Short-run price elasticity | Marginal significance level of restriction | $P_t$ | $C_{t-1}$ | Long-run price elasticity | Short-run price elasticity |
| 0.70 | (ii) | 0.727 | -1.220 | 0.360 | -0.742 | -0.445 | 0.000 | -1.105 | 0.385 | -0.755 | -0.426 |
| | (iv) | 0.054 | -0.925 | 0.426 | -0.792 | -0.395 | 0.000 | -0.822 | 0.449 | -0.820 | -0.376 |
| 0.75 | (ii) | 0.548 | -1.214 | 0.351 | -0.743 | -0.452 | 0.000 | -1.084 | 0.378 | -0.756 | -0.430 |
| | (iv) | 0.021 | -0.919 | 0.415 | -0.792 | -0.404 | 0.000 | -0.803 | 0.440 | -0.824 | -0.384 |
| 0.80 | (ii) | 0.400 | -1.208 | 0.342 | -0.742 | -0.458 | 0.000 | -1.063 | 0.372 | -0.759 | -0.436 |
| | (iv) | 0.008 | -0.913 | 0.404 | -0.790 | -0.413 | 0.000 | -0.781 | 0.432 | -0.829 | -0.391 |
| 0.85 | (ii) | 0.285 | -1.203 | 0.334 | -0.743 | -0.465 | 0.000 | -1.044 | 0.366 | -0.763 | -0.442 |
| | (iv) | 0.003 | -0.908 | 0.394 | -0.791 | -0.421 | 0.000 | -0.761 | 0.424 | -0.833 | -0.398 |
| 0.90 | (ii) | 0.199 | -1.199 | 0.326 | -0.743 | -0.472 | 0.000 | -1.025 | 0.359 | -0.761 | -0.446 |
| | (iv) | 0.001 | -0.904 | 0.385 | -0.795 | -0.431 | 0.000 | -0.743 | 0.416 | -0.837 | -0.405 |
| 0.95 | (ii) | 0.136 | -1.196 | 0.318 | -0.743 | -0.478 | 0.000 | -1.007 | 0.353 | -0.763 | -0.451 |
| | (iv) | 0.000 | -0.901 | 0.375 | -0.791 | -0.439 | 0.000 | -0.725 | 0.409 | -0.845 | -0.414 |

Notes: All price and lagged consumption coefficients and all elasticities are statistically significant at all conventional levels of confidence. For panel A, the instruments in model (ii) are the one-period lag of price, the one-period lead of price, the current state excise tax, the one-period lag of the tax, and the exogenous variables in the demand function. Model (iv) adds the one-period lead of the tax and the two-period lags of the tax and price to the set of instruments. For panel B, the instruments in model (ii) are the one-period lag of price, the current tax, the one-period lag of the tax, and the exogenous variables in the demand function. Model (iv) adds the two-period lags of the tax and price to the set of instruments. The marginal significance levels of the restrictions are based on a Lagrange multiplier (LM) test.

## 5. Monopoly and Addiction

The organization of the cigarette industry has been studied frequently and shown to be highly concentrated (Joe S. Bain, 1968; Daniel A. Sumner, 1981; Elie Appelbaum, 1982; Paul A. Geroski, 1983; Robert H. Porter, 1986). Two companies (R. J. Reynolds and Philip Morris) account for about 70 percent of U.S. output, and the studies just cited conclude in general that cigarette companies have significant monopoly power. Discussions of pricing by cigarette companies have not paid attention to the habitual aspects of cigarette smoking, even though that greatly affects optimal monopoly pricing and other company policies.

To illustrate the relation between pricing and addiction, elsewhere we develop a simple monopoly pricing model (see Becker et al., 1990; also see the extensions of our analyses by Gary Fethke and Raj Jagannathan, 1991, and by Mark H. Showalter, 1991). The main implications are quite intuitive. In each period a monopolist sets a price where marginal revenue is below marginal cost, as long as consumption is addictive and future prices tend to exceed future marginal costs due to the monopoly power. The reason is that future profits are higher when current consumption is larger and current price is lower, because greater current consumption raises future consumption. As it were, a monopolist may lower price to get more consumers "hooked" on the addictive good. The optimal marginal revenue is lower relative to marginal cost when the good is more addictive, future demand is stronger, and future price minus cost is bigger. With a sufficiently large positive effect on future demand of a lower current price, a monopolist might choose a current price that is below current cost, or a price in the inelastic region of demand.

This analysis which incorporates addiction into pricing policy may be helpful in understanding the rise in cigarette prices in recent years. Much of the drop in demand for cigarettes since 1981 documented by Jeffrey E. Harris (1987) and others is due to greater information about health hazards, restrictions imposed on smoking in public places, and the banning of cigarette advertising on radio and television. Several studies have commented about the apparent paradox that cigarette companies have been posting big profits while smoking is declining and have documented the faster rise in cigarette prices than in apparent costs (see Harris, 1987; Amy Dunkin et al., 1988). Indeed, according to Stephen J. Adler and Alix M. Freedman (1990, p. 1), "One of the great magic tricks of market economics . . . [is] how to force prices up and increase profits in an industry in which demand falls by tens of billions of cigarettes each year."

Incorporation of the addictive aspects of smoking into the analysis resolves this paradox if cigarette companies have some monopoly power. An increase in current prices would raise cigarette companies' profits in the short run if they were pricing below the current profit-maximizing point (in order to raise future demand through the addictive effect of greater current smoking). Addictive behavior can also explain why current prices rise: the decline in future demand for smoking reduces the gains from maintaining a lower price to stimulate future consumption.

Incorporation of the addictive aspects of smoking also leads to a test of whether the cigarette industry is oligopolistic or competitive. If smokers are addicted and if the industry is oligopolistic, an expected rise in future taxes and hence in future prices induces a rise in current prices even though current demand falls when future prices are expected to increase. This cannot happen in simple models of competitive behavior.

A higher federal excise tax on cigarettes was widely expected to go into effect at the beginning of 1983—an example of an instance where consumers had prior information about future tax increases. Cigarette prices increased sharply not only in 1983, but also prior to the tax increase during 1982. The price increase in 1982 has been taken as evidence that "the tax increase served as a focal point [or coordinating device] for an oligopolistic price increase" (Harris, 1987, p. 101). That is possible, but a price increase in 1982 may have occurred even if oligopolistic cigarette producers had no such coordinating problems, because the higher future cigarette tax reduced future demand and, hence, the gain from lowering current price.

## Appendix 5A: Solution of Difference Equation and Price Effects

The solution of the difference equation (5.4) is

$$C_t = \frac{1}{\theta\phi_1[\phi_2 - \phi_1]} \sum_{s=1}^{\infty} \phi_1^s h(t + s)$$

(5.A1)
$$+ \frac{1}{\theta\phi_2[\phi_2 - \phi_1]} \sum_{s=0}^{\infty} \phi_2^{-s} h(t - s)$$

$$+ \frac{1}{\phi_2^t}\left( C^0 - \frac{1}{\theta\phi_1[\phi_2 - \phi_1]} \sum_{s=1}^{\infty} \phi_1^s h(s)\right)$$

where

$$h(t) = \theta_0 + \theta_1 P_{t-1} + \theta_2 e_{t-1} + \theta_3 e_t$$

$$\phi_1 = \frac{1 - (1 - 4\theta^2\beta)^{1/2}}{2\theta}$$

$$\phi_2 = \frac{1 + (1 - 4\theta^2\beta)^{1/2}}{2\theta}$$

with $4\theta^2\beta < 1$ for stability.

Equation (5.A1) determines the sign of the effects of changes in the price of cigarettes in period $\tau$ on cigarette consumption in period $t$. These effects, which are temporary in nature since prices in other periods are held constant, are

(5.A2a)
$$\left.\frac{dC_t}{dP_\tau}\right|_{\tau > t} = \frac{\theta_1 \phi_1^{\tau-t}}{\theta[\phi_2 - \phi_1]}\left[1 - \left(\frac{\phi_1}{\phi_2}\right)^t\right] \lessgtr 0 \text{ as } \theta \gtrless 0$$

(5.A2b)
$$\left.\frac{dC_t}{dP_\tau}\right|_{\tau < t} = \frac{\theta_1 \phi_2^{\tau-t}}{\theta[\phi_2 - \phi_1]}\left[1 - \left(\frac{\phi_1}{\phi_2}\right)^\tau\right] \lessgtr 0 \text{ as } \theta \gtrless 0$$

(5.A2c)
$$\frac{dC_t}{dP_t} = \frac{\theta_1}{\theta[\phi_2 - \phi_1]}\left[1 - \left(\frac{\phi_1}{\phi_2}\right)^t\right] < 0$$

To obtain the completely unanticipated price effect, set $t$ or $\tau$ on the right-hand side of equation (5.A2) equal to 1. To obtain the fully anticipated price effect, let $t$ or $\tau$ approach infinity.

The effect on consumption in period $t$ of a permanent reduction in price beginning in period $t$, which we denote as $dC_t/dP_t^*$, is given by

(5.A3)
$$\frac{dC_t}{dP_t^*} = \frac{\theta_1\left[1 - (\phi_1/\phi_2)^t\right]}{\theta\left(1 - \phi_1\right)\left(\phi_2 - \phi_1\right)}$$

With $t$ equal to 1, the equation gives the effect on current consumption of a completely unanticipated permanent reduction in price. This effect is

(5.A4)
$$\frac{dC_t}{dP_t^*} = \frac{\theta_1}{\theta\left(1 - \phi_1\right)\phi_2}$$

Equation (5.A4) shows the short-run price effect, defined as the impact on consumption of a reduction in current price and all future prices, with past consumption held constant.

Finally, the effect of a permanent reduction in price in *all* periods on consumption in period $t$ is

$$(5.A5) \qquad \frac{dC_t}{dP} = \frac{\theta_1 \phi_2^{-t}}{\theta(\phi_2 - \phi_1)} \times \left[ \frac{\phi_2^t}{\phi_2 - 1} - \frac{1 - \phi_1^t}{1 - \phi_1} \right] + \frac{\theta_1 \left[ 1 - (\phi_1/\phi_2)^t \right]}{\theta(1 - \phi_1)(\phi_2 - \phi_1)}$$

The limit of equation (5.A5) as $t$ goes to infinity equals the long-run effect of a permanent reduction in price:

$$(5.A6) \qquad \frac{dC_\infty}{dP} = \frac{\theta_1}{\theta(1 - \phi_1)(\phi_2 - 1)}$$

## Appendix 5B: Data

Cigarette sales were missing for nine states in the years specified below:

> Alaska, 1955–1959
> Hawaii, 1955–1960
> California, 1955–1959
> Colorado, 1955–1964
> Maryland, 1955–1958
> Missouri, 1955
> North Carolina, 1955–1969
> Oregon, 1955–1966
> Virginia, 1955–1960.

The price of cigarettes was missing for Alaska and Hawaii in each year in which sales were missing. In addition, price was not reported for the former state in 1960 and for the latter state in 1961.

The state excise tax on a pack of cigarettes is a weighted average of the tax rates in effect during the fiscal year, where the weights are the fraction of the year each rate was in effect. The Tobacco Tax Council gives the price of cigarettes as of November. The price used in our regressions in fiscal year $t$ equals five-sixths of the price in November of year $t - 1$ plus one-sixth of the price in November of year $t$, adjusted for changes in the state excise tax rate during the fiscal year. In particular, the state excise tax as of the date of the price was subtracted from the price; the average price exclusive of tax was computed from the preceding formula; and the average excise tax was added back to the price. The algorithm was modified in certain years in which price was reported in October. The price variable published by the Tobacco Tax Council (1986) excludes municipal excise taxes imposed on cigarettes by one or more municipalities in certain states. We created a state-specific average municipal excise tax rate (the sum of revenues from municipal cigarette excise taxes for the state as reported by the Tobacco Tax Council [various years] divided by state cigarette sales in packs) and added this variable to the price. Note that the state excise tax rate defined in Table 5.1 and used as an instrumental variable for past and future consumption in Tables 5.2, 5.3, 5.5, and 5.7 is inclusive of the average municipal excise tax rate.

In every state except Hawaii and New Hampshire, the excise tax on cigarettes was a specific tax (fixed amount per pack) during our sample period. In Hawaii the tax was 40 percent of the wholesale price throughout the period. In New Hampshire the tax was 42 percent of retail price until fiscal 1976. Equivalent taxes per pack in these two states were computed by the Tobacco Tax Council.

Short-distance smuggling or casual bootlegging refers to out-of-state purchases by residents of a neighboring state with a higher excise tax. The short-distance importing and exporting incentive measures are used as separate regressors because consumption in an importing state (defined as sales plus imports) depends on the difference between the own state and the out-of-state price or tax. Consumption in an exporting state does not depend on this difference. Of course, both imports and exports respond to the tax difference. Long-distance smuggling or organized bootlegging refers to systematic attempts to ship cigarettes from North Carolina, Virginia, or Kentucky to other states. These cigarettes are sold at the retail prices prevailing in the relevant states without paying the excise tax, which is imposed at the wholesale level. Consumption in the importing state does not depend on the difference between that state's tax and the tax in North Carolina, Virginia, or Kentucky. Hence, long-distance importing and exporting incentives can be summarized by a single variable since imports summed over all states in a given year must equal exports summed over all states in that year. Given the definitions of the three smuggling variables in Table 5.1, their regression coefficients all should be negative.

The effects of short-distance casual smuggling are measured by two variables: one for imports and one for exports. The importing variable is

$$\text{sdtimp}_i = \sum_j k_{ij}(T_i - T_j)$$

where $k_{ij}$ is the fraction of the population of state $i$ (the higher-tax state) living within 20 miles of state $j$ (the lower-tax state), and $T_i$ and $T_j$ are the cigarette excise tax rates in each state. The weights are computed from the 1970 Census of Population (United States Bureau of the Census, 1973), and the summation is taken over neighboring states with lower tax rates. This is equivalent to setting the tax differential equal to zero if $T_i \leq T_j$. The exporting variable is given by

$$\text{sdtexp}_i = \sum_j k_{ji}(T_i - T_j)(\text{POP}_j/\text{POP}_i)$$

where $k_{ji}$ is the fraction of the higher-taxed state's population living within 20 miles of the exporting state (state $i$) and $\text{POP}_j$ denotes the population of state $j$. Here the summation is taken over neighboring states with higher tax rates. This is equivalent to setting the tax differential equal to zero if $T_i \geq T_j$. The reason that the population ratio is used in the export variable is that *total* exports from state $i$ to state $j$ should depend on the part of the population of state $j$ living near state $i$ or $\text{POP}_j$ multiplied by $k_{ji}$. Since the dependent variable in the regression model is state-specific per capita sales, the population of state $i$ enters the denominator.

The tax differentials in the preceding formulas include or exclude municipal excise taxes depending on the border area at issue. The population figures are year-specific. They were taken from the 1960, 1970, and 1980 Censuses of Population for census years and from the United States Bureau of the Census (1985) for other years (see the reference just cited for the complete list of sources). For noncensus years, the population was given as of July 1, and for census years, it was given as of April 1. The latter was interpolated to July 1 using state-specific exponential-growth trends between, for example, April 1, 1980, and July 1, 1981. Then population in fiscal year $t$ was defined as a simple average of population as of July 1 in years $t - 1$ and $t$.

The construction of the long-distance smuggling variable is based on several assumptions. It is assumed that Virginia and North Carolina share the long-distance exporting to all states in the Northeast and Southeast as well as any state within 500 miles of either. All Western states within 1,000 miles of Kentucky are assumed to import from Kentucky. States more than 1,000 miles from Kentucky, Virginia, or North Carolina are assumed to do no long-distance smuggling. The long-distance smuggling variable based on these assumptions is given by

$\ell\text{dtax}_i = (T_i - T_{KY})$ if importing from KY

$$= z_{NC}(T_i - T_{NC}) + z_{VA}(T_i - T_{VA}) \quad \text{if importing from NC and VA}$$

$$= \sum_j (T_{KY} - T_i)(POP_j/POP_{KY}) \quad \text{for KY}$$

$$= z_i \left[ \sum_j (T_i - T_j)(POP_j/POP_i) \right] \quad \text{for } i = \text{NC, VA}$$

The weights used for states that import from North Carolina and Virginia are the shares of value added accounted for by each in the production of cigarettes in these two states combined. That is,

$$z_{NC} = \frac{\text{(value added in NC)}}{\text{(value added in NC + value added in VA)}}$$

Note that total imports from Kentucky, North Carolina, or Virginia to state $i$ depend on population of $i$, which cancels when imports are expressed on a per capita basis. If state $i$'s excise tax was lower than the exporting state's excise tax, which occurred in a few states prior to fiscal 1967, the tax difference was set equal to zero.

State-specific money-per-capita income in fiscal year $t$ is a simple average of money-per-capita income in calendar years $t - 1$ and $t$. The consumer price index in fiscal year $t$, which is not state-specific, is defined in a similar manner. Per capita income by state was taken from the United States Bureau of Economic Analysis (various years).

# Habits, Addictions, and Traditions

6

## 1. Introduction

The usual assumption in most discussions of behavior over time is that choices today are not directly dependent on choices in the past. J. R. Hicks expressed strong disapproval of this assumption: "It is nonsense that successive consumptions are independent; the normal condition is that there is a strong complementarity between them" (1965, p. 261). It is ironic that this sentence comes at the end of a rather lengthy monograph on economic growth that relies throughout on the independence assumption.

The assumption of independence is not "nonsense," for it usefully simplifies many problems that are not crucially affected by dependence over time. But the assumption has discouraged economists from grappling with other issues of considerable significance—including addictions, work habits, preference formation, why children support their elderly parents, preference solutions to the problem of future commitments, and the evolution and stability of institutions. These are the kinds of questions I address in this chapter.

A growing literature during the past two decades has assumed instead of independence that current consumption is affected by past consumption. The most influential work has been by Boyer (1978), Houthakker and Taylor (1966), Kydland and Prescott (1982), Phlips (1974), Pollak (1970), Ryder and Heal (1973), Spinnewyn (1981), von Weizsäcker (1971), and various colleagues and students at Chicago: Iannoccone, Murphy, Hansen, Stigler, Constantinides, Heaton, and Hotz. I will not try to

Originally published in *Kyklos*, 45, no. 3 (1992): 327–345.

review, summarize, or reference these contributions, but will concentrate on the issues that have interested me.

## 2. Habits

Some influences of past consumption on present behavior are obvious. If I just ate a filling dinner, I do not want to eat another dinner in the near future—not even a Persian delight cooked by my wife. Essentially all goods are substitutes if the time intervals are sufficiently close and the quantities consumed are big enough. Even lovers of potato chips or those most hooked on crack do not want any more now if they consumed large quantities during the past hour.

But for many goods, when the time periods compared are not very close, greater consumption earlier stimulates greater, not lesser, consumption later. Following common usage, I define *habitual* behavior as displaying a positive relation between past and current consumption; economists call these goods complements. Well-known examples include smoking, using heroin, eating ice cream or Kellogg's Corn Flakes, jogging, attending church, telling lies, and often intimacy with a lover.

A full discussion needs to consider both short-term substitutions in consumption and the longer-term complementarities. In Chapter 3 Murphy and I present a model of cycles or binges in the amount of eating that has both substitutions and complementarities over time in food consumption, and Heaton (1991) finds both types of relations in the time series on aggregate consumption in the United States. This paper concentrates on the complementary relations because these are responsible for the habitual behavior I want to highlight.

Of course, there are vast differences in the degree of habituation to the same activity: most people can drink or work regularly without ever becoming alcoholics or workaholics. And the likelihood that a person becomes habituated to any activity varies with circumstances and age. Soldiers who became addicted to drugs while in Viet Nam usually stopped the habit soon after returning to civilian life, while former smokers and alcoholics often resume their habits after becoming unemployed or when their marriages break up.

Habits are *harmful* or "bad" if greater present consumption lowers future utility, as in the detrimental effects on future health of heavy smoking or drinking. Similarly, habits are *beneficial* if greater present consumption raises future utility; regular swimming or regular church attendance may be examples. It is natural that bad habits get more attention than good ones, but as we will see, rational behavior also implies that the observed strong habits are more likely to be harmful than beneficial.

If greater past consumption of a good increased the marginal utility of present consumption, myopic persons who do not consider the future consequences of their actions would increase their present consumption. But higher current utility does not guarantee that rational forward-looking persons consume more than in the past. Rational consumers also consider how greater current consumption affects the marginal utilities or disutilities in the future.

Chapter 3 provides a necessary and sufficient condition for a rational forward-looking consumer to develop a habit (for earlier derivations, see Ryder and Heal, 1973, and Iannaccone, 1986). It is indeed necessary for greater past consumption to raise the marginal utility from present consumption—this corresponds to what is called "reinforcement" in the addiction literature. But several other parameters are also important, including the rate of discount on future utilities, and the rate of decay or depreciation in the contribution of past consumption to current utility. The larger the rate at which either the future or past is discounted, the more likely that a good with a given amount of reinforcement is habitual, and the stronger is the habit (see Appendix 6A). This conclusion is intuitive, for the bigger are these discount rates, the smaller are the effects on future utility of greater present consumption. Then reinforcement has the more dominating effect.

An *addiction* is defined simply as a strong habit. Technically, a habit becomes an addiction when the effects of past consumption on present consumption are sufficiently strong to be destabilizing (see Appendix 6A). Therefore, a shock to an individual, such as unemployment, may lead for a while to larger and larger increases over time in the amount consumed of addictive goods. Demand for addictive goods tends to be bifurcated: people either consume a lot, or they abstain because they anticipate that they will become "hooked" if they begin to consume. Smoking is a good example of bifurcation, for 70 percent of adults in the United States do not smoke, while person who do smoke generally consume at least half a pack a day.

A habit may be raised into an addiction by exposure to the habit itself. Certain habits, like drug use and heavy drinking, may reduce the attention to future consequences—there is no reason to assume discount rates on the future are just given and fixed (elsewhere I have developed an analysis of endogenous discount rates; see Becker, 1990). Since an increase in the discount rate strengthens the commitment to all habits, there would be further induced increases in discount rates. The result may be an explosive expansion of certain habits into powerful addictions.

The presumption from the theory that addictions are partly caused by heavy decay rates on past consumption in a way is consistent with the medical evidence. For the damage to lungs, liver, and other organs declines rather quickly after a person stops heavy drinking or smoking, unless the point of no return had been reached.

Since people who heavily discount the future and past would place little weight on the future consequences of their behavior, they are less likely to be deterred from "harmful" activities that reduce future utility, even when these are not habitual. And they would be less attracted by "beneficial" activities that raise utility in the future, even when these are not habitual, such as limiting cholesterol intake. But since high discount rates on the future and past also foster strong habits and addiction, people with high rates would be *especially* attracted by harmful activities that are addictive, or at least highly habitual.

Therefore, we expect addictions to be associated with harmful activities. This can explain why addictions usually cause duress—declines in well-being over time. It can also explain why drug addictions and crime tend to go together, and why religious people tend to be law-abiders, even if drug use and religion do not affect the propensity to engage in crime, and even if crime and religion are not addictive.

Nothing in the analysis of forward-looking utility-maximizing behavior presumes that people know for sure whether they will become habituated or addicted to a substance or activity, although that is sometimes claimed by critics of this approach. An individual may have considerable uncertainty about whether she would become an alcoholic if she begins to drink regularly. A troubled teenager who begins to experiment with drugs may expect, but not be certain, that his life will begin to straighten out, perhaps because of a good job or marriage, before he becomes addicted. Since these and other choices are made under considerable uncertainty, some persons become addicted simply because events turn out to be less favorable than was reasonable to anticipate—the good job never rescued the drug user. Persons who become addicted because of bad luck may regret their addictions, but that is no more a sign of irrational behavior than is any regret voiced by big losers at a race track that they bet so heavily.

I define *traditional* behavior as habits that are sensitive to choices in the more distant past—including sometimes choices made by parents and others in the past—because the effects of the past decay slowly. Tradition-related habits are unlikely to be addictive because low depreciation rates reduce the strength of a habit. Such habits are especially important for understanding culture and institutions, as I will try to show later.


## 3. Invidious Comparisons

Economists usually do not consider why preferences are what they are, but it is advisable to discuss habit formation since many writers have claimed that habitual behavior is not fully rational. Although little is known about the mechanisms behind the development of habits, it is not obvious to me that they are less rational than other preferences.

Alcohol, heroin, cocaine, smoking, and certain other drugs have well-documented biological-pharmacological effects on consumers that raise their desire for the drugs. Habit helps economize on the cost of searching for information, and of applying the information to a new situation (see Chapter 2, Section 3). And most people get mental and physical comfort and reassurance in continuing to do what they did in the past. Thomas Jefferson was surely right when he asserted in a letter to an acquaintance that "He who permits himself to tell a lie once, finds it much easier to do it a second and third time, till at length it becomes habitual" (1785).

Another promising lead in understanding the formation of habit comes from recognizing that the utility of many goods depends on how present consumption of these goods compares with the amounts consumed in the past. For example, a given standard of living usually provides less utility to persons who had grown accustomed to a higher standard in the past. It is the decline in health, rather than simply poor health, that often makes elderly persons depressed. And what appeared to be a wonderful view from a newly occupied house may become boring and trite after living there for several years.

Goods that involve such invidious comparisons with the past are "harmful" in the sense I am using this term because greater consumption now lowers future utility by raising the future standard of comparison. What is more interesting for present purposes and less obvious is that such goods also tend to be habitual: current consumption is encouraged by greater past consumption in order to come closer to the standard set by past behavior.

Indeed, a good *must* be habitual if utility from the good depends on the difference between current consumption and a weighted sum of the amounts consumed in the past. Note that in such cases the effect of comparisons with the past is so powerful that a good must be habitual *regardless* of the discount rate on future utilities or the decay rate on past consumption. The habit is stronger when past consumption has a bigger weight, and it is an addiction when past consumption is weighted more heavily than present consumption (see Appendix 6B).

If utility depends on comparisons between present and past consumption, it would be highest just after consumption rose to a permanently higher level, and it would decline over time as the person became accustomed to that level. Similarly, utility would be lowest just after consumption fell to a permanently lower level.

If the standard of living itself involved such comparisons with the past, the *nouveau riche* would tend to be the happiest of people, the new poor the most miserable, and the long-term rich may not be so much happier than the long-term poor. Indeed, the long-term rich are only a little happier than the long-term poor when the weight on past consumption almost equals the weight on present consumption (see Appendix 6B, and Ryder and Heal, 1973). Suicides might be more closely related to declines in the living standard—perhaps due to a loss of wealth or health—than to the level itself.

Adam Smith has a few wonderful paragraphs in *The Theory of Moral Sentiments* on the transitory gains in utility from a higher standard of living: "The poor man's son, whom heaven in its anger has visited with ambition . . . pursues the idea of a certain artificial and elegant repose . . . which, if in the extremity of old age he should at last attain to it, he will find to be in no respect preferable to that humble security and contentment which he has abandoned for it" (1976, pp. 299–300; I owe this reference to George Stigler). Rapid economic growth raises the level of happiness partly by increasing the number of new rich and reducing the number of new poor. Indeed, a mere slowing of the growth rate could lower utility even when incomes continue to rise if the habitual component to the standard of living were sufficiently powerful.

## 4. Price and Wealth Effects

It is often claimed that habitual and traditional behavior, especially addictions, do not respond much to changes in prices and wealth. The explanation sometimes offered is that habits influence behavior in ways that are independent of calculation, or that habits are locked in by the past. I will consider only the responses of rational habitual behavior since I am claiming that habitual behavior does not imply a reluctance to "calculate."

An unexpected fall in the price of a habitual good may have only a slight impact on demand as long as past consumption has not changed much. This is probably the basis for the claim that habits get locked in by the past. But the magnitude of the response to, say, a permanent fall in price would grow over time as consumption continues to increase, even if it only increased slightly at first. By the definition of highly habitual goods, each increase in consumption of these goods raises future consumption by relatively large amounts. Therefore, it is not surprising that the long-run price elasticity of demand between steady states is *larger, not* smaller, for the more strongly habitual goods (see Chapter 3). Moreover, short-run changes in demand are misleading since the ratio of short-run to long-run elasticities is smaller for the stronger habits (see Chapter 4).

Grossman, Murphy, and I (Chapter 5) used the rational-habit model to study empirically the demand for cigarettes in the United States. We find cigarette demand to be rather strongly habitual, a not very surprising conclusion. The responses to price changes are not small: a 10 percent permanent fall in the price of a pack of cigarettes increases smoking by 4 percent one year later, and by almost 8 percent after a few years. Perhaps more surprising is the evidence that smokers are not myopic—they do try to anticipate the future, as measured by the effects of future prices on current consumption.

There are strong differences of opinion in the United States about whether drug use should be legalized, differences that cut across political labels of liberal or conservative. Everyone agrees that legalization would greatly reduce the retail price of drugs, but much of the disagreement comes from different views about how legalization will affect the demand for drugs. Since many drugs are strongly habitual and even addictive, the analysis of rational addiction suggests that the demand for drugs may not increase much shortly after legalization, but that it would increase by a lot in the long run—especially by the poor (see Chapter 4)—unless legalization has other effects than simply lowering price.

One important other effect concerns peer pressure, which induces some teenagers to smoke, drink heavily, and experiment with drugs. Although I do not know of convincing reasons why strongly habitual and addictive behavior is *generally* more subject to pressure from peers than other behavior, it is straightforward to show that habitual behavior is more *vulnerable*, in the sense that a given level of peer pressure has an especially large effect on habitual behavior. Strong peer pressure can convert moderately habitual behavior into what appears to be a strong habit or even an addiction.

Consider a fall in price of a habitual good subject to peer pressure. Each consumer would increase his demand, partly because price is lower, and partly because other consumers have raised their demands. Habit increases demand over time, and so too does the pressure to consume more when peers also do. This synergy between peer pressure and habit implies that peer pressure has a larger effect on the elasticity of demand when the habit is stronger; similarly, a stronger habit has more of an effect on the long-run elasticity where there is greater peer pressure (see Appendix 6C). Consequently, it may only appear that peer pressure is stronger for habitual behavior since such pressure has greater effects on demand when habits are stronger.

The importance of peer pressure in the market for drugs generally strengthens the conclusion that legalization would greatly increase the use of drugs. One qualification would be if pressure to use drugs declined when they became legal. Another would if the synergy between peer pressure and habits produced sections of positively sloped demand curves (see Appendix 6C), and hence multiple equilibria in the drug market. Legalization might then lower both price and drug use by shifting the market to a wholly different equilibrium. As yet, however, there is no evidence that the drug market is characterized by such multiple equilibria.

Econometric studies usually find that high taxes on incomes and other taxes on work effort do not have large effects on the hours worked by men. Yet more than fifty years of weak work incentives under communist rule in Eastern Europe and elsewhere had a shattering effect on work effort in these countries. The commitment to hard work apparently has also eroded in countries like Sweden that greatly raised the effective tax on work effort during the past quarter-century.

The econometric findings can be reconciled with these other observations by recognizing that work is a tradition-habit that builds up very slowly over time, perhaps partly under the influence of examples set by parents and others. As Victor Hugo said, "Nothing is more dangerous than discontinued labor—it is habit lost. A habit easy to abandon, difficult to resume" (1909, p. 159). The long time it takes for high taxes and other policies to break down slowly accumulated work habits is not easily captured by econometric studies, even by studies that use a few years of panel data to discover some effects of work habits (see, e.g., Bover, 1991).

Countries can take advantage of the slow decay of good work habits by imposing heavy *temporary* taxes on effort. But the pessimistic side of the story is that the new countries emerging from Eastern Europe and the Soviet Union will have difficulty rebuilding the good work habits eroded during the many decades of mismanagement and weak work incentives.

Being on welfare may create a bad habit if children and parents lose their initiative by becoming dependent on government handouts. Then many families may refuse to go on welfare, even when eligible—as is the case in the United States—because the cost of dependency exceeds the value of the payments. Although a sizable fall in welfare payments might greatly increase the number who decline to go on, it could *initially* have only a minor impact on the number of families who remain on welfare since they have become habituated to the welfare payments (see Sanders, 1991).

The permanent-income model explains why total consumption often does not respond much to income shocks by assuming that many shocks have a large temporary component. Yet some critics have argued that aggregate consumption in the United States is too stable—the "excess stability" issue—to be explained by the permanent-income story because aggregate shocks are alleged to have a small transitory component. Even if they are right about aggregate shocks, and there is considerable disagreement, the problem is not with the permanent-income concept—which is surely basically correct—but with the assumption that preferences are separable over time. If current consumption depends on past consumption, even a permanent shock to income may initially have only a small effect on consumption.

Habit-driven responses to permanent shocks can explain most of the behavior usually explained since Friedman's work (1957) by nonhabitual responses to transitory shocks. For example, Friedman showed that higher-income groups would save a larger fraction of their incomes than lower-income groups if only because these groups contain relatively many persons who received positive transitory income shocks. However, higher-income groups save a lot also because they contain relatively many persons who are *newly* rich. I believe that the effects of habits as well as the distinction between permanent and transitory income are needed for a satisfactory explanation of aggregate consumption behavior (see Heaton, 1991, and Ferson and Constantinides, 1991).

## 5. Preference Formation

Each person is born perhaps not as a *tabula rasa*—an empty slate—but with limited experiences that get filled in by childhood and later experiences. These experiences influence teenage and adult desires and choices partly by creating habits, addictions, and traditions. The habits acquired as a child or young adult generally continue to influence behavior even when the environment changes radically. For example, Indian adults who migrate to the United States often eat the same type of cuisine they had in India, and continue to wear the same style of clothing. A woman who was badly sexually abused as a child may forever fear and dislike men, including those who would treat her with consideration and respect. A person may remain an alcoholic until he dies mainly because he started drinking heavily as a teenager.

Childhood experiences can greatly influence behavior over a person's entire life because it may not pay to try to greatly change habits when the environment changes. Childhood-acquired habits then continue, even though these would not have developed if the environment when growing up had been the same as the environment faced as an adult.

The Freudian emphasis on the crucial influence of early childhood on later behavior would be consistent with utility-maximizing forward-looking behavior if behavior were highly habitual. For then experiences while a child could have a very large effect on adult preferences and choices.

Children spend their early years under the care of parents and close relatives who determine what they eat, read, observe, and hear. The enormous influence this has on children's preferences explains the close link between parents and children in many attitudes and choices, including religious and political party affiliations, the propensities to smoke, eat breakfast, or divorce, and the taste for Chinese, Iranian, or Southern-style cuisine.

A natural way in a utility-maximizing framework to model the influence of parents on children is to assume that the preferences of children and adults evolve from early childhood and later experiences under the influence of habitual, including addictive and traditional, behavior. Indeed, some of my remarks will go well beyond habitual behavior to other recursive influences of early childhood and other past experiences on present and future preferences.

Altruistic parents maximize their own utility in part by maximizing their children's. They would try to direct the evolution of children's preferences toward raising the utility of children. For example, parents may refrain from smoking even when that gives them much pleasure because their smoking raises the likelihood that the children will smoke. Or they may take their children to church, even when not religious, because they believe exposure to religion is good for children. Indeed, many parents stop going after their children leave home.

Selfish parents do not care about the welfare of children, but they too are often concerned about the evolution of children's preferences. They may want to be taken care of when old or ill, but cannot have a contract with their children to help out. However, they can try to shape the formation of children's preferences to raise the chances their children will help voluntarily.

The preferences children get when young, in effect, can *precommit* them to helping out much later when they are adults and their parents are elderly. Parents can help make the children altruistic, or can make grown children feel "guilty" when they do not help. Propensities toward guilt may lower the lifetime utility of children—selfish parents do not care—but helping out of guilt may raise the utility of adult children, *conditional on their past experiences.*

Therefore, even selfish parents do not necessarily neglect or abuse children, for they might spend considerable time, money, and emotional resources on children to rig the evolution of preferences in their own favor. This sounds calculating and selfish. It is. Yet the opportunity to "commit" children to helping out when parents need it can induce selfish parents to treat their children much better than they would if adult preferences and behavior did not evolve from childhood experiences and treatment. It also implies that selfish parents become meaner when they need not rely on their children, perhaps because the government becomes committed to helping out the elderly in need.

Children carry along into adulthood the baggage of experiences they had only a limited role in shaping. Therefore, a rational person can meaningfully state that she does not "like" her preferences in the sense that she doesn't like the inherited baggage: the guilt, the sexual fears, the propensity to smoke or drink heavily, and so forth. She can change the stock of experiences over time, but how much a rational person wants to change depends on how long she expects to live, the strength of the influence of the past on present choices, and other factors. We all are to some extent prisoners of experiences we wish we never had.

Economists are so conditioned to identifying rational choice with separable preferences that we often call "irrational" quite rational behavior that is the result of past experiences. We have trouble understanding the people who take good care of elderly parents even when not forced by social norms or altruism—I have tried to indicate why this can be utility-maximizing behavior once the importance of guilt and other results of past experiences is recognized.

A prominent example is the literature on "endowment" effects (see Kahneman, Knetsch, and Thaler, 1990). A family may refuse to sell for half-a-million dollars the house it has lived in for twenty years, even though it would be unwilling to spend anywhere near that amount for an otherwise equivalent house. Of course, the qualifier "otherwise" is crucial since twenty years in the same house presumably built up memories and attachments to *that* particular house, not to a seemingly "equivalent" house that is really not equivalent.

A more difficult example of the endowment effect concerns a person like Sherwin Rosen who stores a young bottle of wine that cost a few bucks. By luck the bottle turns out to be worth several hundred dollars after ten years. But Sherwin refuses to sell, even though he would never contemplate paying that much for an otherwise equivalent bottle. Irrational? Or like the family that refuses to sell its house, a case where the experience of "consuming" a particular bottle for a long time raised the value attached to *that* bottle, not to an otherwise equivalent bottle?

Other "rational" interpretations of the refusal are possible; e.g., Sherwin may get pleasure from bragging about his shrewdness in acquiring such a bottle. And an interpretation that uses the effects of owning the bottle for ten years on present demand for it may seem forced since the bottle was not "consumed" during the decade. But such a reaction partly reflects the economist's narrow conception of "consumption." People consume paintings and old rugs and coins simply by looking at them occasionally, and they may value such objects more over time as they grow attached to them.

## 6. Commitment, Institutions, and Culture

Game theory has shown the crucial importance of commitment in the strategic interactions over time of two or more participants. The equilibria that emerge are often highly sensitive to whether players can commit to future behavior. Yet it may be difficult to enforce commitment since people can renege on promises or slip out of contractual obligations. Still, I believe the difficulty of obtaining binding commitments has been exaggerated because of the common assumption that preferences are independent of the past, so that a person's utility-maximizing choices at any moment do not directly depend on past choices.

For habits, addictions, traditions, and other preferences that are directly contingent on past choices partly control, and hence commit, future behavior in predictable ways. Indeed, habits and the like may be very good substitutes for long-term contracts and other explicit commitment mechanisms.

Consider, for example, a firm that would charge consumers a lower price now if they agree to buy more of the good for some time into the future. Unfortunately, it is not possible to write a contract that ensures future purchases. But a contract may not be necessary if the good is habitual since habituated consumers are automatically committed to buying more in the future when they buy more now.

A firm may help finance investments in a worker's general skills if the worker will remain with the firm. A written contract that commits the worker to stay is not enforceable, but the firm may know that the worker is likely to remain after he has been there for a while since the job becomes a habit.

I have already shown how parents may be reasonably confident that their children will help out when they become adults and the parents are elderly because the parents help structure the children's adult preferences by controlling childhood experiences.

Such influences of habitual and other recursive preference relations on behavior get incorporated into the optimal strategies of players in sequential games. For example, a parent may save less to support herself when elderly if her children are conditioned to help out. A boss may exploit his workers' attachments to their jobs, or society may punish crimes more severely now because that raises social support for punishments in the future.

In Chapter 5 Grossman, Murphy, and I consider the optimal pricing of a monopolist who sells an habitual good. We show that wealth-maximizing prices are below the prices where current marginal revenue equals marginal cost since a lower price now, in effect, "commits" consumers to increase their future consumption (for a more complete analysis of optimal pricing, see Fethke and Jagannathan, 1991). Therefore, the optimal prices will be higher if consumers are prevented from raising their future consumption.

This analysis can explain the rise in price-cost margins, and hence "profits," of cigarette companies during the past few years. The continuing growth in legislation that restricts smoking is a major observable obstacle to future increases in the demand for cigarettes. Producers are induced to raise cigarette prices and current "profits," even though they are obviously hurt by legislated restrictions on smoking.

These examples of the effects of preferences on commitment are rather straightforward, although some of you may be dubious. You will then be far more dubious of the following examples, which extend the analysis of habits and traditions to include institutions and culture. I was led to this line of argument by reading in the *Federalist Papers* James Madison's criticisms of Jefferson's proposal for temporary constitutions that are rewritten by each succeeding generation. Madison did more than just claim that a constitution protects fundamental rights and helps commit the actions of future generations. He recognized that a basic problem is whether people are willing to obey a constitution: the world is strewn with wonderful constitutions that are ignored or evaded.

Madison argued in effect that a constitution is more likely to be followed out of habit and tradition the longer it has been around. The frequent changes advocated by Jefferson would deprive a constitution of—I can do no better than quote Madison's words—"that veneration, which time bestows on everything, and without which perhaps the wisest and freest governments would not possess the requisite stability," and "when the examples which fortify opinion are ancient as well as numerous, they are known to have a double effect" (Madison, 1787).

Madison and others—he apparently was following Hume (1748)—claim that preferences are formed not simply by what a person did in the past, what his parents did, and what contemporary peers are doing, but also by the behavior of past generations of "peers." This extensive influence of the past on present beliefs and behavior helps stabilize older institutions and cultures. As Madison argued in rejecting Jefferson's suggestion for frequent change, the ultimate strength of the support for an institution depends on whether there is time to cumulate the support over several generations.

Sometimes, support for an institution or ethic—such as the belief in honesty—is called "unthinking" attachment to a culture or ethic. Wordsworth claimed that "habit rules the unreflecting herd" (1822). But this is no more "unthinking" than other preferences that are formed by what happened in the past.

Obedience to institutions often can be utilized in social decision making. The armed forces try to instill the habit of obedience to commands during fighting by emphasizing military traditions, rigid rules, and response to peer pressure. Young people asked to contribute heavily to social security may not have to worry that the next generation will refuse to support them when they become elderly, even though it might *appear* to be in the next generation's self-interest to do so. Indeed, this generation's support of the elderly may well strengthen the tradition-habit that will induce the next generation to support the elderly.

I readily admit that I do not know how far one can push this point of view. And the stress on institutions influenced by tradition-habits and peer pressure may seem to be an *ad hoc* trick invented to solve intractable commitment and collective choice problems. But this approach does come out of an attention to more straightforward problems, such as heavy drinking, drug use, and brand preferences. And the evolution of preferences out of past experiences seems far more intuitive, even when extended to institutions and culture, than the opposite assumption so dominant in economics that preferences are independent of the past.

Some of you might be surprised to hear a co-author of the *"de gustibus"* point of view, with its emphasis on stable preferences, waxing enthusiastically about the formation of preferences. But what *de gustibus* assumes is that *meta*-preferences are stable. Meta-preferences include past choices and choices by others as arguments in a person's current utility function. In fact, addictive behavior and social interactions were two of the major examples analyzed by Stigler and myself (Chapter 2).

The message of Chapter 2 is not that preferences at time $t$ for different people depend in the same way on their consumption at $t$. Rather, it is that common rules determine the way different variables and experiences enter the meta-preferences that motivate most people at most times. And that forward-looking rational factors maximize the utility from their meta-preferences, not from current preferences alone, because they recognize that choices today affect their utilities in the future.

## 7. Conclusion

My concluding remarks can be brief. I have tried to show that the past casts a long shadow on the present through its influence on the formation of present preferences and choices. These links between the past and the present do not simply provide a technical generalization of the independence assumption regarding preferences that permits a few more wiggles in the data to be explained.

The systematic analysis of habitual, addictive, and traditional behavior, and of other ways the past influences present preferences, has profound implications for the analysis of many kinds of economic and social phenomena. These surely include the demand for branded goods, how income shocks affect aggregate consumption, and short- and long-run changes in smoking due to higher taxes on a pack of cigarettes. They also include a better understanding of how legalization would change drug use, the effect of income and other taxes on effort and work habits in the long run, and why the *nouveau riche* and new poor are so different from the long-term rich and long-term poor.

With a still bolder vision and a lot of luck, the link between the past and present choices may also explain why and how parents influence the formation of children's preferences, how people get committed to future decisions, and the formation and support of institutions and culture.

## Appendix 6A

Let the utility function at time $t$ be

(6.A1) $$U(t) = U(y(t), c(t), S(t))$$

where $y$ is a nonhabitual good, $c$ is habitual, and $\dot{S} = c(t) - \delta S(t)$, where $\delta$ is the depreciation rate on past consumption of $c$. The overall utility function at $t = 0$ is the discounted value of the $U(t)$, where $\sigma$ is the rate of discount. I assume that overall utility is maximized subject to a wealth constraint, where the amount of wealth is given.

A good is *habitual* if

(6.A2) $$\frac{dc(t)}{dS(t)} > 0$$

when the marginal utility of wealth is held constant. That is, when a "compensated" increase in past consumption raises present consumption. Since at a steady state, $c = \delta S$, it is natural to define an *addiction* as a habit strong enough that

(6.A3) $$\frac{dc(t)}{dS(t)} > \delta$$

This implies that a steady state is unstable if $c$ is addictive near this state.

Becker and Murphy (Chapter 3) show that a necessary and sufficient condition for a good to be habitual near a steady state is that

(6.A4) $$(\sigma + 2\delta)U_{cs} > -U_{ss}$$

where $U_{cs} = \partial^2 U / \partial c \partial S$, and $U_{ss} = \partial^2 U / \partial S^2$.

## Appendix 6B

Let utility from the habitual good $c$ at time $t$ be separable from the other goods ($y$), and expressible as

(6.B1) $$V(t) = V[c(t) - \alpha \delta S(t)]$$

where $\alpha$ is a constant $> 0$. Since $\delta$ is the depreciation rate on past consumption of $c$, $\delta S(t) = \bar{c}(t)$, a weighted average of past consumption. Then

$$V_{cc} = V''$$

$$V_{cs} = -\alpha\delta V''$$

$$V_{ss} = (\alpha\delta)^2 V''$$

and

$$2\delta V_{cs} = -2\alpha\delta^2 V'' > -V_{ss} = -\alpha^2\delta^2 V'' \quad \text{for all } \alpha < 2$$

Therefore, for all $\sigma$ and $\delta > 0$, the modified Stone-Geary utility function in equation (6.B1) satisfies the condition in equation (6.A4) for $c$ to be a habit. It can be shown that the habit is stronger when $\alpha$ is greater, and it is an addiction when $\alpha > 1$.

Equation (6.B1) implies that in a steady state where $c = \delta S = \bar{c}$,

$$V = V[\bar{c}(1 - \alpha)]$$

(6.B2)

$$V_c = V'(1 - \alpha)$$

Therefore, a rise in $c$ between steady states has a smaller effect on utility when the habit ($\alpha$) is stronger (given the value of $V'$).

The effect on steady-state consumption of a permanent change in the price of $c$ compensated to hold the marginal utility of wealth ($\lambda$) constant is

(6.B3)
$$\frac{dc}{dp_c} \cong \frac{\lambda}{V''(1 - \alpha)^2} \quad \text{if } \sigma \cong 0$$

(This is a special case of equation 3.18; see Chapter 3.) Clearly, the effect on $c$ is greater when $\alpha$—the strength of the habit—is bigger.

### Appendix 6C

I now expand the utility function in equation (6.B1) to include peer pressure:

(6.C1)
$$V(t) = [c(t) - \alpha\delta S(t) - \gamma \overline{C}(t)]$$

where $\gamma > 0$ measures the strength of the pressure, and $\overline{C} = \sum \frac{c_j}{N} = c$ when all $N$ consumers are identical. Peer pressure alters the effects of a change in the price of $c$ on its steady-state consumption to

(6.C2)
$$\frac{dc}{dp_c} \cong \frac{\lambda}{V''(1 - \alpha)(1 - \alpha - \gamma)} \quad \text{if } \sigma \cong 0$$

A proof is straightforward. The first-order condition for each consumer near a steady state is

$$V_c + \frac{V_s}{\sigma + \delta} = \lambda p_c$$

Differentiating with respect to $p_c$ while holding $\lambda$ constant, assuming $c = \delta S$, and $\overline{C} = c$, we get

$$\left\{ V_{cc} + \frac{V_{cs}}{\delta} + V_{c\overline{c}} + \left( \frac{V_{ss}}{\delta} + V_{sc} + V_{s\overline{c}} \right) \frac{1}{\sigma + \delta} \right\} \cdot \frac{dc}{dp_c} = \lambda$$

Substituting $V'' = V_{cc}$, $-\alpha\delta V'' = V_{cs}$, $\alpha^2\delta^2 V'' = V_{ss}$, $-\gamma V'' = V_{c\overline{c}}$, and $\alpha\gamma\delta V'' = V_{sc}$, and setting $\sigma = 0$, we get

$$V''(1 - 2\alpha - \gamma + \alpha^2 + \alpha\gamma)\frac{dc}{dp_c} = \lambda$$

which is equation (6.C2).

Clearly, $[d/d(\gamma)][(dc)/(dp_c)]$ is greater in absolute value when $\alpha$ is greater. Moreover, the demand curve becomes unstable $[(d_c)/(dp_c) > 0]$ when $\alpha + \gamma > 1$.

# PART II

# Social Capital

# The Economic Way of Looking at Life

## 1. The Economic Approach

My research uses the economic approach to analyze social issues that range beyond those usually considered by economists. Here I will describe the approach and illustrate it with examples drawn from past and current work.

Unlike Marxian analysis, the economic approach I refer to does not assume that individuals are motivated solely by selfishness or material gain. It is a *method* of analysis, not an assumption about particular motivations. Along with others, I have tried to pry economists away from narrow assumptions about self interest. Behavior is driven by a much richer set of values and preferences.

The analysis assumes that individuals maximize welfare *as they conceive it,* whether they be selfish, altruistic, loyal, spiteful, or masochistic. Their behavior is forward-looking, and it is also assumed to be consistent over time. In particular, they try as best they can to anticipate the uncertain consequences of their actions. Forward-looking behavior, however, may still be rooted in the past, for the past can exert a long shadow on attitudes and values.

Actions are constrained by income, time, imperfect memory and calculating capacities, and other limited resources, and also by the opportunities available in the economy and elsewhere. These opportunities are largely determined by the private and collective actions of other individuals and organizations.

Revised version of Nobel Lecture, delivered December 9, 1992, in Stockholm, Sweden; originally published in *Journal of Political Economy,* 101, no. 3 (June 1993): 385–409. © The Nobel Foundation, 1992.

Different constraints are decisive for different situations, but the most fundamental constraint is limited time. Economic and medical progress have greatly increased length of life, but not the physical flow of time itself, which always restricts everyone to twenty-four hours per day. So while goods and services have expanded enormously in rich countries, the total time available to consume has not.

Thus wants remain unsatisfied in rich countries as well as in poor ones. For while the growing abundance of goods may reduce the value of additional goods, time becomes more valuable as goods become more abundant. The welfare of people cannot be improved in a utopia where everyone's needs are fully satisfied, but the constant flow of time makes such a utopia impossible. These are some of the issues analyzed in the literature on time allocation (for two early studies, see Becker, 1965, and Linder, 1970).

The following sections illustrate the economic approach with four very different subjects. To understand discrimination against minorities, it is necessary to widen preferences to accommodate prejudice and hatred of particular groups. The economic analysis of crime incorporates into rational behavior illegal and other antisocial actions. The human capital perspective considers how the productivity of people in market and non-market situations is changed by investments in education, skills, and knowledge. The economic approach to the family interprets marriage, divorce, fertility, and relations among family members through the lens of utility-maximizing forward-looking behavior.

## 2. Discrimination against Minorities

Discrimination against outsiders has always existed, but with the exception of a few discussions of the employment of women (see Edgeworth, 1922, and Fawcett, 1918), economists wrote little on this subject before the 1950s. I began to worry about racial, religious, and gender discrimination while a graduate student, and used the concept of discrimination coefficients to organize an approach to prejudice and hostility to members of particular groups.

Instead of making the common assumptions that employers only consider the productivity of employees, that workers ignore the characteristics of those with whom they work, and that customers only care about the qualities of the goods and services provided, discrimination coefficients incorporate the influence of race, gender, and other personal characteristics on tastes and attitudes. Employees may refuse to work under a woman or a black even when they are well paid to do so, or a customer may prefer not to deal with a black car salesman. It is only through *widening* of the usual assumptions that it is possible to being to understand the obstacles to advancement encountered by minorities.

Presumably, the amount of observable discrimination against minorities in wages and employment depends not only on tastes for discrimination, but also on other variables, such as the degree of competition and civil rights legislation. In the 1950s, a systematic analysis of how prejudice and other variables interact could begin with the important theory of compensating differentials originated by Adam Smith, and Gunnar Myrdal's pioneering *American Dilemma* (1944), but much remained to be done. I spent several years working out a theory of how actual discrimination in earnings and employment is determined by tastes for discrimination, along with the degree of competition in labor and product markets, the distribution of discrimination coefficients among members of the majority group, the access of minorities to education and training, the outcome of median voter and other voting mechanisms that determine whether legislation favors or is hostile to minorities, and other considerations. My advisors encouraged me to convert my doctoral dissertation into a book (1957, 1971). I have continued over my career to write books rather than only articles, a practice which has become uncommon in economics.

Actual discrimination in the market place against a minority group depends on the combined discrimination of employers, workers, consumers, schools, and governments. The analysis shows that sometimes the environment greatly softens, while at other times it magnifies, the impact of a given amount of prejudice. For example, the discrepancy in wages between equally productive blacks and whites, or women and men, would be much smaller than the degree of prejudice against blacks and women when many companies can efficiently specialize in employing mainly blacks or women.

Indeed, in a world with constant returns to scale in production, two segregated economies with the same distribution of skills would completely bypass discrimination, and they would have equal wages and equal returns to other resources, regardless of the desire to discriminate against the segregated minorities. Therefore, discrimination by the majority in the marketplace is effective because minority members cannot provide various skills in sufficient quantities to companies that would specialize in using these workers.

When the majority is very large compared to the minority—in the United States whites are nine times as numerous and have much more human and physical capital per capita than blacks—market discrimination by the majority hardly lowers its incomes, but may greatly reduce the incomes of the minority. However, when minority members are a sizable fraction of the total, discrimination by members of the majority injures them as well.

This proposition can be illustrated with an analysis of discrimination in South Africa, where blacks are some five times as numerous as whites. Discrimination against blacks has also significantly hurt whites, although some white groups have benefitted (see Becker, 1971, pp. 30–31; Hutt, 1964; and Lundahl, 1992). Its sizable cost to whites suggests why Apartheid and other blatant forms of Afrikaner discrimination eventually broke down.

Many economists have the impression that my analysis of prejudice implies market discrimination disappears in the "long run" (Arrow, 1972, seems to be the first to make this claim). This impression is erroneous because I had shown that whether employers who do not want to discriminate compete away all discriminating employers depends not only on the distribution of tastes for discrimination among potential employers, but critically also on the nature of firm production functions (see Becker, 1971, pp. 43–45).

Of greater significance empirically is the long-run discrimination by employees and customers, who are far more important sources of market discrimination than employers. There is no reason to expect discrimination by these groups to be competed away unless it is possible to have enough efficient segregated firms and effectively segregated markets for goods (for a good review of this and other issues regarding discrimination, see Cain, 1986).

A novel theoretical development in recent years is the analysis of the consequences of stereotyped reasoning or statistical discrimination (see Phelps, 1972, and Arrow, 1973). This analysis suggests that the *beliefs* of employers, teachers, and other influential groups that minority members are less productive *can* be self-fulfilling, for these beliefs may cause minorities to underinvest in education, training, and work skills, such as punctuality. The underinvestment does make them less productive (see a good recent analysis by Loury, 1992).

Evidence from many countries on the earnings, unemployment, and occupations of blacks, women, religious groups, immigrants, and others has expanded enormously during the past twenty-five years. This evidence more fully documents the economic position of minorities and how that changes in different environments. However, the evidence has not dispelled some of the controversies over the source of lower incomes of minorities.

## 3. Crime and Punishment

I began to think about crime in the 1960s after driving to Columbia University for an oral examination of a student in economic theory. I was late and had to decide quickly whether to put the car in a parking lot or risk getting a ticket for parking illegally on the street. I calculated the likelihood of getting a ticket, the size of the penalty, and the cost of putting the car in a lot. I decided it paid to take the risk and park on the street. (I did not get a ticket.)

As I walked the few blocks to the examination room, it occurred to me that the city authorities had probably gone through a similar analysis. The frequency of their inspection of parked vehicles and the size of the penalty imposed on violators should depend on their estimates of the type of calculations potential violators like me would make. Of course, the first question I put to the hapless student was to work out the optimal behavior of both the offenders and the police, something I had not yet done.

In the 1950s and '60s, intellectual discussions of crime were dominated by the opinion that criminal behavior was caused by mental illness and social oppression, and that criminals were helpless "victims." A book by a well-known psychiatrist was entitled *The Crime of Punishment* (see Menninger, 1966). Such attitudes began to exert a major influence on social policy, as laws changed to expand criminals' rights. These changes reduced the apprehension and conviction of criminals, and provided less protection to the law-abiding population.

I was not sympathetic to the assumption that criminals had radically different motivations from everyone else. I explored instead the theoretical and empirical implications of the assumption that criminal behavior is rational (see the early pioneering work by Bentham, 1931, and Beccaria, 1986), but again "rationality" did not mean to imply narrow materialism. It recognized that many people were constrained by moral and ethical considerations, and they did not commit crimes even when these were profitable and there was no danger of detection.

However, police and jails would be unnecessary if such attitudes always prevailed. Rationality implied that some individuals become criminals because of the financial and other rewards from crime compared to legal work, taking account of the likelihood of apprehension and conviction, and the severity of punishment.

The amount of crime is determined not only by the rationality and preferences of would-be criminals, but also by the economic and social environment created by public policies, including expenditures on police, punishments for different crimes, and opportunities for employment, schooling, and training programs. Clearly, the type of legal jobs available as well as law, order, and punishment are an integral part of the economic approach to crime.

Total public spending on fighting crime can be reduced, while keeping the mathematically expected punishment unchanged, by offsetting a cut in expenditures on catching criminals with a sufficient increase in the punishment to those convicted. However, risk-preferring individuals are more deterred from crime by a higher probability of conviction than by severe punishments. Therefore, optimal behavior by the State would balance the reduced spending on police and courts from lowering the probability of conviction against the preference of risk-preferring criminals for a lesser certainty of punishment. The State should also consider the likelihood of punishing innocent persons.

In the early stages of my work on crime, I was puzzled by why theft is socially harmful since it appears merely to redistribute resources, usually from wealthier to poorer individuals. I resolved the puzzle (Becker 1968a, fn. 3) by pointing out that criminals spend on weapons and on the value of the time in planning and carrying out their crimes, and that such spending is socially unproductive—it is what is now called "rent-seeking"—because it does not create wealth, only forcibly redistributes it. I approximated the social cost of theft by the dollars stolen since rational criminals would be willing to spend up to that amount on their crimes. I should have added the resources spent by potential victims protecting themselves against crime.

One reason why the economic approach to crime became so influential is that the same analytic apparatus can be used to study enforcement of all laws, including minimum wage legislation, clean air acts, insider trader and other violations of security laws, and income tax evasions. Since few laws are self-enforcing, they require expenditures on conviction and punishment to deter violators. The United States Sentencing Commission has explicitly used the economic analysis of crime to develop rules to be followed by judges in punishing violators of Federal statutes (United States Sentencing Commission, 1992).

Studies of crime that use the economic approach have become common during the past quarter century. These include analysis of the optimal marginal punishments to deter increases in the severity of crimes—for example, to deter a kidnapper from killing his victim (the modern literature starts with Stigler, 1970), and the relation between private and public enforcement of laws (see Becker and Stigler, 1974, and Landes and Posner, 1975).

Fines are preferable to imprisonment and other types of punishment because they can deter crimes effectively if criminals have sufficient financial resources—if they are not "judgment proof," to use legal jargon. Moreover, fines are more efficient than other methods because the cost to offenders is also revenue to the State. My discussion of the relations between fines and other punishments has been clarified and considerably improved (see, e.g., Polinsky and Shavell, 1984, and Posner, 1986).

Empirical assessments of the effects on crime rates of prison terms, conviction rates, unemployment levels, income inequality, and other variables have become more numerous and more accurate (the pioneering work is by Ehrlich, 1973, and the subsequent literature is extensive). The greatest controversies surround the question of whether capital punishment deters murders, a controversy that arouses much emotion, but is far from being resolved (see, e.g., Ehrlich, 1975, and National Research Council, 1978).

## 4. Human Capital

Until the 1950s economists generally assumed that labor power was given and not augmentable. The sophisticated analyses of investments in education and other training by Adam Smith, Alfred Marshall, and Milton Friedman were not integrated into discussions of productivity. Then T. W. Schultz and others began to pioneer the exploration of the implications of human capital investments for economic growth and related economic questions.

Human capital analysis starts with the assumption that individuals decide on their education, training, medical care, and other additions to knowledge and health by weighing the benefits and costs. Benefits include cultural and other non-monetary gains along with improvement in earnings and occupations, while costs usually depend mainly on the foregone value of the time spent on these investments.

Human capital is so uncontroversial nowadays that it may be difficult to appreciate the hostility in the 1950s and 1960s toward the approach that went with the term. The very concept of *human* capital was alleged to be demeaning because it treated people as machines. To approach schooling as an investment rather than a cultural experience was considered unfeeling and extremely narrow. As a result, I hesitated a long time before deciding to call my book *Human Capital* (1964, 1975), and hedged the risk by using a long subtitle that I no longer remember. Only gradually did economists, let alone others, accept the concept of human capital as a valuable tool in the analysis of various economic and social issues.

My work on human capital began with an effort to calculate both private and social rates of return to men, women, blacks, and other groups from investments in different levels of education. After a while it became clear that the analysis of human capital can help explain many regularities in labor markets and the economy at large. It seemed possible to develop a more general theory of human capital that includes firms as well as individuals, and that could consider its macroeconomic implications.

The empirical analysis tried to correct data on the higher earnings of more educated persons for the fact that they are abler: they have higher I.Q.'s and score better on other aptitude tests. It also considered the effects on rates of return to education of mortality, income taxes, foregone earnings, and economic growth. Ability corrections did not seem very important, but large changes in adult mortality and sizable rates of economic growth did have big effects. Meltzer (1992) recently has argued that the high death rates, especially from AIDS, to young males in many parts of Africa greatly discourage investments in human capital there.

The empirical study of investments in human capital received a major boost from Mincer's classic work (1974). He extended a simple regression analysis that related earnings to years of schooling (Becker and Chiswick, 1966) to include a crude but very useful measure of on-the-job training and experience—years after finishing school; he used numerous individual observations rather than grouped data, and he carefully analyzed the properties of residuals from earnings-generating equations. There are now numerous estimated rates of return to education and training for many countries (for a summary of some of this literature, see Psacharopoulos, 1985); indeed, the earnings equation is probably the most common empirical regression in microeconomics.

The accumulating evidence on the economic benefits of schooling and training also promoted the importance of human capital in policy discussions. This new faith in human capital has reshaped the way governments approach the problem of stimulating growth and productivity, as was shown by the emphasis on human capital in the recent presidential election in the United States.

One of the most influential theoretical concepts in human capital analysis is the distinction between general and specific training or knowledge (see Becker, 1962, and Oi, 1962). By definition, firm-specific knowledge is useful only in the firms providing it, whereas general knowledge is useful also in other firms. Teaching someone to operate an IBM-compatible personal computer is general training, while learning the authority structure and the talents of employees in a particular company is specific knowledge. This distinction helps explain why workers with highly specific skills are less likely to quit their jobs and are the last to be laid off during business downturns. It also explains why most promotions are made from within a firm rather than through hiring—workers need time to learn about a firm's structure and "culture"—and why better accounting methods would include the specific human capital of employees among the principal assets of most companies.

Firm-specific investments produce rents that must be shared between employers and employees, a sharing process that is vulnerable to "opportunistic" behavior because each side may try to extract most of the rent after investments are in place. Rents and opportunism due to specific investments play a crucial role in the modern economic theory of how organizations function (see Williamson, 1985), and in many discussions of principle-agent problems (see, for example, Grossman and Hart, 1983). The implications of specific capital for sharing and turnover have also been used in analyzing marriage "markets" to explain divorce rates and bargaining within a marriage (see Becker, Landes, and Michael, 1977, and McElroy and Horney, 1981), and in analyzing political "markets" to explain the low turnover of politicians (see Cain, Ferejohn, and Fiorina, 1987).

The theory of human capital investment relates inequality in earnings to differences in talents, family background, and bequests and other assets (see Becker and Tomes, 1986). Many empirical studies of inequality also rely on human capital concepts, especially differences in schooling and training (see Mincer, 1974). The sizable growth in earnings inequality in the United States during the 1980s that has excited so much political discussion is largely explained by higher returns to the more educated and better trained (see, e.g., Murphy and Welch, 1992).

Human capital theory gives a provocative interpretation of the so-called gender gap in earnings. Traditionally, women have been far more likely than men to work part-time and intermittently partly because they usually withdrew from the labor force for a while after having children. As a result, they had fewer incentives to invest in education and training that improved earnings and job skills.

During the past twenty years all this changed. The decline in family size, the growth in divorce rates, the rapid expansion of the service sector where most women are employed, the continuing economic development that raised the earnings of women along with men, and civil rights legislation encouraged greater labor force participation by women, and hence greater investment in market-oriented skills. In practically all rich countries, these forces significantly improved both the occupations and relative earnings of women.

The United States' experience is especially well-documented. The gender gap in earnings among full-time men and women remained at about 35 percent from the mid-fifties to the mid-seventies. Then women began the steady economic advance which is still continuing; it narrowed the gap to under 25 percent (see, for example, O'Neill, 1985; Goldin, 1990). Women are flocking to business, law, and medical schools, and are working at skilled jobs that they formerly shunned, or were excluded from.

Schultz and others (see, e.g., Schultz, 1963, and Denison, 1962) early on emphasized that investments in human capital were a major contributor to economic growth. But after a while the relation of human capital to growth was neglected, as economists became discouraged about whether the available growth theory gave many insights into the progress of different countries. The revival of more formal models of endogenous growth has brought human capital once again to the forefront of the discussions (see, e.g., Romer, 1986; Lucas, 1988; Becker, Murphy, and Tamura, 1990; and Barro and Sala-i-Martin, 1992).

## 5. Formation, Dissolution, and Structure of Families

The rational choice analysis of family behavior builds on maximizing behavior, investments in human capital, the allocation of time, and discrimination against women and other groups. The rest of this chapter focuses on this analysis since it is still quite controversial, and I can discuss some of my current research.

Writing *A Treatise on the Family* (1981, 1991) is the most difficult sustained intellectual effort I have undertaken. The family is arguably the most fundamental and oldest of institutions—some authors trace its origin to more than 40,000 years ago (Soffer, 1990). The *Treatise* tries to analyze not only modern Western families, but those in other cultures and changes in family structure during the past several centuries.

Trying to cover this broad subject required a degree of mental commitment over more than six years, during many nighttime as well as daytime hours, that left me intellectually and emotionally exhausted. In his autobiography, Bertrand Russell says that writing the *Principia Mathematica* used up so much of his mental powers that he was never again fit for really hard intellectual work. It took about two years after finishing the *Treatise* to regain my intellectual zest.

The analysis of fertility has a long and honorable history in economics, but until recent years marriage and divorce, and the relations between husbands, wives, parents, and children had been largely neglected by economists (although see the important study by Mincer, 1962). The point of departure of my work on the family is the assumption that when men and women decide to marry, or have children, or divorce, they attempt to raise their welfare by comparing benefits and costs. So they marry when they expect to be better off than if they remained single, and they divorce if that is expected to increase their welfare.

People who are not intellectuals are often surprised when told that this approach is controversial since it seems obvious to them that individuals try to improve their welfare by marriage and divorce. The rational choice approach to marriage and other behavior is in fact often consistent with the instinctive economics "of the common person" (Farrell and Mandel, 1992).

Still, making intuitive assumptions about behavior is only the *starting point* of systematic analysis, for alone they do not yield many interesting implications. Marquise du Deffand said, when commenting on the story that St. Dennis walked two leagues while carrying his head in his hands, that the most remarkable was the first step. The first one in new research is also important, but it is of little value without second, third, and several additional steps (I owe this reference to the Marquise and the comparison with research to Richard Posner). The rational choice approach takes further steps by using a framework that combines maximizing behavior with analysis of marriage and divorce markets, specialization and the division of labor, old age support, investments in children, and legislation that affects families. The implications of the full model are often not so obvious, and sometimes run sharply counter to received opinion.

For example, contrary to a common belief about divorce among the rich, the economic analysis of family decisions shows that wealthier couples are *less* likely to divorce than poorer couples. According to this theory, richer couples tend to gain a lot from remaining married, whereas many poorer couples do not. A poor woman may well doubt whether it is worth staying married to someone who is chronically unemployed. Empirical studies for many countries do indicate that marriage of richer couples are much more stable (see, e.g., Becker, Landes, and Michael, 1977, and Hernandez, 1992).

Efficient bargaining between husbands and wives implies that the trend in Europe and the United States toward no-fault divorce during the past two decades did not raise divorce rates, and, therefore, contrary to many claims, that it could not be responsible for the rapid rise in these rates. However, the theory does indicate that no-fault divorce hurts women with children whose marriages are broken up by their husbands. Feminists initially supported no-fault divorce, but some now have second thoughts about whether it has favorable effects on divorced women.

Economic models of behavior have been used to study fertility ever since Malthus's classic essay; the great Swedish economist, Knut Wicksell, was attracted to economics by his belief in the Malthusian predictions of overpopulation. But Malthus's conclusion that fertility would rise and fall as incomes increased and decreased was contradicted by the large decline in birth rates after some countries became industrialized during the latter part of the nineteenth century and the early part of this century.

The failure of Malthus's simple model of fertility persuaded economists that family-size decisions lay beyond economic calculus. The neoclassical growth model reflects this belief, for in most versions it takes population growth as exogenous and given (see, for example, Cass, 1965, or Arrow and Kurz, 1970).

However, the trouble with the Malthusian approach is not its use of economics per se, but an economics inappropriate for modern life. It neglects that the time spent on child care becomes more expensive when countries are more productive. The higher value of time raises the cost of children, and thereby reduces the demand for large families. It also fails to consider that the greater importance of education and training in industrialized economies encourages parents to invest more in the skills of their children, which also raises the cost of large families. The growing value of time and the increased emphasis on schooling and other human capital explain the decline in fertility as countries develop, and many other features of birth rates in modern economies.

In almost all societies married women have specialized in bearing and rearing children and in certain agricultural activities, whereas married men have done most of the fighting and market work. It should not be controversial to recognize that the explanation is a combination of biological differences between men and women—especially differences in their innate capacities to bear and rear children—and legal and other discrimination against women in market activities, partly through cultural conditioning. However, large and highly emotional differences of opinion exist over the relative importance of biology and discrimination in generating the traditional division of labor in marriages.

Contrary to allegations in many attacks on the economic approach to the gender division of labor (see, e.g., Boserup, 1987), this analysis does not try to weight the relative importance of biology and discrimination. Its main contribution is to show how sensitive the division of labor is to *small* differences in either. Since the return from investing in a skill is greater when more time is spent utilizing the skill, a married couple could gain much from a sharp division of labor because the husband would specialize in some types of human capital and the wife in others. Given such a large gain from specialization within a marriage, only a *little* discrimination against women or *small* biological differences in child-rearing skills would cause the division of labor between household and market tasks to be strongly and systematically related to gender. The sensitivity to small differences explains why the empirical evidence cannot readily choose between biological and "cultural" interpretations. This theory also explains why many women entered the labor force as families became smaller, divorce more common, and earning opportunities for women improved.

Relations among family members differ radically from those among employees of firms and members of other organizations. The interactions between husbands, wives, parents, and children are more likely to be motivated by love, obligation, guilt, and a sense of duty than by self-interest narrowly interpreted.

It was demonstrated about twenty years ago that altruism within families enormously alters how they respond to shocks and public policies that redistribute resources among members. It was shown that exogenous redistributions of resources from an altruist to her beneficiaries (or vice-versa) may not affect the welfare of anyone because the altruist would try to reduce her gifts by the amount redistributed (see Chapter 8). Barro (1974) derived this result in an intergenerational context, which cast doubt on the common assumption that government deficits and related fiscal policies have real effects on the economy.

The "Rotten-Kid Theorem"—the name is very popular even when critics disagree with the analysis—carries the discussion of altruism further, for it shows how the behavior of selfish individuals is affected by altruism. Under some conditions, even selfish persons—of course, most parents believe that the best example of selfish beneficiaries and altruistic benefactors is selfish children with altruistic parents—are induced to act *as if* they are altruistic toward their benefactors because that raises their own selfish welfare. They act this way because otherwise gifts from their benefactors would be reduced enough to make them worse off (see Chapter 8, and the elaboration and qualifications to the analysis in Lindbeck and Weibull, 1988, Bergstrom, 1989, and Becker, 1991, pp. 9–13).

The Bible, Plato's *Republic,* and other early writings discussed the treatment of young children by their parents, and of elderly parents by adult children. Both the elderly and children need care—in one case because of declining health and energy, and in the other because of biological growth and dependency. A powerful implication of the economic analysis of relations within families is that these two issues are closely related.

Parents who leave sizable bequests do not need old-age support because instead they help out their children. I mentioned earlier one well-known implication of this: under certain conditions, budget deficits and social security payments to the elderly have no real effects because parents simply offset the bigger taxes in the future on their children through larger bequests.

It is much less appreciated that altruistic parents who leave bequests also tend to invest more in their children's skills, habits, and values. For they gain from financing all investments in the education and skills of children that yield a higher rate of return than the return on savings. They can indirectly save for old age by investing in children, and then reducing bequests when elderly. Both parents and children would be better off when parents make all investments in children that yield a higher return than that on savings, and then adjust bequests to the efficient level of investment (see Appendix 7A for a formal demonstration).

However, even in rich countries many parents do not plan on leaving bequests. These parents want old-age support, and they "underinvest" in their children's education and other care. They underinvest because they cannot compensate themselves for greater spending on children by reducing bequests since they do not plan on leaving any.

Both the children and parents would be better off if the parents agreed to invest more in the children in return for a commitment by the children to care for them when they need help. But how can such a commitment be enforced? Economists and lawyers usually recommend a written contract to insure commitment, but can you imagine a society that will enforce contracts between adults and ten-year-olds or teenagers?

Part of my current research considers an indirect way to generate commitments when promises and written agreements are not binding. I will describe briefly some of this new work because it carries the economic approach to the family onto uncharted ground related to the rational formation of preferences within families.

Parental attitudes and behavior have an enormous influence on their children. Parents who are alcoholic or are addicted to crack create a bizarre atmosphere for impressionable youngsters, whereas parents with stable values who transmit knowledge and inspire their children favorably influence both what their children are capable of and what they want to do. The economic approach can contribute insights to the formation of preferences through childhood experiences without necessarily adopting the Freudian emphasis on the primacy of what happened during the first few months of life.

Again, I am trying to model a commonsense idea; namely, that the attitudes and values of adults are enormously influenced by their childhood experiences. An Indian doctor living in the United States may love curry because he acquired a strong taste for it while growing up in India, or a woman may forever fear men because she was sexually abused as a child.

Through its assumptions of forward-looking behavior, the economic point of view implies that parents try to anticipate the effect of what happens to children on their attitudes and behavior when adults. These effects help determine the kind of care parents provide. For example, parents worried about old-age support may try to instill in their children feelings of guilt, obligation, duty, and filial love that indirectly, but still very effectively, can "commit" children to helping them out.

Economists have too narrow a perspective on commitments. "Manipulating" the experiences of others to influence their preferences may appear to be inefficient and fraught with uncertainty, but it can be the most effective way available to obtain commitment. Economic theory, especially game theory, needs to incorporate guilt, affection, and related attitudes into preferences in order to have a deeper understanding of when commitments are "credible" (see Appendix 7B for a formal discussion).

Parents who do not leave bequests may be willing to make their children feel guiltier precisely because they gain more utility from greater old-age consumption than they lose from an equal reduction in children's consumption. This type of behavior may be considerably more common than suggested by the number of families that actually do leave bequests, for parents with young children often do not know whether they will be financially secure when they are old. They may try to protect themselves against ill health, unemployment, and other hazards of old age by instilling in their children a willingness to help out if that becomes necessary.

This analysis of the link between childhood experiences and adult preferences is closely related to work on rational habit formation (see Chapter 3; also see the discussion by Kandel and Lazear, 1992, of the creation of guilt among employees). The formation of preferences is rational in the sense that parental spending on children partly depends on the anticipated effects of childhood experiences on adult attitudes and behavior. I do not have time to consider the behavior of children—such as crying and acting "cute"—that tries in turn to influence the attitudes of parents.

Many economists, including myself, have excessively relied on altruism to tie together the interests of family members. Recognition of the connection between childhood experiences and future behavior reduces the need to rely on altruism in families. But it does not return the analysis to a narrow focus on self-interest, for it partially replaces altruism by feelings of obligation, anger, and other attitudes usually neglected by models of rational behavior.

If children are expected to help out in old age—perhaps because of guilt or related motivations—even parents who are not very loving would invest more in the children's human capital, and save less to provide for their old age. (For a proof, see Appendix 7C.) But equation (7.B12) shows that altruistic parents always prefer small increases in their own consumption when old to equal increases in their children's *if* they have made their children feel guilty. This means that such parents always underinvest in the children's human capital. This shows directly why creating guilt has costs and is not fully efficient.

Altruistic family heads who do not plan to leave bequests try to create a "warm" atmosphere in their families, so that members are willing to come to the assistance of those experiencing financial and other difficulties. This conclusion is relevant to discussions of so-called family values, a subject that received attention during the recent presidential campaign in the United States. Parents help determine the values of children—including their feelings of obligation, duty, and love—but what parents try to do can be greatly affected by public policies and changes in economic and social conditions.

Consider, for example, a program that transfers resources to the elderly, perhaps especially to poorer families who do not leave bequests, that reduces the elderly's dependence on children. According to the earlier analysis I gave, parents who do not need support when they become old do not try as hard to make children more loyal, guiltier, or otherwise feel as well-disposed toward their parents. This means that programs like social security that significantly help the elderly would encourage family members to drift apart emotionally, not by accident but as maximizing responses to those policies.

Other changes in the modern world which have altered family values include increased geographical mobility, the greater wealth that comes

with economic growth, better capital and insurance markets, higher divorce rates, smaller families, and publicly funded health care. These developments have generally made people better off, but they also weakened
the personal relations within families between husbands and wives, parents and children, and among more distant relatives, partly by reducing
the incentives to invest in *creating* closer relations.

## 6. Concluding Comments

An important step in extending the traditional analysis of individual
rational choice is to incorporate into the theory a much richer class of
attitudes, preferences, and calculations. This step is prominent in all the
examples I consider. The analysis of discrimination includes in preferences
a dislike of—prejudice against—members of particular groups, such as
blacks or women. In deciding whether to engage in illegal activities, potential criminals are assumed to act as if they consider both the gains and
the risks—including the likelihood they will be caught and severity of punishments. In human capital theory, people rationally evaluate the benefits
and costs of activities, such as education, training, expenditures on health,
migration, and formation of habits that radically alter the way they are.
The economic approach to the family assumes that even intimate decisions
like marriage, divorce, and family size are reached through weighing the
advantages and disadvantages of alternative actions. The weights are determined by preferences that critically depend on the altruism and feelings
of duty and obligation toward family members.

Since the economic, or rational choice, approach to behavior builds
on a theory of individual decisions, criticisms of this theory usually concentrate on particular assumptions about how these decisions are made.
Among other things, critics deny that individuals act consistently over
time, and question whether behavior is forward-looking, particularly
in situations that differ significantly from those usually considered by
economists—such as those involving criminal, addictive, family, or political behavior. This is not the place to go into a detailed response to the
criticisms, so I simply assert that no approach of comparable generality
has yet been developed that offers serious competition to rational choice
theory.

I have intentionally chosen certain topics—such as addiction—to
probe the boundaries of rational choice theory. William Blake said that
you never know what is enough until you see what is more than enough
(Jon Elster brought this proverb to my attention). My work may have

sometimes assumed too much rationality, but I believe it has been an antidote to the extensive research that does not credit people with enough rationality.

While the economic approach to behavior builds on a theory of individual choice, it is not mainly concerned with individuals. It uses theory at the micro level as a powerful tool to derive implications at the group or macro level. Rational individual choice is combined with assumptions about technologies and other determinants of opportunities, equilibrium in market and nonmarket situations, and laws, norms, and traditions to obtain results concerning the behavior of groups. It is mainly because the theory derives implications at the macro level that it is of interest to policymakers and those studying differences among countries and cultures.

None of the theories considered in this lecture aims for the greatest generality; instead, each tries to derive concrete implications about behavior that can be tested with survey and other data. Disputes over whether punishments deter crime, whether the lower earnings of women compared to men is mainly due to discrimination or lesser human capital, or whether no-fault divorce laws increase divorce rates, all raise questions about the empirical relevance of predictions derived from a theory based on individual rationality.

A close relation between theory and empirical testing helps prevent both the theoretical analysis and the empirical research from becoming sterile. Empirically oriented theories encourage the development of new sources and types of data, the way human capital theory stimulated the use of survey data, especially panels. At the same time, puzzling empirical results force changes in theory, as models of altruism and family preferences have been enriched to cope with the finding that parents in Western countries tend to bequeath equal amounts to different children.

I have been impressed by how many economists want to work on social issues rather than those forming the traditional core of economics. At the same time, specialists from fields that do consider social questions are often attracted to the economic way of modelling behavior because of the analytical power provided by the assumption of individual rationality. Thriving schools of rational choice theorists and empirical researchers are active in sociology, law, political science, and history, and to a lesser extent, in anthropology and psychology. The rational choice model provides the most promising basis presently available for a unified approach to the analysis of the social world by scholars from different social sciences.

## Appendix 7A

To develop a formal analysis, suppose that each person lives for three periods: youth ($y$), middle age ($m$), and old age ($o$), and has one child at the beginning of period $m$. A child's youth overlaps his parent's middle age, and a child's middle age overlaps his parent's old age. The utility parents get from altruism is assumed to be separable from the utilities produced by their own consumption.

A simple utility function of parents ($V_p$) incorporating these assumptions is

$$(7.A1) \qquad\qquad V_p = u_{mp} + \beta u_{op} - \beta a V_c$$

where $\beta$ is the discount rate, and the degree of altruism rises with $a$. For selfish parents, $a = 0$. I do not permit parents to be sadistic toward children ($a < 0$), although the analysis is easily generalized to include sadists.

Each person works and earns income only during middle age. It is possible to save then to provide consumption for old age ($Z_{op}$) by accumulating assets with a yield of $R_k$. Parents influence children's earnings by investing in their human capital. The marginal yield on these investments ($R_h$) is defined as

$$(7.A2) \qquad\qquad R_h = \frac{dE_c}{dh}$$

where $E_c$ is the earnings of children at middle age, and $h$ is the amount invested. This yield is assumed to decline as more is invested in children: $dR_h/dh \leq 0$.

Parents must also decide whether to leave bequests, denoted by $k_c$. If parents can consume at different ages, leave bequests, or invest in the child's human capital, their budget constraint is

$$(7.A3) \qquad\qquad Z_{mp} + h + \frac{Z_{op}}{R_k} + \frac{k_c}{R_k} = A_p$$

where $A$ is the present value of resources.

One first order condition to maximize parental utility determines their optimal consumption at middle and old age

$$u'_{mp} = \beta R_k u'_{op} = \lambda_p$$

where $\lambda_p$ is the parents' marginal utility of wealth. Another condition determines whether they give bequests:

$$(7.A5) \qquad\qquad \beta a V_c' \leq \frac{\lambda_p}{R_k} = \beta u_{op}'$$

and the last determines investments in the human capital of children

$$(7.A6) \qquad\qquad R_h \beta a V_c' = \lambda_p$$

Equation (7.A6) assumes that the first-order condition for investment in human capital is a strict equality; that some human capital is always invested in children. This can be justified with an Inada-type condition that small investments in human capital yield very high rates of return. In rich economies like Sweden or the United States, investments in basic knowledge and nutrition of children presumably do yield a very good return. As long as parents are not completely selfish—as long as $a > 0$—then such a condition does always imply positive investment in human capital. For completely selfish parents, equation (7.A6) would be an inequality.

Equation (7.A4) determines the accumulation of assets to finance old-age consumption. Whether parents leave bequests or want old-age support from their children is determined by the inequality in (7.A5). If this is a strict inequality, parents want support and would not leave bequests.

That inequality can be written in a more revealing way. If children also maximize their utility, then the envelope theorem implies that

$$(7.A7) \qquad\qquad a u_{mc}' < u_{op}' \text{ whenever } a V_c' < u_{op}' \text{ since } V_c' = u_{mc}'$$

Equation (7.A7) has the intuitive interpretation that parents do not give bequests when the utility the parents get from their children consuming a dollar more at middle age is less than the utility they get from a dollar more of their own consumption at old age. Obviously, such an inequality holds for completely selfish parents since the left-hand side of equations (7.A5) and (7.A7) are zero when $a$ is zero. The weaker the altruism (the smaller $a$) the more parents want from children.

Combining equations (7.A5) and (7.A6) gives

$$(7.A8) \qquad\qquad \frac{\lambda_p}{R_h} \leq \frac{\lambda_p}{R_k}, \text{ or } R_h \geq R_k$$

Equation (7.A8) implies that the marginal rate of return on human capital equals the return on assets when parents give bequests, and it is greater than the asset return when parents do not give bequests. Parents can help children either by investing in their human capital or by leaving them assets. Since they want to maximize the advantage to children, given the cost to themselves—parents are not sadistic—they help in the most efficient form.

Consequently, if strict inequality holds in equation (7.A8), they would not give bequests, for the best way to help children when the marginal return on human capital exceeds that on assets is to invest only in human capital. They leave bequests only when they get the same marginal return on both (some of these results have been derived in Becker and Tomes, 1986).

*Appendix 7B*
To analyze in a simple way the influence of parents over the formation of children's preferences, suppose parents can take actions $x$ and $y$ when children are young that affect their preferences when adults. I use the assumption of separability to write the utility function of middle-aged children as

(7.B9) $$V_c = u_{mc} + H(y) - G(x, g) + \beta u_{oc} + \ldots$$

I assume that $H' > 0$ and $G_x > 0$, which means that an increase in $y$ raises the utility of children, but an increase in $x$ lowers their utility. Interpret $H$ for concreteness as "happiness," and $G$ as the "guilt" children feel toward their parents, so that greater $x$ makes children feel guiltier. The question is why would nonsadistic parents want to make their children feel guilty?

The variable $g$ is the key to understanding why. This measures the contribution of children to the old-age support of parents; let us assume that children feel less guilty when they contribute more ($G_g < 0$). If $G_{gx} > 0$, then greater $x$ both raises children's guilt and stimulates more giving by them.

The budget constraint of parents becomes:

(7.B10) $$Z_{mp} + h + x + y + \frac{Z_{op}}{R_k} + \frac{k_c}{R_k} = A_p + \frac{g}{R_k}$$

The first-order condition for the optimal $y$ is

(7.B11) $$\beta a H' \leq \lambda_p$$

Since $H' > 0$, it is easy to understand why an altruistic parent may try to affect children's preferences through $y$ since an increase in $y$ makes children happier.

The first-order condition for $x$ is more interesting, for even altruistic parents may want to make their children feel guilty if that sufficiently raises old-age support. This first-order condition can be written as

$$(7.B12) \qquad \frac{dV_p}{dx} = \frac{dg}{dx} \beta (u'_{op} - au'_{mc}) - \beta a \frac{dG}{dx} \le \lambda_p$$

where $dG/dx$ incorporates the induced change in $g$. The second term in the middle expression is negative to altruistic parents because greater $x$ does raise children's guilt, which lowers the utility of these parents ($a > 0$). However, guilt also induces children to increase old-age support, as given by $dg/dx$. The magnitude of this response determines whether it is worthwhile for parents to make children guiltier.

Increased old-age support from children has two partially offsetting effects on the welfare of altruistic parents. On the one hand, it raises their old-age consumption and utility, as given by $u'_{op}$. On the other hand, it lowers children's consumption, and hence the utility of altruistic parents, as given by $-au'_{mc}$. This means that altruistic parents who leave bequests never try to make children guiltier, for $u'_{op} = au'_{mc}$ for these parents. Since $dG/dx > 0$, they must be worse off when their children feel guiltier.

Equations (7.A5) and (7.B12) imply that

$$(7.B13) \qquad \frac{dg}{dx} - \frac{aG_x}{u'_{op}} = R_x \le R_k$$

The marginal rate of return to altruistic parents from making children feel guiltier (given by $R_x$) nets out the parents' evaluation of the loss in children's utility from their guilt. Selfish parents ($a = 0$) ignore this loss, and simply compare the effects of $x$ and $k$ on their consumption at old age.

## Appendix 7C

Combine the first-order conditions in equations (7.A5) and (7.A6) to get

$$(7.C14) \qquad \frac{u'_{op}}{au'_{mc}} = \frac{R_h}{R_k}$$

   Both sides of this equation exceed unity when parents do not give bequests. Since greater old-age support from children lowers the left-hand side by lowering the numerator and raising the denominator, the right-hand side must also fall to be in a utility-maximizing equilibrium. But since $R_k$ is given by market conditions, the right-hand side can fall only if $R_h$ falls, which implies greater investment in children when parents expect greater old-age support from children. Even completely selfish parents ($a = 0$) might invest in children if that would sufficiently increase the expected old-age support from guilty children.

# A Theory of
# Social Interactions

# 8

No Man is an Island.
—Donne, *Devotions upon
Emergent Occasions*

Man is a social animal.
—Seneca, *De beneficiis*

## 1. Introduction

Before the theory of consumer demand began to be formalized by
Jevons, Walras, Marshall, Menger, and others, economists frequently discussed what they considered to be the basic determinants of wants. For
example, Bentham (1789, chap. 5) discusses about 15 basic kinds of pleasures and pains—all other pleasures and pains are presumed to be com-
binations of the basic set—and Marshall (1962, bk. 3, chap. 2) briefly
discusses a few basic determinants of wants before moving on to his well-
known presentation of marginal utility theory. What is relevant and important for present purposes is the prominence given to the interactions
among individuals.

Bentham mentions "the pleasures . . . of being on good terms with
him or them," "the pleasures of a good name," "the pleasures resulting
from the view of any pleasures supposed to be possessed by the beings
who may be the objects of benevolence," and "the pleasures resulting from
the view of any pain supposed to be suffered by the beings who may become the objects of malevolence." Nassau Senior said that "the desire
for distinction . . . is a feeling which if we consider its universality, and
its constancy, that it affects all men and at all times, that it comes with
us from the cradle and never leaves us till we go into the grave, may be
pronounced to be the most powerful of all human passions" (quoted by
Marshall, 1962, p. 87). Marshall also stresses the desire for distinction and

Originally published in *Journal of Political Economy*, 82, no. 6 (1974): 1063–
1093. © 1974 by the University of Chicago. All rights reserved.

illustrates its influence by discussing food, clothing, housing, and productive activities.[1]

As greater rigor permeated the theory of consumer demand, variables like distinction, a good name, or benevolence were pushed further and further out of sight. Each individual or family generally is assumed to have a utility function that depends directly on the goods and services it consumes. This is not to say that interactions between individuals have been completely ignored. Pigou (1903), Fisher (1926, p. 102), and Panteleoni (1898)[2] included attributes of others in utility functions (but did nothing with them). In recent literature, "demonstration" and "relative income" effects on savings and consumption,[3] "bandwagon" and "snob" influences on ordinary consumption theory,[4] and the economics of philanthropic contributions[5] have been discussed. But these efforts have not been unified and, more significantly, have not captured the dominance attributed to social interactions by nineteenth-century economists.

Of course, sociologists have for a long time emphasized the central role of interactions and their importance in the basic structure of wants or personality. Veblen's conspicuous consumption and conspicuous leisure (if for this purpose he is classified as a sociologist) have entered ordinary discourse. At one point he said: "But it is only when taken in a sense far removed from its naive meaning that the consumption of goods can be said to afford the incentive from which accumulation invariably proceeds. The motive that lies at the root of ownership is emulation," and "the usual basis of self-respect is the respect accorded by one's neighbors" (Veblen, 1934, pp. 25, 30). Interactions were also emphasized by Durkheim, Simmel, Freud, and Weber, as well as in modern discussions of "social exchange" and the "theory of action" (see Blau, 1968; Parsons, 1968).

My interest in interactions can probably be traced to a study of dis-

---

1. He limits his discussion of consumer demand to the largely formal theory of marginal theory because of the importance he attaches to the interaction between activities, consumer behavior and the basic wants: "Such a discussion of demand as is possible at this stage of our work must be confined to an elementary analysis of an almost purely formal kind" (1962, p. 90). He never developed the more complicated and less formal analysis.

2. I owe this reference to George Stigler.

3. See, e.g., Brady and Friedman (1947), Duesenberry (1949), or Johnson (1952).

4. See Leibenstein (1950).

5. See Vickery (1962), Schwartz (1970), Alchian and Allen (1967, pp. 135–42), and Boulding (1973).

UNIVERSITY COLLEGE Library CORK

crimination and "prejudice" where I analyzed discriminatory behavior by incorporating the race, religion, sex, or other personal characteristics of employees, fellow workers, customers, dealers, neighbors, etc., into utility functions (Becker, 1957, 1971). Subsequently, in order to provide a theoretical framework for a study of philanthropy by the National Bureau of Economic Research, I incorporated the standard of living of "poorer" persons into the utility functions of "richer" ones (Becker, 1961). Further reflection gradually convinced me that the emphasis of earlier economists deserved to be taken much more seriously because social interactions had significance far transcending the special cases discussed by myself[6] and others.

This chapter incorporates a general treatment of interactions into the modern theory of consumer demand. In Section 2, various characteristics of different persons are assumed to affect the utility functions of some persons, and the behavioral implications are systematically explored. Section 3 develops further implications and applications in the context of analyzing intrafamily relations, charitable behavior, merit goods and multiperson interactions, and envy and hatred. The variety and significance of these applications is persuasive testimony not only to the importance of social interactions but also the feasibility of incorporating them into a rigorous analysis.

## 2. Theoretical Framework

### 2A. Equilibrium for a Single Person

According to the modern (and very old!) theory of household behavior,[7]

$$(8.1) \qquad\qquad U_i = U_i(Z_1, \ldots, Z_m)$$

is the utility function of the $i$th person, and $Z_1, \ldots, Z_m$ are the basic wants or commodities. As indicated earlier, Bentham mentions about 15 basic wants, whereas Marshall and Senior stress an even smaller number. Each person also has a set of production functions that determine how much of these commodities can be produced with the market goods, time, and other resources available to him:

$$(8.2) \qquad\qquad Z_j = f_j^i(x_j, t_j, E^i, R_j^1, \ldots, R_j^r)$$

---

6. Other drafts that were also circulated include Becker (1968b).
7. For an exposition of this theory, see Michael and Becker (1973).

where $x_j$ are quantities of different market goods and services; $t_j$ are quantities of his own time, $E^i$ stands for his education, experience, and "environmental" variables; and $R_j^1, \ldots, R_j^r$ are characteristics of other persons that affect his output of commodities. For example, if $Z_1$ measures $i$'s distinction in his occupation, $R_1^1, \ldots, R_1^r$ could be the opinions of $i$ held by other persons in the same occupation. Presumably, characteristics of others affect the production of a significant fraction of commodities.

If the $R_j$ were completely outside $i$'s control—that is, unaffected by what he does with his resources—$i$ would maximize $U$ taking the $R_j$ as given. This is one way to justify the usual neglect of interactions. They are considered beyond the control of the persons being studied and are therefore taken as given when one is analyzing their reactions to changes in resources and prices.

The point of departure of my approach is to assume the contrary, namely, that $i$ can change $R_j$ by his own efforts. For example, he can avoid social opprobrium and perhaps ostracism by not engaging in criminal activities; achieve distinction by working diligently at his occupation, giving to charities, or having a beautiful house; or relieve his envy and jealousy by talking meanly about or even physically harming his neighbors. These effects can be formalized in a production function for the $(R_j^1, \ldots R_j^r)$ that depends partly on the efforts of $i$ and partly on other variables.

To simplify the discussion,[8] I follow Senior and assume only a single commodity (distinction?) that is produced with a single good (the input of time is ignored) and a single characteristic of others. Then maximizing utility is equivalent to maximizing the output of this commodity, and one can write

(8.3) $$U_i = Z(x, R)$$

I assume also (until Section 3C) that the effect of other variables (including the efforts of others) on this characteristic is not dependent on $i$'s own efforts. Therefore, $R$ can be written as the additive function

(8.4) $$R = D_i + h$$

where $h$ measures the effects of $i$'s efforts, and $D_i$ the level of $R$ when $i$ makes no effort; that is, $D_i$ measures $i$'s "social environment."

---

8. I have also developed the analysis assuming many commodities and many characteristics.

His budget constraint for money income can be written as

$$(8.5) \qquad\qquad p_x x + p_R h = I_i$$

where $I_i$ is his money income, $p_R h$ is the amount he spends on $R$, and $p_R$ is the price to him of a unit of $R$. Substitute $R - D_i$ for $h$ in equation (8.5) to get

$$(8.6) \qquad\qquad p_x x + p_R R = I_i + p_R D_i = S_i$$

The right-hand side gives the sum of $i$'s money income and the value to him of his social environment, and will be called his social income. The left-hand side shows how his social income is "spent": partly on his "own" goods ($x$) and partly on the characteristics of others ($R$).[9]

If $i$ maximizes the utility-output function given by equation (8.3) subject to the constraint on social income given by equation (8.6), the equilibrium condition is[10]

$$(8.7) \qquad\qquad \frac{\partial U_i}{\partial x} \Big/ \frac{\partial U_i}{\partial R} = \frac{p_x}{p_R}$$

If I did not want to purchase any $R$, $p_R$ would be a "shadow" price, measured by the monetary equivalent of the marginal utility (equal to the marginal product) of $R$ to $i$ when $R = D_i$ (or when $h = 0$).

His equilibrium position is shown in Figures 8.1 and 8.2. The first figure assumes that $R$ has a positive marginal product in the production of $Z$ (a positive marginal utility); that $R$ refers, for example, to the respect accorded $i$ rather than to his envy of others. The quantity $0D$ measures his social environment, and $0x_0$ his own income (measured in terms of $x$), so that the "endowed" point $E_0$ gives his utility when he spends nothing on $R$. If $E_0 S_0$ measures the opportunities available for purchasing additional $R$,[11] he would maximize his utility by moving along $E_0 S_0$ to point

---

9. Sociologists sometimes assert that variables like social approval and respect "do not have any material value on which a price can be put" (see Blau, 1968). But prices measure only scarcity and have nothing intrinsically to do with "material value"; $p_R$, for example, only measures the resource cost to $i$ of changing social approval, respect, etc.

10. I assume for simplicity in this formula that $p_R$ measures the marginal as well as average price of $R$.

11. If he can also reduce $R$ by giving up own goods, the curve $E_0 S_0$ would continue in the southwest direction (see $E S_0'$ in the figure). However, this section would be irrelevant if $R$ had positive marginal utility.

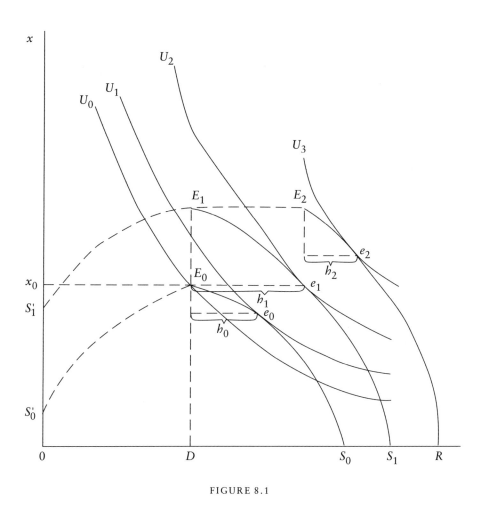

FIGURE 8.1

$e_0$, where the slope of this opportunity curve equaled the slope of his indifference curve. His equilibrium purchase of $R$ is measured by the line segment $h_0$.

Figure 8.2 assumes that $R$ has a negative marginal product (or utility) because, say, it measures the income or prestige of persons that $i$ envies. The section of the opportunity curve to the southeast of point $E_0$ is now irrelevant, and he moves along the southwest section $E_0 S_0'$ to point $e_0$. He

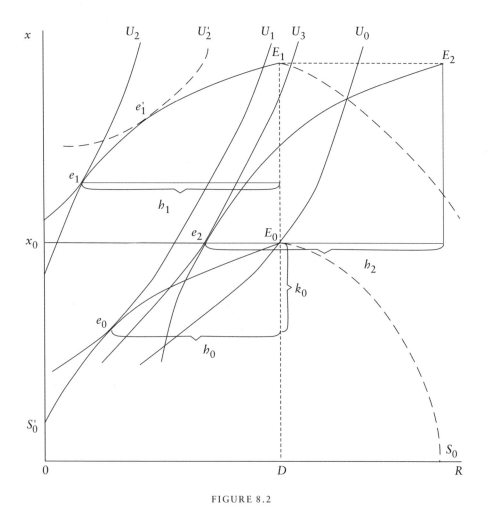

FIGURE 8.2

is willing to give up resources to reduce $R$ because his utility is raised by a reduction in $R$; at point $e_0$, he spends enough resources to reduce $R$ by $h_0$.

Note that since the marginal (and average) price of $R$ is negative in Figure 8.2, $i$'s social income is *less* than his own income because the value of his social environment is subtracted from his own income. That is, he is made worse off by his social environment if it is dominated by characteristics of others that are distasteful to him. Note too that as long as the marginal utility of $R$ is not zero at the socially endowed position, his social income would differ from his own income even if he did not want to spend anything on $R$. He would add to (or subtract from) his own income the product of $D$ and the (monetary equivalent of the) marginal utility of $R$ at the endowed position $E_0$. In other words, the traditional income concept is incomplete even when no resources are spent trying to influence the attitudes or situation of others.

The analysis developed for social interactions in these figures and in equations (8.3), (8.6), and (8.7) is also applicable whenever there is a physical environment that either can be altered directly or can have its effects augmented or diminished. For example, the human capital of a person is the sum of the amount inherited and that acquired through investments; moreover, the amount invested is partly determined by the inheritance. Or the temperature in a house is determined by the weather and expenditures on fuels, insulation, etc., that reinforce or offset the natural environment.

A more general analysis, therefore, would assume that every term entering the utility function has both an environmental and acquired component. The general analysis could readily be developed, but I have chosen to simplify the discussion by ignoring the nonsocial environment. The results are consistent with those from the general analysis as long as the contribution of the social environment is, on the whole, significantly more important than that of the physical environment. This is assumed to be true. (I am indebted to Gilbert Ghez and especially Robert Barro for stressing the general nature of the analysis.)

## 2B. INCOME AND PRICE EFFECTS

An increase in $i$'s own income alone—without any change in prices or the social environment—would increase both $x$ and $R$ unless one were inferior. The average percentage response in $x$ and $R$ per 1 percent change in his own income is not unity, but is less by the fraction $\alpha$, where $\alpha$ is the share of the social environment in his social income.[12] Therefore, the effect

---

12. By differentiating equation (8.6) with respect to $I_i$ alone, $\bar{n} \equiv w_x n_x + w_R n_R = 1 - \alpha$, where

$$w_x = \frac{p_x x}{S_i}, w_R = \frac{p_R R}{S_i} = 1 - w_x, n_x = \frac{dx}{dI_i} \cdot \frac{I_i}{x}, n_R = \frac{dR}{dI_i} \cdot \frac{I_i}{R}, \alpha = \frac{p_R D_i}{S_i}$$

and I am assuming that $p_R$ is given (not dependent on $h$, $x$, etc.). Of course, the weighted average of income elasticities with respect to a change in $S_i$ must equal unity, as in the usual analysis.

of a change in his own income on his utility-output is smaller the more important his social environment is.

Put differently, the greater the contribution of his social environment to his social income, the more his welfare is determined by the attitudes and behavior of others rather than by his own income. Traditional models of choice by economists assume that own efforts and access to property income and transfer payments determine welfare. On the other hand, those who stress the social environment, its normative requirements and sanctions for compliance and noncompliance, and the helplessness of the individual in the face of his environment naturally see society dominating individual efforts and, consequently, see little scope for important choices by individuals.

The relative importance of the social environment, as well as other implications of the theory of social interactions, can be empirically estimated from information on expenditures motivated by these interactions. If $i$'s social environment did not change when his own income changed, the induced absolute change in the characteristics of others would equal the change in his contribution to these characteristics. However, the relative change in his contribution would differ from the relative change in these characteristics because the level of the latter is partly determined by the social environment.

Consider again Figures 8.1 and 8.2, where an increase in $i$'s own income with no changes in the environment is shown by a vertical increase in the endowed position from $E_0$ to $E_1$. Since his equilibrium position changes from $e_0$ to $e_1$, the change in $R$ is exactly equal to $h_1 - h_0$, the change in $i$'s contribution to $R$. The percentage change in $R$ in Figure 8.1 is clearly less than that in $h$, since $R$ is the sum of $h$ and (a fixed) $D$. Since the percentage change in $R$ in Figure 8.2 is negative, it is also less than the percentage change in $h$, which is positive (since $h$ is negative). However, if $R$ had been increased by the increase in $i$'s own income—if, say, the new equilibrium position was at point $e_1'$—the percentage change in $R$ would be positive and would clearly exceed in algebraic value the negative percentage change in $h$.

The own-income elasticity of demand for contributions is related to the elasticity of demand for characteristics by the following formula:[13]

---

13. Since $dh/dI_i = dR/dI_i$,

$$(8.8')\qquad n_h = \frac{dh}{dI_i} \cdot \frac{I_i}{h} = \frac{dR}{dI_i} \cdot \frac{I_i}{R} \cdot \frac{R}{h} = n_R \cdot \frac{R}{h}$$

(8.8)
$$n_h \equiv \frac{dh}{dI_i} \cdot \frac{I_i}{h} = \frac{n_R}{\bar{n}(=1-\alpha)}\left[1+\alpha\left(\frac{1}{\beta}-1\right)\right]$$

where $0 \leq \beta \leq 1$ is the fraction of own income that is spent on contributions to $R$. If $\alpha > 0$, if the social environment adds to $i$'s social income, then clearly $n_h > n_R$.[14] Moreover, if $n_R \geq \bar{n} = 1-\alpha < 1$, necessarily $n_h > 1$ even when $n_R < 1$; that is, contributions to the characteristics of others could have a "high" income elasticity even when the characteristics themselves had a "low" elasticity. Of couse, if $n_h > 1$, the own-income elasticity of demand for own consumption $(n_x)$ would be less than unity. That is, social interaction implies a relatively *low* income elasticity for own consumption even without introducing transitory changes in income, errors in variables, and the like.

Equation (8.8) further implies that an increase in $\alpha$, an increase in the social environment, with no change in the own-income elasticity of demand for characteristics relative to the average elasticity $(n_R/\bar{n})$,[15] would increase the own-income elasticity of demand for contributions.[16] In other words, the more that $i$'s social income was determined by his social environment, the greater would be the percentage change in his contributions to the characteristics of others as his own income changed.

If, on the other hand, $\alpha < 0$—the social environment subtracted from $i$'s social income—then equation (8.8) implies that $n_h < n_R$ when $n_R > 0$, and $n_h > n_R$ when $n_R < 0$ (these different cases are shown in Fig. 8.2). His demand for characteristics would probably be reduced by an increase in his own income (i.e., $n_R < 0$) if these characteristics have a negative marginal utility to him. Again, an increase in $\alpha$, with $n_R/\bar{n}$ held constant, would raise $n_h$ (the argument in fn. 16 fully applies).

---

But
$$\frac{R}{h} = \frac{p_R R}{p_R h} = 1 + \frac{p_R D_i}{p_R h} = 1 + \frac{S_i - I_i}{\beta I_i} = 1 + \frac{1/(1-\alpha)-1}{\beta} = \frac{(1-\alpha)+\alpha/\beta}{1-\alpha}$$

Since $1 - \alpha = \bar{n}$ (see fn. 12 above), $n_h = (n_R/\bar{n})(\alpha/\beta + 1 - \alpha)$.

14. For $[1 + \alpha(1/\beta - 1)]/(1-\alpha) > 1$, since $1/\beta > 1$, and $1 - \alpha < 1$.

15. An increase is $\alpha$ lowers $\bar{n}$ because the relative contribution of own income to social income is reduced.

16.
$$\frac{dn_h}{d\alpha}\left(\frac{n_R}{\bar{n}} = \text{constant}\right) = \frac{n_R}{\bar{n}}\left(\frac{1}{\beta}-1\right) - \frac{n_R}{\bar{n}}\alpha\,\beta^{-2}\frac{d\beta}{d\alpha}$$

Both terms are greater than zero because $\beta < 1$, and $d\beta/d\alpha < 0$ (this is shown shortly); therefore, $dn_h/d\alpha > 0$.

Since the social environment to any person cannot be readily observed, an indirect method of estimating at least its sign would be useful. If $n_R/\bar{n}$ were known, that is, if the relative income elasticity of demand for characterisitics were known, the sign of $\alpha$ could be estimated simply from information on the own-income elasticity of demand for contributions to the environment, and its magnitude from additional information on the fraction of own income spent on these contributions. Equation (8.8) implies that

$$(8.9) \qquad \alpha = \frac{n_h(\bar{n}/n_R) - 1}{1/\beta - 1}$$

Therefore, $\alpha \gtreqless 0$ as $n_h(\bar{n}/n_R) \gtreqless 1$, and information on $n_h$, $\bar{n}/n_R$, and $\beta$ would be sufficient to estimate $\alpha$.

An increase in a social environment that adds to $i$'s social income would increase his demand for own goods if they had positive income elasticities. If his own income were unchanged, his increased expenditure on own goods would have to be "financed" by reduced contributions to the characteristics of others. Similarly, an increase in a social environment that subtracts from his social income would increase his expenditures on others and reduce his expenditures on own goods. Consequently, the effect of a change in the environment is always (i.e., as long as own goods are not inferior) partly offset by induced changes in $i$'s contributions in the opposite direction, regardless of whether the environment adds to or subtracts from $i$'s social income.

Geometrically, a change in the social environment is shown by a horizontal movement of the endowed position. An increase in the environment shifts the endowment in Figure 8.1 from point $E_1$ to $E_2$; the equilibrium position is changed from point $e_1$ to a point on a higher indifference curve ($e_2$), and $i$'s contribution declines from $h_1$ to $h_2$. In Figure 8.2, the equilibrium is changed from point $e_1$ to a point on a lower indifference curve ($e_2$), and $i$'s contribution increases from $h_1$ to $h_2$.[17]

If both the own and environment incomes of $i$ changed, the effect

---

17. The endowment-income elasticity of demand for contributions can easily be shown to equal

$$N_h = \frac{dh}{dD} \cdot \frac{D}{h} = (N_R - 1) \left\{ \frac{1}{1-\alpha} \left[ 1 + \alpha \left( \frac{1}{\beta} - 1 \right) \right] \right\} + 1$$

Clearly, when $\alpha > 0$, $N_h < 0$ if $N_R \le \alpha = \bar{N}$, the average endowment-income elasticity of demand; and when $\alpha < 0$, $N_h > 0$ if $N_R \ge \alpha$.

would be a combination of those when each alone changed. For example, if both incomes increased, the effect on his contributions of the increase in the environment would at least partly offset the effect of the increase in his own income. In particular, if both incomes increased by the same percentage, the percentage change in contributions would be greater than, equal to, or smaller than that percentage as his demand for characteristics exceeded, equaled, or was less than unity.

Through the assumption that $p_R$ is constant, I have been assuming, in effect, that expenditures and the social environment are perfect substitutes in producing characteristics of others. However, the qualitative implications of this assumption can also be derived if they are simply better substitutes for each other than for own consumption—if $p_R$ rises as $h$ rises, but not "too" rapidly. For example, a rise in the environment would reduce contributions, and a rise in own income would increase contributions by a relatively large percentage if the environment and expenditures on these characteristics are simply relatively close direct substitutes.

A rise in the cost of changing the characteristics of others ($p_R$) would induce the usual substitution (and perhaps income) effects away from these characteristics. If the environment were given, the absolute change in contributions would equal the absolute change in these characteristics, while the percentage changes would differ according to equation (8.8) in the following way:

$$(8.10) \qquad E_h = -\frac{dh}{dp_R}\frac{p_R}{h} = E_R\left[\frac{1+\alpha(1/\beta - 1)}{1-\alpha}\right]$$

(same proof as in fn. 13 above). Therefore, when $\alpha > 0$, $E_h$ would exceed $E_R$ by an amount that would be greater, the greater $\alpha$ and the smaller $\beta$. Similarly, when $\alpha < 0$, $E_h$ would be less than $E_R$[18] by an amount that would be greater, the greater the absolute value of $\alpha$ and the smaller $\beta$.

## 3. Applications

Three specific applications of the general analysis of social interaction are now considered: interactions among members of the same family, charity, and envy and hatred. These applications not only provide empirical support for the income and price implications just derived, but also bring out a number of other implications of social interaction.

---

18. I assume that an increase in the absolute value of $p_R$ reduces the demand for $R$, so that $E_h > 0$.

## 3A. THE FAMILY

Assume that $i$ cares about his spouse $j$ in the sense that $i$'s utility function depends on $j$'s welfare.[19] I assume until much later in this section that $j$ does not care positively or negatively about $i$. For simplicity, define the variable measuring this dependence, $R_i$, as follows:

$$(8.11) \qquad R_i = \frac{I_j + h_{ij}}{p_x} = \frac{S_j}{p_x} = x_j$$

where $I_j$ is $j$'s own income, $h_{ij}$ are the contributions from $i$ to $j$, $S_j$ is $j$'s social income, and $x_j$ are the goods consumed by $j$. The social income of $i$ can be derived by substituting equation (8.1) into equation (8.6):

$$(8.12) \qquad p_x x_i + p_R R_i = S_i = I_i + \frac{p_R I_j}{p_x}$$

where $p_R$ is the price to $i$ of transferring resources to $j$. If $i$ can transfer resources to $j$ without any "transactions" costs—presumably, these costs are reduced by sharing a common household—and if $i$ cares sufficiently about $j$ to have $h_{ij} > 0$, then $p_R = p_x$, and

$$(8.13) \qquad S_i = p_x x_i + p_x x_j = I_i + I_j = I_{ij}$$

The social income of $i$ equals the combined own incomes of $i$ and $j$, or the "family's" own income. Moreover, the equilibrium condition given by equation (8.7) implies that

$$(8.14) \qquad \frac{\partial U_i}{\partial x_i} \bigg/ \frac{\partial U_i}{\partial (R_i = x_j)} = \frac{p_x}{p_R} = 1$$

or $i$ would receive equal marginal utility from $j$'s and his own consumption.

Conditions (8.13) and (8.14) are shown in Figure 8.3. Resources can be transferred from $i$ to $j$ by moving along $i$'s budget line in a southeast direction from the endowed position at point $E_0$. The equilibrium position is at point $e$, where the slope of $i$'s indifference curves equals the slope of his budget line $(= -1)$. The vertical (or horizontal) intercept gives the family's own income—$i$'s social income—deflated by the price of $x$.

---

19. Caring is not simply a *deus ex machina* introduced to derive the following implications, since I have shown elsewhere (Becker, 1974) that the marriage market is more likely to pair a person with someone he cares about than with an otherwise similar person that he does not care about.

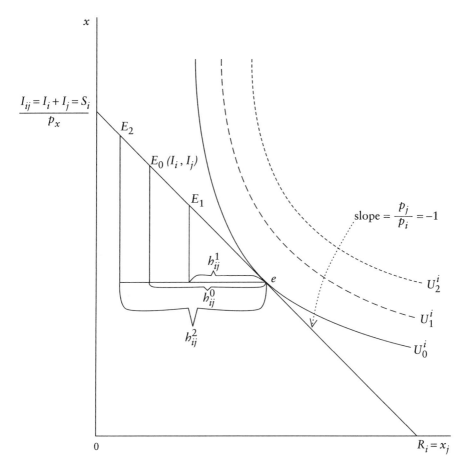

FIGURE 8.3

An important implication of this analysis is that a change in the distribution of family income between $i$ and $j$ has no effect at all on the consumption or welfare of either, as long as $i$ continues to transfer resources to $j$. A change in the distribution would be on the same budget line as $E_0$ if total family income is unchanged: the change from $E_0$ to $E_1$ is nominally more favorable to $j$, whereas the change to $E_2$ is nominally more favorable to $i$. Since there is only one point of tangency between $i$'s budget line and an indifference curve, the equilibrium position must be unchanged at $e$. A shift in favor of $j$'s income to $E_1$ simply induces an equal reduction in $i$'s contributions to $j$ (from $h_{ij}^0$ to $h_{ij}^1$ in the figure), whereas a shift against $j$'s income to $E_2$ induces an equal increase in his contributions (from $h_{ij}^0$ to $h_{ij}^2$).[20]

This discussion has assumed a two-person family but is equally applicable to larger families that include grandparents, parents, children, uncles, aunts, or other kin. If one member, call him the "head," cares sufficiently about all other members to transfer general resources to them,[21] redistribution of income among members would not affect the consumption of any member, as long as the head continues to contribute to all.

The head's concern about the welfare of other members provides each, including the head, with some insurance against disasters. If a disaster reduced the income of one member alone, $k$, by say 50 percent, the head would increase his contributions to $k$, and thereby offset to some extent the decline in $k$'s income. The head would "finance" his increased contribution to $k$ by reducing his own consumption and his contributions to other members; in effect each member shares $k$'s disaster by consuming less. If $k$'s share of family income were negligible, he would essentially be fully insured against his own disasters because even a 50 percent decline in his income would have a negligible effect on family income, and thus on the consumption of each member. Since the share contributed by any member would tend to be inversely related to family size, large families, including the extended kinship family found in certain societies, can provide self-insurance especially when old-age, health, and other kinds of market insurance are not available or are very costly.[22] Note that insurance is automatically provided when resources are voluntarily transferred, without

---

20. If the utility of $i$ also partly depended directly on the amounts he transferred to $j$, perhaps because $i$'s "prestige" or "approval" partly depended on these tranfers, then redistribution of family income *would* have a net effect on the consumption of both $i$ and $j$.

21. A somewhat weaker assumption is that the family is "fully connected" through a series of transfers between members; for example, $a$ transfers resources to $b$ because $a$ cares about $b$, $b$ transfers to $c$ because $b$ cares about $c$, and so on until $m$ transfers to the last member, $n$, and $n$ transfers to no one (this assumption is made in an intergenerational context by Barro, 1974). Indirectly, $a$ (or any other member but $n$) would be transferring to all members because an increase in his contributions to $b$ would induce an increase in the contributions to all other members.

22. The interaction between self and market insurance is analyzed in Ehrlich and Becker (1972).

the need for any member to have dictatorial control over the family's allocation of resources.

The result on the unimportance of the distribution of income among persons linked by transfers can also be used to understand the interaction among generations.[23] Suppose that the resources of the present generation are changed at the expense of or to the benefit of the resources accruing to future generations. For example, increased government debt or social security payments are financed by increased taxes on future generations, or increased public investment, perhaps in schools, with benefits accruing to future generations is financed by taxes on the present generation. If present and future generations are fully connected by a series of intergenerational transfers, called "bequests," then each of these apparent changes in the relative resources of present and future generations would tend to be offset by equal but opposite changes in bequests. In particular, increased public debt would not raise the real wealth or consumption of the present generation or reduce that of future generations because increased taxes on future generations would be matched by increased bequests to them. Similarly, increased public investment in education would be matched by reduced private investment in education.[24]

The budget constraint of the head is determined by total family income, not his own income alone—equation (8.13) for a two-person family can be readily generalized to many persons. Since the head maximizes his utility subject to his budget constraint, anything that increased family income would increase his utility. Therefore, the head would consider the effect on total family income of his different actions, and would forfeit own income if the incomes of other family members were increased even more. For example, he would not move to another city if his spouse's or children's income would be decreased by more than his own income would be increased. Or, although children usually eventually set up their own households and fully control their own incomes, the head would guide and help finance their investments in education and other human capital to maximize the present value of the real income yielded by these investments.[25]

---

23. This application is taken from the detailed discussion in Barro (1974).

24. The empirical evidence does strongly suggest that most of the investment in higher education by state governments has been offset by reduced private investment (see Peltzman, 1973; McPherson, 1974).

25. The incentive that parents have to invest in their children is discussed in several places (see, e.g., De Tray, 1973; Parsons, 1978).

Put differently, the head automatically internalizes the "external" effects of his actions on other family members.[26] Indeed, because the head maximizes family income, he *fully* internalizes these externalities not only when the income of different members but also when their consumption, the other side of the budget constraint, is directly affected. He would take an action directly affecting consumption only when either the value of any increase in his consumption exceeded the value (to him) of any decrease in other members' consumption, or when any decrease in his own was less valuable than the increase in theirs.[27]

For example, he would read in bed at night only if the value of reading exceeded the value (to him) of the loss in sleep suffered by his wife, or he would eat with his fingers only if its value exceeded the value (to him) of the disgust experienced by his family. The development of manners and other personal behavior "rules" between family members well illustrates how apparent "external" effects can be internalized by social interaction between members.

Note too that not only is the head better off when his utility is raised, but so too are other members of his family, even if his actions directly reduce their consumption or increase their discomfort and disgust. For if his utility is raised and if their welfare has a positive income elasticity to him, he would increase his contributions to them by more than enough to

---

26. The Coase Theorem proves that when "bargaining costs" are negligible, each family member could always be induced to maximize family opportunities through bargaining with and side payments from other members. I have proved that the head (and, as shown later, other members too) has this incentive and, in effect, makes or receives "side payments" without bargaining with other members. The word "automatically" is used to distinguish this theorem from the Coase Theorem.

27. Although this is a rather immediate implication of his interest in maximizing family opportunities, a direct proof may be instructive. Suppose that a particular action changed the utility of the head by

(8.1')
$$dU_h = mu^h dx_h + \sum_{j=1,\neq h}^{n} mu^j dx_j$$

where $mu^j = \partial U_h/\partial x_j$, and $dx_j$ measures the change in consumption of the $j$th family member. If the head can transfer resources to other members dollar for dollar, in equilibrium,

(8.2')
$$mu^j = \lambda_h p_j \quad \text{all } j$$

where $\lambda_h$ is the marginal utility of income to the head, and $p_j$ is the cost of $x_j$. Substitution of eq. (8.2') into (8.1') gives offset their initial losses. For example, if he benefits from reading at night, his wife does too because he more than compensates her for her loss of sleep.[28]

The head maximizes a utility function that depends on the consumption of all family members subject to a budget constraint determined by family income and family consumption. Therefore, the effect of a change in relative prices of goods, or in aggregate family income (as well as in its distribution) on a family's consumption of different goods, could be predicted solely from the head's utility function and a budget constraint on family variables. The usual substitution and income effects of demand theory would be fully applicable.

In this sense, then, a family with a head can be said to maximize "its" consistent and transitive utility function of the consumption of different members subject to a budget constraint defined on family variables. The "family's" utility function is identical with that of one member, the head, because his concern for the welfare of other members, so to speak, integrates all the members' utility functions into one consistent "family" function.

That is, a "family's" utility function is the same as that of one of its members not because this member has dictatorial power over other members, but because he (or she!) cares sufficiently about all other members to transfer resources voluntarily to them. Each member can have complete freedom of action; indeed, the person making the transfers would not change the consumption of any member even with dictatorial power! For example, if $i$ had dictatorial power, he could move the equilibrium po-

---

(8.3′)
$$dU^h = \lambda_h\left(p_h dx_h + \sum_{j=1,\neq h}^{n} p_j dx_j\right) = \lambda_h \sum_{\text{all } j} p_j dx_j$$

Since the head takes an action if and only if $dU_h > 0$, eq. (8.3′) implies (since $\lambda_h > 0$) that he takes an action if, and only if,

(8.4′)
$$\sum_{\text{all } j} p_j dx_j > 0$$

which was to be proved.

28. Recall that I have been assuming that only a single good is consumed by each person, although this analysis presupposes many goods. The transition to many goods is straightforward if the head's utility depends on a function of the various goods consumed by another member that is monotonically related to the utility function of that member (see the discussion later in this section).

sition $e$ in Figure 8.3 to the vertical axis (or anywhere else), but would not choose to move it because his utility partly depends on $j$'s consumption.[29]

Nothing much has yet been said about the preferences of members who are not heads. The major, and somewhat unexpected, conclusion is that if a head exists, *other members also are motivated to maximize family income and consumption, even if their welfare depends on their own consumption alone.* This is the "rotten kid" theorem (I owe this name to the Barro family). For consider a selfish member $j$ who can take an action that would reduce his income by $b$, but increase that of another member $k$ by $c$. Initially, $j$ would be worse off by $b$, since the gain to $k$ is of no direct concern to him. However, if $c = b$, the head would transfer enough additional resources to $j$ from $k$ to leave him (and $k$) equally well off, since intrafamily reallocations of income do not affect the consumption of any member. Moreover, if $c > b$—if family income were raised by $j$'s action—and if $j$'s welfare were a superior "good" to the head, then he would transfer enough additional resources to $j$ to make $j$ better off. Consequently, even a selfish $j$ would only undertake actions that raised family income or consumption, regardless of the initial impact on him.

In other words, when one member cares sufficiently about other members to be the head, all members have the same motivation as the head

---

29. It is difficult to contrast my derivation of a "family" utility function with a traditional derivation, since explicit derivations are rare. The most explicit appears to be in a well-known article on social indifference curves by Samuelson (1956). He considers the problem of relating individual and family utility functions, but his discussion is brief and the arguments sometimes are not spelled out. Without sufficient elaboration, he refers to a consistent "family welfare function" being grafted onto the separate utility functions of different family members (p. 10). In addition, he says that a family member's "preferences among his own goods have the special property of being independent of the other members' consumption. But since blood is thicker than water, the preferences of the different members are interrelated by what might be called a 'consensus' or 'social welfare function' which takes into account the deservingness or ethical worths of the consumption levels of each of the members." How are these preferences interrelated by a "consensus," and should not the "deservingness" of the consumption levels of different members simply be incorporated into different members' preferences (as in my approach)? Incidentally, at one point (p. 9), Samuelson appears to believe that if the family utility function is the same as the head's, he must have sovereign power, which I have shown is not necessary. He later (p. 20) says that "if within the family there can be assumed to take place an optimal reallocation of income so as to keep each member's dollar expenditure of equal ethical worth, then there can be derived for the whole family a set of well-behaved indifference contours relating the totals of what it consumes: the family can be said to *act as if* it maximizes such a group preference function" (italics in original). In my analyses, the "optimal reallocation" results

to maximize family opportunities and to internalize fully all within-family "externalities," regardless of how selfish (or, indeed, how envious) these members are. Even a selfish child receiving transfers from his parents would *automatically* consider the effects of his actions on other siblings as well as on his parents. Put still differently, sufficient "love" by one member guarantees that all members act as if they loved other members as much as themselves. As it were, the amount of "love" required in a family is economized: sufficient "love" by one member leads all other members by "an invisible hand" to act as if they too loved everyone.

Armed with this theorem, I do not need to dwell on the preferences of nonheads. Of course, just as there may be no head if all members are sufficiently selfish, so there may be none if they are all sufficiently altruistic. Each would want to transfer resources to other members, but no one would want to accept transfers. Aside from that, mutual interaction or mutual interdependence of welfare raises no particular problems.[30]

By assuming in Figure 8.3 and in formal development given by equations (8.11)–(8.14) that only a single good is consumed by each person, I eliminated any distinction between transferring general purchasing power and transferring particular goods to another member. If each member consumes many goods, the conclusions in this section about family utility functions, internalization of within-family externalities, and so on fully hold only if the head is content to transfer general purchasing power. He

---

from interdependent preferences and voluntary contributions, and the "group preference function" is identical with that of the "head."

30. It frequently has been alleged to me that mutual interaction of the form

$$U_i = U_i[x_i, g_i(U_j)]$$

$$U_j = U_j[x_j, g_j(U_i)]$$

where $x_i$ and $x_j$ are the own consumption of $i$ and $j$, and $g_i$ and $g_j$ are monotonic functions of the utility indexes $U_i$ and $U_j$, results in instability and unbounded utility levels. For it is argued, an increase in $x_i$ by one unit directly raises $i$'s utility, which raises $j$'s utility through $g_j$, which in turn further raises $i$'s utility, and so on, until $U_i$ and $U_j$ approach infinity. Mathematically, there is an infinite regress, since, by substitution,

$$U_i = U_i[x_i, g_i\{x_j, g_j\{x_i, g_i\{x_j, g_j\{\ldots\}\}]$$

However, with appropriate restrictions on the magnitude of the interactions, the infinite regress has a finite effect, and the "reduced forms" of $U_i$ and $U_j$ on $x_i$ and $x_j$ are well defined. Consider, for example, the Cobb Douglas functions would transfer in this form if his utility function depended on the utility of other members—that is, if his utility function could be written in the form

(8.15)    $U_h = U_h[x_{h1}, \ldots, x_{hm}, g_1(x_{21}, \ldots, x_{2m}), \ldots, g_n(x_{n1}, \ldots, x_{nm})]$

where $x_{ij}$ is the quantity of the $j$th good consumed by the $i$th person, and

$$dg_i = 0 \left( = \sum_{j-1}^{m} \frac{\partial g_i}{\partial x_{ij}} dx_{ij} \right)$$

implies that the utility of the $i$th person is unchanged. If he is concerned not about the utility of other members but about their consumption of particular "merit" goods, the conclusions can be quite different. The systematic discussion of merit goods is postponed to Section 3C.

If parents are transferring resources to their children in the form, say, of gifts and expenditures on education and other human capital or after they die in the form of bequests, then an increase in the income of parents by a given percentage would tend to increase contributions to children by a still larger percentage, certainly by one exceeding the increased welfare of their children (see the discussion in Section 2). In other words, contributions to children can be very responsive to a change in parental income without the welfare of children being so responsive.

Empirical evidence on bequests, gifts, and many other transfers to

------------------------

$$U_i = x_i^{a_i} U_j^{b_i}$$

$$U_j = x_j^{a_j} U_i^{b_j}$$

where $a_i$ and $a_j$ presumably are greater than zero, and $b_i$ and $b_j$ can either be greater than or less than zero. By substitution,

$$U_i = x_i^{a_i/(1-b_i b_j)} x_j^{a_j b_i/(1-b_i b_j)} = x_i^{\alpha_i} x_j^{\beta_i}$$

$$U_j = x_i^{a_i b_j/(1-b_i b_j)} x_j^{a_j/(1-b_i b_j)} = x_i^{\alpha_j} x_j^{\beta_j}$$

where $b_i b_j$ is independent of monotonic transformations on $U_i$ and $U_j$. A finite sum to the regress requires that $|b_i b_j| < 1$; essentially, that the marginal utilities or disutilities due to interdependence are less than unity. Note that although it is possible for $a_i = b_i$ and $a_j = b_j$, for own consumption and the welfare of the other person to be equally "important," the condition $|b_i b_j| < 1$ implies that either $|\alpha_i| > |\beta_i|$, or $|\beta_j| > |\alpha_j|$, or both; that is, for at least one of the persons, own consumption has to be more important than the other person's consumption in the "reduced forms."

children is seriously deficient. The general impression is, however, that bequests have a very high income elasticity. Moreover, the elasticity of expenditures on children's education with respect to parental income does appear to be above unity (Schultz, 1963, p. 9), which is consistent with the implications of the theory.

The responsiveness of expenditures on children's education and other training and skills to parental income has often been noted, and lamented as evidence of immobility and rigid "class" structure. Yet my analysis implies that the welfare of children—a measure of their "class"—rises by a smaller percentage than parent expenditures on them, and possibly even by a smaller percentage than parental income. Put differently, considerable regression toward the mean across generations—that is, the expected income or other measure of the position of children would be much closer to the average position than is that of their parents—can be observed at the same time that contributions to children are very responsive to parental income.[31]

The crucial point is that considerable regression toward the mean across generations would occur partly because of genetic factors and luck if all parents spent an equal amount on their children. As a result of this,

---

31. In one study, the elasticity of children's years of schooling with respect to parental income is a sizable +1.2, at the same time that the elasticity of children's *income* with respect to parental income is only +0.3, or a 70 percent regression toward the mean (unpublished calculations by Jacob Mincer from the Eckland Sample). Note in this regard, however, that parents cannot easily prevent considerable regression toward the mean by investing in their children. For let the relation between the human captial invested in children and parental income be

$$S_c = a + b \log I_p + u$$

where $b$ is the elasticity of parental response, and $u$ represents other determinants of $S_c$. According to the theory of investment in human capital (Mincer, 1974; Becker, 1975),

$$\log I_c = \alpha + r S_c + v$$

where $r$ is the rate of return on human capital, and $v$ represents other determinants of $\log I_c$. Then by substitution,

$$\log I_c = (\alpha + ra) + rb \log I_p + (ru + v)$$

Even if $r$ were as large as 0.2, and $b$ as large as 2.0, $rb$ would only be 0.4: the regression toward the mean would be 60 percent. If $v = c \log I_p + v'$, where $1 - c$ measures the degree of "intrinsic" regression to the mean, then by substitution,

$$\log I_c = (\alpha + ra) + (rb + c) \log I_p + (ru + tv')$$

and given interdependent preferences, higher-income parents tend to spend considerably more on their children than lower-income ones. However, these expenditures would only tend to dampen but not eliminate the regression toward the mean. Therefore, the elastic response of contributions to children can give a very biased picture of the degree of immobility or inheritance of "class" position. Indeed, contributions would be more responsive to parental income the stronger are the basic forces producing mobility because parents attempt to offset these forces. In other words, an elastic response of contributions to parental income may be evidence of sizable *mobility!*[32]

## 3B. CHARITY

If someone makes contributions of time or goods to unrelated persons or to organizations, he is said to be "charitable" or "philanthropic." The discussion of contributions within a family indicates that charitable behavior can be motivated by a desire to improve the general well-being of recipients.[33] Apparent "charitable" behavior can also be motivated by a desire to avoid the scorn of others or to receive social acclaim. Not much generality is sacrificed, however, by only considering charity motivated by a desire to improve well-being.[34]

The numerous implications about family behavior developed in the

---

Since the analysis in the text implies that $b$ would be positively related to $1 - c$ as parents try to offset the "intrinsic" regression, the "observed" regression to the mean,

$$1 - \gamma = 1 - (c + rb) = (1 - c) - rb$$

may be only weakly related to and also is less than the "intrinsic" regression $1 - c$. I am indebted to discussions with Jacob Mincer on the issues sketchily covered in this footnote.

32. It is generally believed that the United States has a more mobile "open" society than European countries do; yet (admittedly crude) comparisons of occupational mobility between fathers and sons do not reveal large differences between the United States and several Western European countries (Lipset and Bendix, 1959). Since the analysis in this paper suggests that parents' contributions to their children's education and other training is more responsive to parental position in "open" societies, more responsive parental contributions are probably offsetting the greater "openness" of American society.

33. *The Random House Dictionary of the English Language* (unabridged, 1967) defines charity as "the benevolent feeling, especially toward those in need or in disfavor."

34. The utility function of a charitable person who desires to improve the general well-being of recipients can be written as

previous section fully apply to the synthetic "family" consisting of a charitable person $i$ and all recipients of his charity. For example, no member's well-being would be affected by a redistribution of income among them, as long as $i$ continued to give to all of them. For he would simply redistribute his giving until everyone losing income was fully compensated and everyone gaining was fully "taxed." Moreover, all members, not simply $i$, would try to maximize "family" opportunities and "family" consumption, instead of their own income or consumption alone. In addition, each member of a synthetic "family" is at least partly "insured" against catastrophes because all other members, in effect, would increase their giving to him until at least part of his loss were replaced. Therefore, charity is a form of self-insurance that is a substitute for market insurance and government transfers. Presumably, the rapid growth of these latter during the last 100 years discouraged the growth of charity.

According to the analysis in Section 2, an increase in the income of a charitable person would increase his charitable giving by a greater percentage than the increase in the well-being of recipients. Indeed, his income elasticity of demand for giving would exceed unity, possibly by a substantial amount, as long as his elasticity of demand for their well-being (which I will call his demand for charity) was not much below his average income elasticity. The available evidence on charitable giving clearly supports this implication of the theory: income elasticities estimated by Taussig (1965) from giving in different income classes in 1962 are all well above unity,

$$ U_i = U_i \left[ x_i, x_j \left( = \frac{I_j + h}{p_j} \right) \right] $$

where $h$ is his charitable giving, $x_j$ measures the well-being of recipients, and $\partial U_i / \partial I_j = \partial U_i \big| \partial h > 0$; that is, a unit increase in the own income of recipients has the same effect on the utility of a charitable person as a unit increase in his giving. The utility function of a person who makes "charitable" contributions to win social acclaim can be written as

$$ U_i = U_i \left( x_i, \frac{I_j}{p_j}, \frac{h}{p_j} \right) $$

where still $\partial U_i / \partial h > 0$—an increase in his contributions would increase his acclaim—but now the sign of $\partial U_i / \partial I_j$ is not so obvious. If, however, contributions and the income of recipients were much closer substitutes for each other than for the own consumption of the contributor, which is plausible, then these utility functions have similar implications. Not much generality is sacrificed, therefore, by only considering charity motivated by a desire to improve the well-being of recipients.

ranging from a low of +1.3 in the under $25,000 class to a high of +3.1 in the $100,000–$200,000 class.[35]

A crucial implication of charitable giving in terms of social interaction between the giver and others is that an increase in the incomes of recipients would reduce giving. Therefore, an increase in the incomes of both recipients and givers should not increase giving by as much as an increase in the incomes of givers alone. These implications are tested and confirmed by Schwartz (1970), who analyzes aggregate time series on incomes and charitable giving in the United States between 1929 and 1966 and also compares his findings with the cross-sectional findings of Taussig (1965) reported above.[36]

The usual theory of consumer choice ignores social interactions, and would consider charitable giving simply as a "good" that enters the giver's utility function along with his other goods:

$$(8.16) \qquad\qquad U_i = U_i(x_i, h)$$

where $h$ measures the amount given by $i$, and $x_i$ are the other goods that he consumes. This "conventional" approach does not imply that an increase in $i$'s income would increase his giving by a particularly large percentage, or that an increase in the incomes of recipients would lower his giving. Therefore, considerable ad hocery would be required if the "conventional" approach were to explain the evidence on charitable giving that is more readily explained by an approach that incorporates social interactions.

These findings can be used to make very crude, but instructive, calculations of the share of recipient's own incomes in the social incomes of contributors. If the own-income elasticity of demand for giving is taken from Taussig as +2.0, the share of own income spent on giving as 0.04 (see Schwartz, 1970, p. 1278), and the income elasticity of demand for charity

---

35. These estimates are net of differences in tax rates. Note, however, that charitable giving is estimated from itemized deductions in personal income tax returns. Since only giving to (certain) institutions and not to individuals can be deducted, since many taxpayers, especially with lower incomes, do not itemize their deductions, and since others inflate their deductions, the response of tax-reported giving may not accurately describe the response of actual giving.

36. Schwartz's study, like Taussig's, is based on personal income tax returns. Both studies also estimate the price elasticity of giving, where price is measured by one minus the marginal tax rate. Schwartz finds considerable response to price, elasticities generally exceeding −0.5, which is consistent with the implications of the theory of social interactions. Taussig, on the other hand, finds only a weak response to price; but Schwartz argues that Taussig's findings are biased downward.

as equal to the average income elasticity (actually, Schwartz's findings suggest that it may be lower than the average), then, according to equation (8.9), charity's share in social income would be $(2 - 1)/(1/0.04 - 1) \approx 0.4$. If the own-income elasticity of giving were taken as $+3.0$ rather than $+2.0$, charity's share would double to 0.08; if, in addition, the income elasticity of charity were only four-fifths of the average elasticity, its share would increase further to 0.11 (a tithe?).

### 3C. Merit Goods and Multiperson Interactions

Contributors are content to transfer general purchasing power to recipients if they are concerned about the general welfare or utility of recipients—as seen by recipients. They want to restrict or earmark their transfers, on the other hand, if they are concerned about particular "merit" goods consumed by recipients. For example, parents may want transfers to their children spent on education or housing, or only the money incomes rather than "full" incomes of children may be of concern to parents, or contributors to beggars may not want their giving spent on liquor or gambling.

Assume, therefore, that $i$ transfers resources to $j$ that are earmarked for particular goods consumed by $j$ because the utility function of $i$ depends not only on his own goods but also on these goods of $j$. If $j$ were permitted to spend his own income as he wished, an assumption modified shortly, he would spend less on these goods as a result of the earmarked transfers from $i$. Clearly, the reduction in his own spending would be greater, the greater the transfer, the smaller the fraction of his social income spent on these goods, and the smaller their income elasticity. For example, if they take 20 percent of his social income and have an income elasticity equal to 2.0, he would reduce his own spending by $0.60 for each dollar earmarked by $i$.[37]

As long as $j$ continues to spend on the merit goods, earmarked transfers are worth as much to $j$ as a transfer of general purchasing power with equal monetary value. Moreover, $i$ would not have a greater effect on $j$'s consumption of these goods with earmarked transfers than with general transfers. Therefore, as long as $j$ continues to spend on these goods, earmarked transfers are equivalent to general transfers; and the results derived for the latter fully hold for the former. For example, a redistribution

---

37. It is easily shown that $r_j = 1 - v_m n_m$, where $v_m$ is the share spent on merit goods; $n_m$, their income elasticity; and $r_j$, the reduction in $j$'s own spending per unit increase in $i$'s contribution. Therefore, if $v_m = 0.2$, and $n_m = 2.0$, $r_j = 0.6$.

of income between $i$ and $j$ would have no effect on the consumption of either as long as both continue to spend on the merit goods, or both $i$ and $j$ want to maximize their combined incomes, not their own incomes alone.

On the other hand, if $j$ did not want to spend anything on the merit goods because earmarked transfers were sufficiently large, such transfers would be worth less to $j$ and more to $i$ than would general transfers with equal money value. Moreover, various results derived for general transfers no longer hold: for example, a redistribution of income to $j$ and away from $i$ would reduce $j$'s consumption of merit goods and increase his consumption of other goods.

If $i$ were aware that $j$ reduced his spending on merit goods when transfers increased, $i$ would be discouraged from giving because $j$'s reaction raises $i$'s private price of merit goods to[38]

$$(8.17) \qquad p_m^i = p_m \frac{1}{1 - r_j} = p_m \frac{1}{v_m n_m}$$

where $p_m$ is the market price of merit goods, and the other terms are defined in note 37. Similarly, if $j$ were aware that $i$ reduced his transfers when $j$ increased his spending on merit goods, $j$ would also be discouraged from spending because $i$'s reaction raises the price to $j$. Indeed, $j$ could end up consuming fewer merit goods than he would if $i$ were not concerned! That these induced reactions are not simply hypothetical or always minor is persuasively shown in a recent study of higher education (Peltzman, 1973). States earmark transfers to higher education mainly through highly subsidized public institutions. Private spending was apparently reduced by (at least) $0.75 per dollar of public spending in 1966–67; private spending may have been reduced by more than $1.00 per dollar of public spending in 1959–60, so that *total* spending on higher education in that year would have been reduced by public spending.

Both $i$ and $j$ want to limit the induced reactions of the other because such reactions reflect the incentive to "underreveal" preferences about merit goods and "free-ride" in their consumption. Since equation (8.17) shows that these reactions raise the price of merit goods to $i$ and $j$, in effect, both want to lower these prices. Indeed, it is well known from the theory of public goods, and a merit good is a particular kind of "public" good, that efficient prices to $i$ and $j$ would be less than the market price;

---

38. For example, if $j$ spent $0.60 less for each dollar transferred by $i$, the price to $i$ would be $p_m^i = p_m(1/0.4) = 2.5 p_m$, or more than twice the market price.

indeed, these efficient prices would *sum* to the market price of the merit good.[39] Efficient prices might be achieved, for example, by $i$ and $j$ matching each other's spending in specified proportions, or each might be given a spending quota.

I intentionally say "might" be achieved because any agreement has to be "policed" to insure that each lives up to his commitment. Policing is relatively easy for the consumer of the merit goods, $j$, since he usually automatically knows how much is spent by $i$, but is much more difficult for $i$, since he does not automatically know how much is spent by $j$.[40] Parents may use their children's grades in school to measure the input of time and effort by children that presumably "matches" the money contribution by the parents.[41] Or parents may save a large part of their total transfer to children for a bequest when they die in order to provide an incentive for children to spend "appropriately," at least while their parents are alive.[42] This may explain why the inheritance tax on bequests apparently has induced relatively little substitution toward gifts to children (see Shoup, 1966; Adams, 1974).

The "underrevealing," "free-riding," coordination of efforts, and "policing" discussed for merit goods are common to all multiperson interactions—that is, all situations where two or more persons are affected by the consumption, attitudes, or other behavior of the same person. The analytical issues for multiperson interactions are the same as for other "public" goods: is public intervention desirable—for example, should charitable giving be deductible from personal income in arriving at tax liabilities in order to lower the private price of giving—and do private equilibria without government intervention more closely approximate joint maximization, a Nash noncooperative game solution, or something quite different? Since space is limited, I refrain from discussing further these and related issues.

---

39. A proof of this well-known summation formula can be found in Samuelson (1954).

40. The difficulty of policing "merit" goods is shown amusingly in a recent Wizard of Id cartoon. Two drunks meet, and one says, "Could you spare a buck for a bottle of wine?" The other answers, "How do I know you won't buy food with it?"

41. I owe this example to Lisa Landes.

42. This conclusion about the incentives provided by large bequests is a special case of a more general result proven elsewhere (see Becker and Stigler, 1974) that relatively large pensions discourage employees from acting contrary to the interests of their employers (a bequest serves the same purpose as a pension).

## 3D. Envy and Hatred

An envious or malicious person presumably would feel better off if some other persons become worse off in certain respects. He could "harm" himself (i.e., spend his own resources) in order to harm others: in Figure 8.2, he gives up $k_0$ units of his own consumption in order to harm others by $h_0$ units. The terms of trade between his own harm and the harm to others, given by the curve $E_0 S_0'$ in Figure 8.2, is partly determined by his skill at "predatory" behavior and partly by public and private expenditures to prevent crime, libeling, malicious acts, trespass, and other predatory behavior. Since an increase in these expenditures would increase the cost to him of harming others, he would be discouraged from harming them. The limited evidence available on predatory expenditures supports this implication of the theory. Crimes against persons provide some evidence on predatory behavior, since most assaults and murders probably are motivated by the harm to victims.[43] The frequency of assaults and of murder (and also crimes against property) apparently is strongly negatively related to the probability of conviction, punishment, and other measures of the cost of committing these crimes (see Ehrlich, 1973).

Section 2 suggests that a rise in own income would tend to reduce predatory expenditures. An increase in the social environment,[44] on the other hand, would necessarily increase these expenditures, unless own consumption were an inferior good. Therefore, a rise in the social environment and own income by the same percentage would reduce predatory expenditures by less than would a rise in own income alone, and might even increase them.

Again, the implications of the theory can be tested with evidence on crimes against persons. Since assaults and murders have been more frequent at lower income levels,[45] an increase in own income appears to reduce crimes against persons, if differences in own income alone are measured by differences in the incomes of individuals at a moment in time (as in the discussion of charity in Section 3B). As predicted by the theory, an increase in own income that is accompanied by an increase in the social

---

43. Most robberies, burglaries, and larcenies, on the other hand, probably are motivated by the prospects of material gain.

44. That is, in that part of the social environment that motivates predatory expenditures.

45. Persons committing crimes against other persons as well as against property are much more likely to live in low income areas (see Crime Commission, 1967a, table 9).

environment (as measured by the income of others) does not have such a negative effect on these crimes. Indeed, the frequency of assaults and murders has not been reduced by the sizeable growth in aggregate incomes during the last 40 years, nor do higher-income states presently have fewer crimes against persons than other states.[46]

Over the years, even acute observers of society have differed radically in their assessment of the importance of envy and hatred. Two hundred years ago, for example, Adam Smith recognized these "passions" but shunted them aside with the comment: "Envy, malice, or resentment, are the only passions which can prompt one man to injure another in his person or reputation. But the *greater part of men are not very frequently under the influence of those passions,* and the very worst men are so only occasionally. As their gratification too, how agreeable soever it may be to certain characters, is not attended with any real or permanent advantage it is in the greater part of men commonly restrained by prudential considerations. Men may live together in society with some tolerable degree of security, though there is no civil magistrate to *protect them from the injustice of those passions*" (Smith, 1937; my italics).[47] To Thorstein Veblen, on the other hand, writing many years later, these motives are the very stuff of life that dominate everything else: "The desire for wealth can scarcely be satiated in any individual instance, and evidently a satiation of the average or general desire for wealth is out of the question. However widely, or equally, or 'fouly,' it may be distributed, no general increase of the community's wealth can make any approach to satiating this need, the ground of which is the desire of everyone to excel everyone else in the accumulation of goods" (Veblen, 1934, p. 32).[48]

In principle, the importance of envy and hatred can be measured us-

---

46. The rate of assaults grew significantly from 1933 to 1965 in the United States, and the murder rate remained about the same (Crime Commission, 1967b, figs. 3, 4). Higher-income states do not have fewer crimes against persons even when the probability of conviction, the punishment, and several other variables are held constant (Ehrlich, 1973, tables 2–5). Note that Ehrlich's study, unlike the evidence from the Crime Commission, holds the "price" of crime constant when estimating the effects of income (and holds income constant when estimating the effects of price).

47. Not much later, Jeremy Bentham reached a similar conclusion: "The pleasure derivable by any person from the contemplation of pain suffered by another, is in no instance so great as the pain so suffered" (Bentham, 1952).

48. Similarly, a sociologist recently has argued that envy is a powerful motive in primitive as well as advanced societies, communist as well as capitalist ones, and is critical in determining economic progress and public policy (see Schoeck, 1966).

ing equation (8.9) by the contribution of the relevant social environment to social income; this is done in a crude way in Section 2B for charity. Unfortunately, not enough information is available either on the own-income elasticity of demand or on the fraction of own income spent on "predatory" behavior to make even crude estimates of the relative contribution of envy and hatred.

Still, it may be useful to note several implications of the differing views about the significance of envy and hatred. For example, Veblen's belief that the welfare of a typical person primarily depends on his relative income position implies that social income essentially is zero: that the value of the social environment causing envy would exactly offset the value of own income.[49] For then, and only then, would a rise in this social environment and own income by the same percentage, prices held constant, not affect social income or welfare. That is, a rise in all incomes in a community by the same percentage would not improve anyone's welfare in Veblen's world.[50]

If social income were negative, if the environment causing envy were more important than own income, a rise in the environment and own income by the same percentage would lower social income and welfare. That is, a general rise in incomes in a more extreme Veblenian world would actually lower welfare![51]

On the other hand, Smith's belief that envy is a relatively minor determinant of welfare implies that social income is positive: the environment causing envy is less important than own income. A rise in the environment and own income by the same percentage would then raise social income and welfare. That is, Veblen's general rise in the community's income would raise the welfare of the typical person.


## 4. Summary

This chapter uses simple tools of economic theory to analyze interactions between the behavior of some persons and different characteristics

---

49. "Own" income here includes the value of other aspects of the social environment.

50. If $U_i = U_i(I_i/\bar{I})$, where $\bar{I}$ is the average community income, then $S_i = I_i - p_r\bar{I}$, where $S_i$ is $i$'s social income, and $p_r$ is the price of $\bar{I}$ in terms of $I_i$. If $i$ did not engage in predatory behavior, $p_r$ would simply equal the slope of his indifference curve: slope $= dI_i/d\bar{I} = I_i/\bar{I} = p_r$. Hence $S_i = I_i - I_i/\bar{I} \cdot \bar{I} = 0$.

51. When envy is so important, economic development is undesirable because it lowers welfare. See Schoeck's (1966) discussion of what he calls "the envy-barrier of the developing countries."

of other persons. Although these interactions are emphasized in the contemporary sociological and anthropological literature, and were considered the cornerstone of behavior by several prominent nineteenth-century economists, they have been largely ignored in the modern economic literature.

The central concept of the analysis is "social income," the sum of a person's own income (his earnings, etc.) and the monetary value to him of the relevant characteristics of others, which I call his social environment. The optimal expenditure of his own income to alter these characteristics is given by the usual marginal conditions. By using the concept of social income, I can analyze the effect on these expenditures of changes in different sources of income and in different prices, including the "price" of the social envirnonment. Perhaps the most important implication is that a change in own income alone would tend to cause a relatively large change in these expenditures; in other words, the own-income elasticity of demand for these expenditures would tend to be "large," certainly larger than the elasticity resulting from equal percentage changes in own income and the social environment.

Interactions among members of the same family receive the greatest attention. The "head" of a family is defined not by sex or age, but as that member, if there is one, who transfers general purchasing power to all other members because he cares about their welfare. A family with a head is a highly interdependent organization that has the following properties:

A redistribution of income among members does not affect the consumption of welfare of any member because it simply induces offsetting changes in transfers from the head. As a result, each member is at least partially insured against disasters that may strike him.

Not only the head but other members too act "as if" they "loved" all members, even when they are really selfish, in the sense that they maximize not their own income alone but family income. As it were, the existence of a head economizes on the amount of true love required in a family.

A family acts "as if" it maximized a consistent and transitive utility function subject to a budget constraint that depended only on family variables. This utility function is the same as the head's not because he has dictatorial power, but because his concern for the welfare of other members integrates all their utility functions into one consistent "family" function.

Transfers from parents to children in the form, say, of schooling, gifts, and bequests tend to be negatively related to what the income of children would be relative to their parents in the absence of these transfers. Therefore, the relative income of children *inclusive* of transfers could be unrelated or even negatively related to these transfers. Consequently, one cannot infer anything about the stability across generations of economic or social positions simply from knowing the relation between parental position and the amount transferred.

More briefly treated are charity and envy, with special attention to the effects of different kinds of income change on charitable contributions and expenditures to alleviate envy. For example, the much higher income elasticity of demand for charitable contributions estimated from differences in individual incomes at a moment in time than from aggregate changes in incomes over time is shown to be implied by this theory of social interactions, but not readily by the traditional theory of choice.

From a methodological viewpoint, the aim of the paper is to show how another relation considered important in the sociological and anthropological literature can be usefully analyzed when incorporated into the framework provided by economic theory. Probably the main explanation for the neglect of social interactions by economists is neither analytical intractability nor a preoccupation with more important concepts, but excessive attention to formal developments during the last 70 years. As a consequence, even concepts considered to be important by earlier economists, such as social interactions, have been shunted aside.

# A Note on Restaurant Pricing and Other Examples of Social Influences on Price

.

A popular seafood restaurant in Palo Alto, California, does not take reservations, and every day it has long queues for tables during prime hours. Almost directly across the street is another seafood restaurant with comparable food, slightly higher prices, and similar service and other amenities. Yet this restaurant has many empty seats most of the time.

Why doesn't the popular restaurant raise prices, which would reduce the queue for seats but expand profits? Several decades ago I asked my class at Columbia to write a report on why successful Broadway theaters do not raise prices much; instead they ration scarce seats, especially through delays in seeing a play. I did not get any satisfactory answers, and along with many others, I have continued to be puzzled by such pricing behavior. The same phenomenon is found in the pricing of successful sporting events, such as the World Series and Super Bowls, and in a related way in the pricing of best-selling books. This chapter suggests a possible solution to the puzzle based on social interactions.

The puzzle is easily shown in a supply-demand diagram, in which $S$ in Figure 9.1 is the number of restaurant tables, theater seats, and so forth, and $d_1$ is the usual negatively inclined demand curve. At a price of $p_0$, the $S$ units sold must be rationed, with $D_0 - S$ being the excess demand at that price. Clearly, profits increase if price is raised to $p_e$ since $S$ units are still sold, but at a higher price. The profit-maximizing price is even higher if $d_1$ is inelastic at $p_e$.

Many explanations have been suggested for apparently nonmaximizing prices such as $p_0$. It could be a tax dodge if speculators who sell tickets

---

Originally published in *Journal of Political Economy,* 99, no. 5 (1991): 1109–1116. © 1991 by The University of Chicago. All rights reserved.

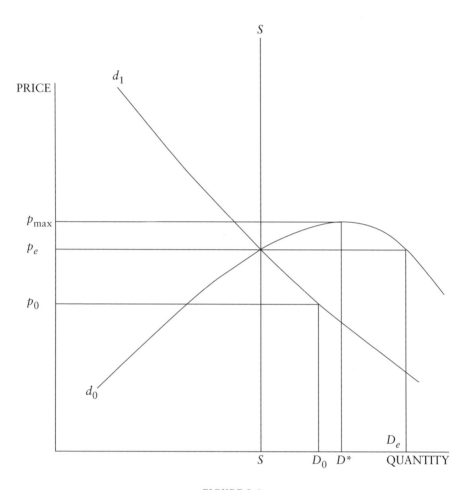

FIGURE 9.1

at a higher price than $p_0$ share profits with owners or employees that are not reported as taxable income. A similar story applies to the maître d' who provides scarce tables to customers willing to pay "under the table." However, it is unclear why such tax evasion or principal-agent conflicts should be more common with successful plays and restaurants than with the sale of steel or oranges. Moreover, nonprice rationing apparently existed on Broadway long before tax considerations were important.

Price increases will be discouraged if consumers believe that they are unfair (see Kahneman, Knetsch, and Thaler, 1986). This may sometimes help explain why prices do not rise to take advantage of temporary shortfalls in supply, but it is not plausible when rationing is more permanent. A series of gradual price increases could eliminate the gap in Figure 9.1 without causing serious complaints about unfair pricing.

Here I provide a different explanation, which assumes that a consumer's demand for some goods depends on the demands by other consumers. The motivation for this approach is the recognition that restaurant eating, watching a game or play, attending a concert, or talking about books are all social activities in which people consume a product or service together and partly in public.

Suppose that the pleasure from a good is greater when many people want to consume it, perhaps because a person does not wish to be out of step with what is popular or because confidence in the quality of the food, writing, or performance is greater when a restaurant, book, or theater is more popular. This attitude is consistent with Groucho Marx's principle that he would not join any club that would accept him.

Formally, I propose that the demand for a good by a person depends positively on the aggregate quantity demanded of the good:

(9.1) $$D = \Sigma d^i(p, D) = F(p, D), \quad F_p < 0, F_d > 0$$

where $d^i(p, D)$ is the demand of the $i$th consumer, and $D$ is the market demand. For each value of $D$, the equilibrium price solves $D = F(p, D)$. Since $F_p < 0$, there is a unique price for each feasible level of demand, given by the inverse demand function, $p = G(D)$. There are formal similarities between the effects of social interactions and the gains from standardization (see, e.g., Farrell and Saloner, 1988).

Social interactions imply that $\partial G / \partial D$ may not be negative. As is well known, $F_d > 0$ can lead to a positive relation between price and aggregate demand. By differentiating equation (9.1), we get

(9.2) $$\frac{dp}{dD} = G_d = \frac{1 - F_d}{F_p}$$

If the social interaction is strong enough—if $F_d > 1$—an increase in aggregate demand would increase the demand price. If $F_d > 1$ for all $D < D^*$, $F_d = 1$ for $D = D^*$, and $F_d < 1$ for $D > D^*$, the demand price rises as $D$ increases for $D < D^*$, it hits a peak when $D = D^*$, and then it falls as $D$ increases beyond $D^*$ (see $d_0$ in Fig. 9.1).

Since $d_0$ is rising at the market-clearing price $p_e$, it obviously pays to raise price above $p_e$: no less is sold and each unit fetches more. Indeed, profits are maximized when the price equals $p_{max}$, the peak demand price. The positively inclined demand curve in the vicinity of $S$ explains why popular restaurants remain popular despite "high" prices. Obviously, demand must be rationed at $p_{max}$ since $D^*$ exceeds $S$. To simplify the discussion, I assume that the method used to ration demand is costless, such as a pure lottery system, so that the money price is the full cost to consumers.

Since a firm that charges $p_{max}$ has a permanent gap measured by the difference between $D^*$ and $S$, shouldn't it raise price still further, cut the gap, and make even more profits? The answer from Figure 9.1 is clear: demand is discontinuous at $p_{max}$ for price increases and falls to zero even for trivial increases. The reason for the discontinuity is clear. If demand fell only a little (say to $D_1$) at $p = p_{max} + \epsilon$, there would be multiple demand prices at $D_1$: $p_1$ and $p_{max} + \epsilon$. We know that demand price is unique at $D_1$ and at all other values of $D$. Hence demand must fall to zero when $\epsilon > 0$, no matter how small $\epsilon$ is.

Of course, demand curves like $d_0$ that first rise and then fall are not the only possible outcome of the positive effect of market demand on the quantities demanded by each consumer. The net effect could be a demand curve that is negatively inclined (when $F_d$ is always less than one, as $d_1$ in Fig. 9.1), or it could be the demand $d$ in Figure 9.2 that is first negatively sloped, becomes positively sloped for some $D$, and then becomes negatively sloped again. The firm would like to charge $p^*$ in Figure 9.2 and sell all $S$ units, with demand at $D_g^*$ and the gap being sizable. This equilibrium is similar to the equilibrium at $p_{max}$ in Figure 9.1.

However, if the firm simply chooses the price $p^*$, demand may be at $D_b^*$ rather than at $D_g^*$ since demand has two values at $p^*$. Moreover, $D_b^*$ is not an attractive equilibrium since the excess capacity $(S - D_b^*)$ is substantial. If the firm must have an inferior equilibrium, it prefers $p_e$ to $p^*$ since marginal revenue is zero when $p = p_e < p^*$ and $D = D_e < S$.

Consequently, there are two competing locally profit-maximizing equilibria: one has excess capacity and a low price $(S - D_e, p_e)$, and the other has excess demand and a high price $(D_g^* - S, p^*)$. The difference between these equilibria corresponds to the difference between a struggling restaurant or play with excess tables or seats and a highly successful one that is "in" and turns away would-be customers.

Obviously, producers prefer the excess demand equilibrium, but how can they help bring that about? Since each consumer demands more when

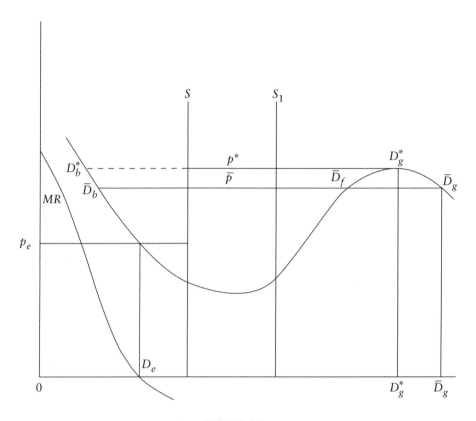

FIGURE 9.2

others do, producers can try to coordinate consumers to induce them to raise their demands together.

Advertising and publicity may help, for these have a multiplier effect when consumers influence each other. Advertising that raises the demands of some consumers also indirectly raises the demands of other consumers since higher consumption by those vulnerable to publicity campaigns stimulates the demands of others. This explains the promotion of new books, and it suggests that goods with bandwagon properties tend to be heavily advertised.

The distinctive equilibria at $D = D_e$ and $D = D_g^*$ are a formal recognition of the well-known fact mentioned at the beginning that one restaurant may do much better than another one, even though they have very similar food and amenities. The success or failure of new books is an equally good example. Stephen Hawking's *A Brief History of Time* was on the *New York Times* best-seller list for over 100 weeks and sold more than 1.1 million hardcover copies. Yet I doubt if 1 percent of those who bought the book could understand it. Its main value to the purchasers has been as a display on coffee tables and as a source of pride in conversations at parties.

The inequality in book sales is large: the coefficients of variation in total sales to August 1989 of books issued in 1987–88 by one publisher exceeded 129 percent and 177 percent for hardcover fiction and nonfiction books, respectively (the data were supplied to me by Eugene Kandel). The success or failure of trade books—like that of restaurants, plays, and other events—often depends on fortuitous factors that help sales snowball when they catch on and sink when they flop.

Figure 9.2 can explain an important characteristic of book pricing: the price of the hardcover edition almost never increases when a book turns out to succeed, nor until remaindering does it fall so much if it flops (see the analysis and evidence in Kandel, 1990). The reason is that $p^*$ is more or less the optimal price whether the book flops or not, assuming that demand is quite inelastic for $p < p^*$ (so that $p_e$ is close to $p^*$). Publishers set a price of $p^*$ and hope for success, but they recognize that they may end up with many unsold copies $(S - D_b^*)$ that are mainly useful in the remainder market and for the paper content.

The "fickleness" of consumers evident in the shift of restaurants between "in" and "out" categories is also captured by this analysis. Although the equilibrium at $(p_e, D_e)$ is locally stable, the one at $(p^*, D_g^*)$ is not stable for shocks that reduce demand, and neither equilibrium is stable for large changes. If consumers at $(p^*, D_g^*)$ lose confidence that other consumers want the good, demand will drop all the way to $D_b^*$.

This analysis explains too another commonly noted phenomenon: it is much easier to go from being "in" to being "out" than from being "out" to being "in." Since the equilibrium at $(p_e, D_e)$ is locally stable in *both* directions, only a large upward shock to demand could shift that "out" equilibrium to the more profitable one at $(p^*, D_g^*)$.

The partial instability of the profitable equilibrium at $(p^*, D_g^*)$ may also explain a puzzle about supply. If price is not raised when demand exceeds supply, why doesn't output expand to close the gap? That does happen for best-sellers, where unexpected heavy demand is usually met by additional printings. Sometimes, too, restaurants faced with excess demand expand seating capacity, but often they do not. One explanation for why they do not expand is that restaurants know customers are fickle and a booming business is very fragile. They might be reluctant to expand capacity if demand at $p^*$ could suddenly fall from $D_g^*$ to $D_b^*$. The cost of an expansion in capacity from, say, $S$ to $S_1$ could then drive a restaurant into bankruptcy.

Another possible explanation of why supply does not grow is that aggregate demand depends not only on price and aggregate demand but also positively on the gap between demand and supply:

$$(9.3) \qquad D = \Sigma d^i \left( p, D, \frac{D}{S} \right) = F \left( P, D, \frac{D}{S} \right), \frac{\partial F}{\partial d/s} > 0$$

Greater supply might not pay because that lowers the gap and, hence, the optimal price available to a producer.

This may explain why customers who have trouble getting into the popular Palo Alto restaurant mentioned at the beginning of this chapter do not switch to the nearby unpopular one. When I suggest doing this to my wife, she usually answers that she prefers the amenities at the popular restaurant. But the main difference in "amenities" is that one restaurant is crowded and has queues, while the other one is partially empty and provides immediate seating!

The gap between what is demanded and what is supplied affects demand when consumers get utility from competing for goods that are not available to everyone who wants them—such as an exclusive club—or when the camaraderie on a queue itself delivers utility. Of course, entering the gap into the demand function to explain why supply does not increase appears to be an ad hoc invention of a "good" to solve a puzzle. Therefore, I do not want to overemphasize the importance of the gap between demand and supply, although I do believe that it is sometimes relevant.

In an insightful comment, Ted Bergstrom was disturbed by the leftward instability of the equilibrium at $(p^*, D_g^*)$ and proposed a somewhat different approach. In his model, typical consumers prefer a larger aggregate demand only up to some fraction of capacity; beyond that they find a restaurant, theater, and so forth "too crowded." He shows that this can lead to a locally *stable* high-price profit-maximizing equilibrium in which demand equals capacity. Bergstrom's suggestion is valuable for some problems, but the model in this note seems better suited to the best-seller phenomenon, persistent excess demand, and the much greater fragility of being an "in" activity than an "out" activity.

Moreover, a restaurant could increase the leftward stability of a high-price equilibrium by lowering price in Figure 9.2 below $p^*$, say to $\bar{p} < p^*$, which has a demand at $\overline{D}_g > D_g^*$. The seller might be willing to trade off a lower price than $p^*$ for a more stable equilibrium: the point $(\bar{p}, \overline{D}_g)$ is stable not only for increases in demand but also for some shocks that lower demand. However, $\bar{p}$ does not avoid but magnifies the multiple equilibrium problem since there is the unstable equilibrium at $\overline{D}_f$ as well as the excess capacity locally stable equilibrium at $\overline{D}_b$.

It may strike some readers as ad hoc to make a person's demand depend on the demands of others in order to explain why restaurants, theaters, publishers, and others do not raise price when demand exceeds supply. But economists have paid insufficient attention to direct social influences on behavior. Fortunately, social interactions finally are being incorporated into economic models to explain residential segregation and neighborhood "tipping," custom, pay structure, gambling, and other behavior (for some examples, see Chapter 8; Schelling, 1978; Akerlof, 1980; Brenner, 1983; Jones, 1984; Frank, 1985; Granovetter, 1985; Bond and Coulson, 1989). Therefore, the analysis here fits well into a growing economic literature that recognizes the influence on consumers and workers of the social world they live in.

# A Simple Theory of Advertising as a Good or Bad

# 10

## 1. Introduction and Summary

Most economists and other intellectuals have not liked advertisements that provide little information. Noninformative advertising is claimed to create wants and to change and distort tastes. Although we agree that many ads create wants without producing information, we do not agree that they change tastes. Our approach may at first blush appear strange: we include advertisements as one of the goods that enter the fixed preferences of consumers.

The usual definition of a "good" is something consumers are willing to pay for, and a "bad" is something consumers pay to have removed or must be compensated to accept. Both goods and bads are part of given utility functions. For example, horror movies are "goods" for the many people who pay to be frightened out of their wits, and garbage is a "bad" because people are willing to pay to have it removed.

The straightforward definitions of goods and bads suggest that non-informative advertisements are "goods" in utility functions if people are willing to pay for them—they need not actually pay in equilibrium—and such advertisements are "bads" if people must be paid to accept them. If advertisements are considered utility and "taste shifters" rather than goods, why aren't horror movies, cars, opera, and many other things that consumers buy?

To be sure, consumers may respond to the social and psychological pressures generated by advertisements. But they also respond to such pres-

By Gary S. Becker and Kevin M. Murphy; originally published in *Quarterly Journal of Economics*, 108, no. 4 (1993): 941–964. © 1993 by the President and Fellows of Harvard College and the Massachusetts Institute of Technology.

sures when considering dinners at prestige restaurants, ownership of Mercedes cars, and many other goods.

Advertisements "give favorable notice" to other goods, such as Pepsi-Cola or cornflakes, and raise the demand for these goods. In consumer theory, goods that favorably affect the demand for other goods are usually treated as complements to those other goods, not as shifters of utility functions. There is no reason to claim that advertisements change tastes just because they affect the demand for other goods.

Our analysis treats advertisements and the goods advertised as complements in stable metautility functions, and generates new results for advertising by building on and extending the general analysis of complements. By assimilating the theory of advertising into the theory of complements, we avoid the special approaches to advertising found in many studies that place obstacles in the way of understanding the effects of advertising. By removing these obstacles, a clearer picture of these effects emerges.

Clearly, very few advertisements are sold separately and directly to consumers. Ads may be given away, as those in direct mail and billboard advertisements, or they may be sold jointly with programs, newspaper articles, comics, sports pages, etc. The special properties of advertising markets are responsible for important differences between the positive and normative analysis of advertisements and that of many other complements.

Section 2 sets out the basic model that treats advertisements with the theory of the demand and supply of goods (or bads) that are complements to consumers. We emphasize two cases: either advertisements are given away free and rationed to consumers; or they are sold to consumers, possibly jointly with other ads and goods, and possibly at subsidized, even negative, prices. This section contrasts our approach with the traditional one that treats advertisements as shifting tastes. Ours has the major advantage that it readily incorporates the demand for advertising into the theory of rational consumer choice, and has the usual implications of utility theory concerning symmetry conditions and negatively inclined demand functions.

Section 3 discusses the relation between advertising and industrial structure. The well-known theorem (Dorfman and Steiner, 1954) that the incentive to advertise rises as the elasticity of demand for the advertised good falls is shown to be highly misleading, for the incentive to advertise may rise, not fall, as a market becomes more competitive. The reason is that the effect of advertising on the price of the good advertised may rise as the elasticity of demand for this good increases. Section 3 also demonstrates that advertising tends to raise elasticities of demand for goods advertised by lifting the demands of marginal consumers.

Section 4 uses our approach to evaluate advertising from a welfare perspective. Whether there is excessive or too little advertising depends on several variables: the effects on consumer utility, the degree of competition in the market for advertised goods, the induced changes in prices and outputs of advertised goods, and whether advertising is sold to consumers. We show that treating advertising as shifting tastes prejudices a welfare analysis toward the conclusion that advertising is excessive. We avoid that prejudice without implying that firms supply the socially optimal amount.

Section 5 considers the properties of radio and television, and shows that advertisements attracted to these media tend to lower the utility of viewers. This may also be true of some advertisements that use other media. Advertisers provide utility-raising programs to compensate viewers for exposing themselves to the ads. Even when the programs compensate viewers fully, we reach the strange-sounding conclusion that advertisers would profit from utility-reducing ads that sufficiently raise marginal demands for the goods advertised.

Many implications of a model of advertisements as goods in stable utility functions are similar to the implications of models where advertising provides information or lies about the goods advertised (see, e.g., Grossman and Shapiro, 1984). But there are differences: for example, the information approach to advertising has trouble explaining advertisements that lower consumer utility (see Section 5).

Moreover, it is also "obvious" that many ads provide essentially no information. Rather, they entertain, create favorable associations between sexual allure and the products advertised, instill discomfort in people not consuming products popular with athletes, beauties, and other elites, and in other ways induce people to want the products. Table 10.1 gives the U.S. companies with the ten largest ratios of advertising expenditures to sales in the first quarter of 1988. Chewing gum, cereal, beer, or cola ads, to take a few of the ads produced by companies on the list, surely usually convey very little information.

Some recent literature agrees that much advertising provides little *direct* information about the goods advertised, but they are said to provide information to consumers *indirectly* by signaling the quality of the goods advertised (Nelson's study, 1974, pioneered this approach; also see

*Table 10.1*  Ten Companies with Largest Advertising to Sales Ratios
Among Major National Advertisers

|  | Advertising/sales | Primary business |
|---|---|---|
| 1. Noxell Corporation | 0.18 | Toiletries |
| 2. William Wrigley, Jr. Co. | 0.17 | Food |
| 3. Kellogg Company | 0.13 | Food |
| 4. Warner-Lambert Company | 0.10 | Pharmaceuticals |
| 5. Alberto-Culver Company | 0.10 | Toiletries |
| 6. Adolph Coors Company | 0.10 | Beer |
| 7. Hasbro, Inc. | 0.09 | Toys |
| 8. Schering-Plough Corp. | 0.09 | Pharmaceuticals |
| 9. Coca-Cola Company | 0.07 | Soft drinks |
| 10. Proctor and Gamble Co. | 0.07 | Soaps and cleaners |

*Source. Advertising Age,* August 22, 1988; advertising/sales is for first quarter, 1988; from set of "100 leading national advertisers."

Kihlstrom and Riordan, 1984, and Horstman and MacDonald, 1987). We do not believe that the intensive advertising for Miller beer, Chevrolet cars, or Marlboro cigarettes, to take a few examples, is signaling exceptionally high product quality. But we shall not try to compare systematically the implications of our model of advertising as a good with a signaling model, beyond pointing out that in the signaling approach, demand can be affected by advertising even when consumers are not exposed to the content of the ads, whereas in our approach demand can be affected only through exposure. Moreover, the pure signaling interpretation implies that companies should advertise how much they spend on advertising, yet almost no companies do that.

Our study builds on important work by others. Dixit and Norman (1978) provide the best formulation of the taste-shifting approach. Telser (1962, 1964) gives a pioneering analysis that includes advertisements as part of given consumer preferences; also see the comment on Dixit and Norman by Fisher and McGowan (1979). The discussion of advertising in Ehrlich and Fisher (1982) stresses the importance of advertising in economizing on time. Kaldor (1949) has a good early analysis of advertising that discusses both positive and normative economic issues. Comanor and Wilson (1974, chap. 2) and Barnett (1966) briefly mention that advertisements on radio and television may be "bads." Stigler and Becker (Chapter 2) show why perfectly competitive firms may advertise. Analytically, our discussion of the complementarity between advertising and goods advertised is closely related in several respects to Spence's (1976) important analysis of product quality; also see Tirole (1988) and Shapiro (1982).

Although some of our discussion can be found in this earlier literature, apparently no one has worked out the many positive and normative implications of treating advertisements as part of the stable preference structure of consumers. This is the goal of our paper.

## 2. A Model of Advertising

### 2A. MODELING CONSIDERATIONS

Consider a single-period utility function that depends on goods $x$ and $y$, and $A$, advertisements for $x$:

$$(10.1) \qquad U = U(x, y, A)$$

By definition, advertising gives "favorable notice" to the good advertised, so that an increase in $A$ raises the relative marginal utility of $x$. We assume that regardless of market structure, consumers can buy all they want of $x$ and $y$ at fixed prices. But this may not be an appropriate assumption for advertisements. Indeed, most discussions of advertising in the economics literature simply assume without much justification that advertisements are given away rather than sold to consumers. They produce revenue indirectly by raising the demand for the good advertised. Therefore, only producers of that good would be willing to pay for the advertisements since they are the only ones who benefit. Producers who give away advertisements want to limit quantities to consumers since they balance the indirect revenue in the market for the good advertised with the cost of supplying additional ads.

Consequently, the dominant model of advertising assumes both that advertisements are given away to consumers, and that quantities are controlled by producers of the goods advertised. This view is so imbedded in thinking about advertising that activities which violate either of these conditions are simply not considered "advertisements," even when they obviously give "favorable notice" about other goods and services. For example, sports columns in newspapers provide plenty of notice about local professional teams, even though sports sections are not free to readers, and team owners do not pay for the columns. The strike of Pittsburgh's two newspapers in mid-May 1992 was said to have reduced sales to games of the Pittsburgh Pirates baseball team by 3,000 to 4,000 tickets a game (Klein, 1992).

In this example, sport analysis and description are produced jointly with advertising for teams. In other cases, firms help advertise certain goods because of complementarities between the goods advertised and the goods supplied by these firms. But whatever the reason, there are many examples of advertising that violate one or the other of the two standard assumptions of advertising models.

The assumption that producers choose the quantity of advertising to consumers is intrinsically tied to the approach that assumes advertising shifts tastes. For such an approach has no way of determining how consumers make their choices about advertising. It resolves what otherwise would be a serious dilemma by assuming that producers determine the quantity of advertising available to consumers at a zero price. By contrast, when advertising is part of stable meta-preferences, consumer demand for advertising is a straightforward implication of utility maximization (see equation 10.6), and it is no longer necessary to assume that advertising is free and that producers control its quantity.

The usual model with a zero price of advertising and quantities controlled by advertisers does apply to direct mail advertisements, although consumers can discard these mailings without looking at what is inside. But it is doubtful how well it explains newspaper ads or those on radio and television.

For example, the quantity of newspaper ads available to consumers is not rationed, and these ads are not necessarily free to readers. The implicit price for these ads is measured by the difference between the actual cost of newspapers to consumers and what it would be if papers did not have the ads.

The implicit price of advertisements in newspapers or on broadcast media may be negative, even if advertisements are part of consumers' stable utility funtions. Advertisers could not charge a positive price for ads that yield zero or negative marginal utility, and consumers are usually indirectly paid to listen to radio ads and to watch those on television (see Section 5).

Of course, the price charged for advertisements would be much more transparent if they were sold separately, the way oranges and fish are. But technological constraints and transactions costs often make it too expensive to sell ads separately. Prior to pay television, ads on radio or television could not be sold directly since there was no way to charge the audience for what they heard or watched. Ads in print could technically be sold on small pieces of paper, but transaction costs are greatly reduced by selling printed ads together in newspapers, along with information and entertainment.

A special problem arises when consumers are paid to take ads. It might not be profitable to allow them to take all they want at a fixed (negative) price per unit. For they might "buy" a large number and ignore as many as possible, as when remote controls are used to switch off ads on television. The difficulties of monitoring these consumers have led advertisers to control the supply as well as the prices of ads with negative prices.

Therefore, transactions costs and technological constraints in some, but far from all, cases support the usual assumption that advertisers rather than consumers determine the amount of advertising. Our discussion in this and the next section treats two polar situations: either advertisements are given away and the quantity is controlled by producers, or they are sold at a fixed (implicit) price per unit to consumers who can buy all they want. Section 5 considers the case where consumers must be paid to accept certain advertisements.

The production of advertisements is generally a very competitive industry, where advertisers hire agencies to prepare copy for them. Competition implies that the marginal cost to advertisers of a unit of advertising would equal the marginal cost of preparing it ($c_a$).

We start the systematic discussion with the conventional case, where advertisements are given away, with the quantity controlled by producers. A firm that determines $x$ and $A$ to maximize net profits $p_x(A)x - c_x x - c_a A = p_x x(A) - c_x x(A) - c_a A$ must satisfy

(10.2) $$p_x(1 - 1/\epsilon_x) = c_x$$

and

(10.3) $$\frac{\partial p_x}{\partial A} x = \frac{\partial x}{\partial A}(p_x - c_x) = c_a$$

where $c_x$ is the unit cost of $x$, $\epsilon_x$ is the elasticity of demand for $x$, $\partial p_x/\partial A$ holds $x$ constant as $p_x$ changes, and $\partial x/\partial A$ holds $p_x$ constant as $x$ changes. Equation (10.3) assumes that consumers are willing to accept the quantity of $A$ given away by producers because the marginal utility of $A$ is not negative (see equation 10.6).

The first condition is the usual one when firms produce a single product ($x$). Since $A$ is given away, the choice of $x$ does not depend on the price of $A$, but, of course, it does depend on the quantity of $A$. The second condition shows that the entire value of $A$ that is given away comes from its effect on the price and quantity of $x$. Although $A$'s market price is zero, it has a shadow price to each consumer that equals the money value of the marginal utility of an additional advertisement (see equation 10.6).

If instead of giving advertisements away, firms allow consumers to buy all they want at a fixed price $p_a$, the first-order conditions for $x$ and $A$ become

(10.4)
$$p_x \left( 1 - \frac{1}{\epsilon_x} \right) + \frac{\partial p_a}{\partial x} A = c_x$$

(10.5)
$$p_a \left( 1 - \frac{1}{\epsilon_a} \right) + \frac{\partial p_x}{\partial A} x = c_a$$

where $\partial p_a / \partial x$ holds $A$ constant, $\partial p_x / \partial A$ holds $x$ constant, and $\epsilon_a$ is the elasticity of demand for $A$. See the relation between $\partial p_x / \partial A x$ and $\partial x / \partial A (p_x - c_x)$ in equation (10.3). If $A$ raises the demand for $x$, the marginal revenue from an increase in $A$ is partly due to an induced increase in $p_x$ at a given $x$. Equation (10.5) shows that if $\partial p_x / \partial A$ is large, then the optimal value of $A$ could be sufficiently large to lower $p_a$ below $c_a$. Advertising would be sold below cost, even when it could be sold at a profit, if its complementarity with the good advertised is sufficiently strong. The complementarity is obvious with beer advertising on television during football games since many people drink beer as they watch a televised game.

A utility-maximizing consumer satisfies the following inequality both when advertising is sold and when it is not:

(10.6)
$$U_A \geq p_a$$

where $U_A$ is the marginal utility of advertising. If advertising is rationed, then $>$ holds; if it is also given away, $p_a = 0$, and $U_A > 0$. If consumers can buy all the ads they would at fixed prices, then equality holds.

When $A$ is sold at a fixed price, nothing formally distinguishes advertising from an analysis of multiproduct firms, where the products are complements in consumption. For example, $x$ and $A$ could also refer to cars and repair services or personal computers and software.

Since in our formulation advertising enters the consumer's utility function along with other goods, rational choice implies that advertising satisfies the symmetry conditions and other implications of utility theory. Therefore, this analysis implies that if advertisements are complements to goods advertised, those goods are complements to the advertisements. That is, greater consumption of advertised goods would raise the marginal utility from, and the demand for, advertising. This is a crucial implication of our approach, although some readers may be dubious about its validity.

We know of little evidence on this implication, but a study by several psychologists did find that people who have recently purchased a new car were more likely to read ads for the same type of car than for other types (see Ehrlich, Guttman, Schönbach, and Mills, 1957). The authors interpret these findings as evidence of cognitive dissonance, but our treatment of advertisements as complements to the goods advertised can explain them, perhaps including the finding that people who owned their cars for a while did not show more interest in ads for their type.

The positive implications of our approach differ in substance and not only in language from a more traditional approach that treats advertising as shifting tastes. Firm behavior is the same, once firms know the demand for advertising and how advertising affects demand for the goods advertised. But since the taste-shifting approach has no theory of consumer choice, it does not imply the various implications of consumer theory, and cannot explain how consumers choose among different ads that require time, money, or other scarce resources. In particular, this approach lacks the equivalent of equation (10.6), which is a first-order condition for consumers that determines their demand for advertising. It does not seem possible even conceptually for the taste-shifting approach to incorporate advertising into the theory of rational consumer choices.

By contrast, when advertisements are treated as part of given meta-tastes, consumer demand for advertising is subject to the same rules of behavior as their demand for other goods. These rules include consistent choices over time, symmetry between cross price effects, results about the effects of rationing on the demand for substitutes and complements, and so forth. Section 4 makes clear that because the theories about behavior are so different, the welfare implications of the taste-shifting and stable tastes approaches to advertising are also very different.

## 2B. ADVERTISING AND CONSUMER SURPLUS

A firm that rations the ads it gives away (so $p_a = 0$ and $\geq$ holds in equation 10.6) can collect the marginal value of $A$ to consumers only through the effect of the ads on the demand for $x$. Therefore, if the firm also charges for advertising, it might collect *more* than the value of $A$ to consumers because the direct revenue from selling $A$ ($p_a A$) is added to the indirect revenue in the market for $x$. Indeed, if the firm is setting market prices that clear the market for both $x$ and $A$, it can collect twice for a small increase in $A$: once directly in the market for $A$ and once in the market for $x$.

The source of the paradox is the effects of advertising on the ability of firms to extract consumer surplus in the market for the advertised goods. If greater advertising raises the demand for $x$ by a constant amount, the entire increase in consumer surplus from the higher $A$ accrues to the firm through the higher price for $x$, assuming that the quantity of $x$ is held fixed (see Figure 10.1). Additional revenue from the direct sale of $A$ takes away some of the initial surplus. This conclusion about consumer surplus is not unique to advertising and applies to any complements produced by a firm (such as computers and their software) as long as increased quantities of

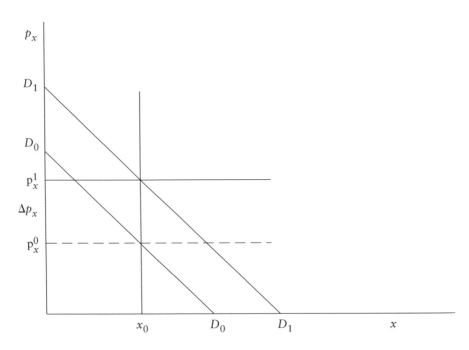

FIGURE 10.1

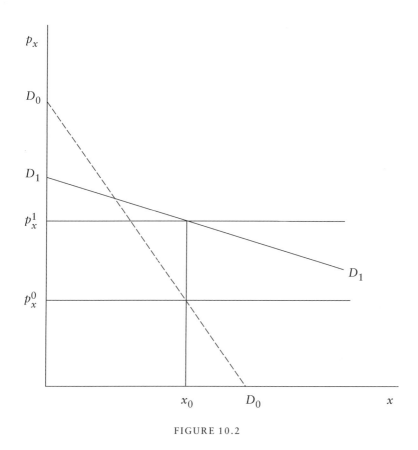

FIGURE 10.2

one of them raises by a constant amount the negatively sloped downward curve for the other.

If the effect of higher $A$ on the marginal utility of $x$ is not constant but is larger when $x$ is bigger (compare $D_1$ and $D_0$ in Figure 10.2), the greater revenue in the $x$ market from an increase in $A$ exceeds the increase in consumer surplus. Direct revenue from the sale of $A$ only adds to the surplus extracted from consumers. This case shows that what counts to producers is the effect of advertising on the utility from *marginal* units of $x$. The effect on marginal units determines the effect on profits through its effect on the price and quantity of $x$.

Therefore, a firm that is unable to price discriminate in a market where it has monopoly power may be able to use a complementary product to extract additional consumer surplus. Even if the complement must be sold below its average cost of production—perhaps because its marginal value to consumers is less than the average cost—the complement may increase the firm's profits by sufficiently raising the demand for the monopolized good.

Since the analysis of advertising has much in common with an analysis of product quality, it is not surprising that the same emphasis on marginal units and marginal consumers is found in the literature on product quality (see Spence, 1976; Shapiro, 1982; and Tirole, 1988) and retail price maintenance (see Klein and Murphy, 1988; and Comanor, 1985). For example, the presale services sometimes encouraged by price maintenance may well be valued most by marginal consumers because they know less about the product.

## 3. Advertising, Competition, and the Elasticity of Demand

### 3A. ADVERTISING AND COMPETITION

Over seventy years ago, Pigou (1920) already argued that competitive firms do not advertise because they can more or less sell all they want at a given price even without advertising. This conclusion is repeated often (see, e.g., Kaldor, 1949; or Scherer, 1980, p. 387).

That firms with elastic demand curves do not want to provide free advertising appears to be supported by the first-order profit-maximizing conditions in equations (10.2) and (10.3). The middle term in equation (10.3) seems to indicate that marginal revenue from advertising is low for competitive producers of $x$ since $p_x - c_x$ is close to zero for these producers. If equation (10.2) is substituted into this middle term, one gets an expression that relates the marginal revenue from advertising directly to the elasticity of demand for $x$:

$$(10.7) \qquad MR_A = \frac{p_x}{\epsilon_x}\frac{dx}{dA}$$

Therefore, *if the price of the product ($p_x$) and the increase in demand due to advertising ($dx/dA$) are held fixed,* the marginal revenue from advertising delines as the elasticity of demand for $x$ ($\epsilon_x$) increases. This is the famous theorem of Dorfman and Steiner (1954) that less competitive firms have more incentive to advertise.

Despite the continued reliance on their result,[1] we claim that it is highly misleading. For one thing, the theorem proves too much, for it applies not only to advertising, but to all complements produced by the same firm. If $x$ is quantity of output and $A$ measures quality, the theorem says that producers with more monopoly power have a greater incentive to upgrade their quality. Hence the unreasonable conclusion from the theorem that monopolistic producers make better quality products than competitive producers.

The proof of this theorem crucially depends on the assumption that $dx/dA$ does not change as $\epsilon_x$ increases. What happens to $dx/dA$ depends on why $\epsilon_x$ changes, and often it would increase as $\epsilon_x$ did. For example, the elasticity of demand for the soap industry is much smaller than that for individual soap companies. And the effect of advertising on the quantity demanded at a given price is presumably also much greater when one company alone advertises than when all companies (the industry) do, since advertising by one company attracts customers from competitors. In this example, therefore, the effect of advertising on the quantity demanded of the advertised good is positively related to, not independent of, the elasticity of demand for the product advertised.

It is far more reasonable to assume that $dp_x/dA$ is approximately constant for a given $x$ as $\epsilon_x$ changes than that $dx/dA$ is constant for a given $p_x$. The difference between these assumptions may seem minor, but actually they have very different implications. In particular, if $dp_x/dA$ is held constant, there is no presumption that the incentive to advertise falls as $\epsilon_x$ increases. For the left-hand side of equation (10.3) indicates that the marginal revenue from advertising can be written not only as in equation (10.7) but also as

$$(10.8) \qquad MR_A = x\frac{\partial p_x}{\partial A}$$

Given the output of the product advertised ($x$), the marginal revenue from advertising is greater when the increase in price is greater. A change in the elasticity of demand for the product advertised *has no effect whatsoever* on the marginal revenue from advertising when $x$ and $\partial p_x/\partial A$ are held constant.

It is easy to reconcile the different implications of equations (10.7) and

---

1. Among the numerous favorable references, see Hurwitz and Caves's recent discussion of advertising by pharmaceutical companies (1988) and Tirole's (1988, p. 103) excellent book on modern industrial theory.

(10.8). When the effect of $A$ on $x$ is held fixed as $\epsilon_x$ increases, the effect of $A$ on $p_x$ falls,[2] which explains why the marginal revenue of advertising then also falls. Similarly, when the effect of $A$ on $p_x$ is held fixed as $\epsilon_x$ increases, the effect of $A$ on $x$ rises.

The value of highlighting the effect of advertising on the price of the good advertised is that the marginal revenue from advertising is then directly related to the higher marginal utility from consuming a given amount of the advertised good, as in equation (10.6). By contrast, the effect of advertising on the quantity demanded at a given price has no ready interpretation in terms of marginal utilities. If the effect of advertising on the marginal utility from consuming a given quantity of the good advertised is unrelated to its elasticity of demand, the effect on price and the incentive to advertise would also be unrelated to this elasticity.

For example, it is plausible to assume that the effects of advertising by one soap company on the price and marginal utility of its soap is similar to the effects of advertising by the industry on the average price of all soap. For the effect of advertising on price depends on the sensitivity of marginal demand. This sensitivity may not be very different when one soap company attracts consumers from competing companies through its advertising than when the industry attracts consumers from competing products.

The presumption that oligopolistic industries usually advertise more than monopolistic industries is based on the assumption that demand for an oligopolistic firm's product is more elastic, *and hence more sensitive to advertising,* than is demand for a monopoly's product. Such reasoning contradicts that behind the Dorfman-Steiner result, although it is fully consistent with our approach.

---

2. If

$$x = a(A)p_x^{-\epsilon_x}, \quad \frac{d \log x}{d A} = \frac{a'}{a} \text{(for a given } p_x)$$

Since

$$\frac{d \log p_x}{d A} = \frac{1}{\epsilon_x} \frac{a'}{a} \text{(for a given } x)$$

an increase in $\epsilon_x$ reduces the effect of $A$ on $p_x$ when $a'/a$ (and thus $(d \log x)/da$) is held fixed.

The discussion in Tirole [1988, pp. 100–103] is revealing. Immediately after a good analysis of product quality that uses the effect of quality on the price consumers are willing to pay for a given quantity, he analyzes advertising through its effect on the quantity demanded at a given price.

A different argument for why competitive firms have no incentive to advertise is that many close competitors could free ride on the advertising (see, e.g., Comanor and Wilson, 1974, p. 20). Advertising by a wheat farmer may raise slightly the demand for all wheat, but it is unlikely to raise much the demand for this farmer's wheat relative to that of others.

Of course, firms do not advertise when they cannot differentiate their products from many competing products. Yet the fact is that companies in highly competitive situations often do a lot of advertising. Perdue chickens closely compete with other chickens, Chiquita bananas with other bananas, and Jaffa oranges with other oranges. Yet all these brands have been extensively advertised because say Perdue advertisements convince consumers that a pound of its chickens is worth more than a pound of other chickens. Whether advertising succeeds in differentiating further the product advertised from that of substitutes may be related empirically to the number and closeness of substitutes, but there is no strict analytical connection.

## 3B. ADVERTISING AND PRICES OF ADVERTISED GOODS

That advertising raises the price of the good advertised for a *given* quantity does not in general imply that it raises the *equilibrium* price. Equations (10.2) and (10.4) show that advertising tends to raise or lower the equilibrium price as it lowers or raises the elasticity of demand for the advertised good. Advertising is often said to lower this elasticity because firms expand their monopoly power by differentiating further their products from others. However, we have shown that advertising is profitable not because it lowers the elasticity of demand for the advertised good, but because it raises the level of demand.

We believe that the presumption in fact goes the other way, that advertising tends to *raise* the elasticity of demand at the initial equilibrium quantity of the advertised good. The reason is that firms try to tailor their advertising to bring up the demands of marginal consumers since these drag down the equilibrium price paid by inframarginal consumers: again the analysis is related to discussions of product quality by Spence (1976) and others. In lieu of explicit price discrimination, advertising may help price a good *effectively* lower to marginal consumers.

Assume two classes of consumers, C and D, where each C is willing to pay $10, and each D is willing to pay only $5, for a single unit of x that costs $2 to produce. Suppose that $10 is the profit-maximizing price without price discrimination and advertising, so that only C buys x at this price. Introduce an advertising campaign aimed at D, the marginal

consumers, and assume it costs $7 to raise each D's reservation price for
$x$ to $10. Although the advertising costs more than the increase in D's
reservation price, advertising is profitable because it enables the firm to
collect also the initial reservation price ($5) of the D consumers.

This example illustrates why advertising tends to increase the market
elasticity of demand for the goods advertised in the vicinity of the initial
equilibrium quantity. In the example, advertising is a way to price discriminate that is inferior to free explicit discrimination but may be superior to
feasible alternatives.

The early ads for low-calorie beer were targeted to women because
their weak demand for beer lowered the equilibrium price of beer. Such
advertising could pay even if it reduced demand by inframarginal males.
Similarly, a political candidate's promises are often targeted to undecided
voters even when that lowers the backing of his strong supporters, because
he is likely to get their votes, and he needs undecided votes to win.

The claim that advertising raises prices of the goods advertised is
often supported by evidence that advertised goods are more expensive than
"similar" unadvertised goods (see the review of this evidence in Scherer,
1980, pp. 381–388). But advertised goods may have good qualities that
are not observed by econometricians, as implied by the signaling literature.

Better evidence comes from the consequences of advertising regulations. Several studies find that states which permit advertising for particular goods have lower prices than states which ban the advertising (see
Benham's well-known study, 1972, of eyeglasses and Bond's discussion,
1980, of advertising in the professions). These studies may be exceptional
cases; however, perhaps they only illustrate that advertising raises elasticities of demand for advertised goods.

## 4. Advertising and Welfare

Economists have long been opposed to advertising (see, e.g., Pigou
1920, p. 199; or Galbraith, 1958, pp. 155–156), yet they have been unable to use standard welfare analysis to show that advertising is excessive
because of the peculiar attitude toward how advertising affects consumers.
A major analytical advantage of our approach that treats advertising as
part of given preferences rather than as shifting tastes is that the standard
welfare analysis becomes directly applicable. Indeed, the following discussion is similar to the welfare analysis of product quality by Spence (1976);
also see Tirole (1988). Some differences between the analysis of advertising
and quality are considered at the end.

We use the sum of consumer and producer surplus ($S$) to evaluate the welfare effects of advertising by a firm:

$$(10.9) \qquad V(A, p_x, T) + \Pi(A, p_x, T) = S$$

where $V$ is the money value of the consumer's utility, $\Pi$ is the surplus to the firm producing the advertising ($A$) and the product advertised ($x$), $p_x$ is the price of $x$, and $T$ is any revenue from the sale of $A$. Whether advertising is socially optimal after including induced changes in the output of the good advertised is found by totally differentiating equation (10.9) with respect to $A$:

$$(10.10) \qquad \frac{dS}{dA} = V_A + V_{p_x}\frac{dp_x}{dA} + V_T\frac{dT}{dA} + \frac{d\Pi}{dA}\left(= \Pi_A + \Pi_{p_x}\frac{dp_x}{dA} + \Pi_T\frac{dT}{dA}\right)$$

It is clear that

$$(10.11) \quad V_T = -1, \;\; V_{p_x} = -x, \;\; \Pi_{p_x} = x, \;\; \Pi_T = 1, \;\; \text{and} \;\; \Pi_A\,(p_x - c_x)\frac{dx}{dA} - c_a$$

where $c_a$ and $c_x$ are the marginal costs of $A$ and $x$, respectively. Note that $dp_x/dA$ and $dx/dA$ are the equilibrium changes in $p_x$ and $x$ after taking account of changes in all variables, whereas $\partial p_x/\partial A$ and $\partial x/\partial A$ in the profit-maximizing first-order condition in equation (10.3) are partial changes, holding $x$ or $p_x$ constant. The term $V_A$ gives the marginal utility to consumers from advertisements for $x$, net of any reduction induced by these ads in the utility from other goods.

By substituting (10.11) into (10.10), we see that advertising is excessive, optimal, or underproduced:

$$(10.12) \qquad \frac{dS}{dA} \gtreqless 0 \;\; \text{as} \;\; V_A + (p_x - c_x)\frac{dx}{dA} \gtreqless c_a$$

Since a firm maximizes producer surplus, $d\pi/dA = 0$, and equation (10.10) also simplifies to

$$(10.13) \qquad \frac{dS}{dA} \gtreqless 0 \;\; \text{as} \;\; V_A - x\frac{dp_x}{dA} - \frac{dT}{dA} \gtreqless 0$$

When consumers voluntarily expose themselves to advertisements, $V_A$ has to be $\geq 0$ unless consumers are compensated for any loss in utility from the ads. That is, unless $dT/dA$ is sufficiently $\leq 0$.

Advertising has been said to be excessive when its price is less than marginal cost (see Kaldor, 1949, p. 3; and Comanor and Wilson, 1974, p. 20). But if producers ration advertisements to consumers, the relevant price is not the price charged, but the shadow price to consumers which is measured by $V_A$. Equation (10.12) shows that the difference between the shadow price and marginal cost of advertising ($c_a$) does help determine whether or not advertising is socially excessive.

If the advertised good is perfectly competitive, with price equal to marginal cost ($p_x = c_x$), equation (10.12) gives the usual first-best criterion for welfare maximization; that is, the marginal cost of producing advertisements equals its shadow price to consumers. If $x$ is imperfectly competitive ($p_x > c_x$), advertising also has a "second-best" aspect, for it may change the distortion in the market for the advertised good by raising or lowering output. A second-best incentive to subsidize advertising would appear to exist if advertising stimulates the demand for $x$, for then $(p_x - c_x)dx/dA > 0$. But firms do take this effect into account when they choose their advertising since profits depend on $(p_x - c_x)dx/dA$ (see equation 10.3). Whether firms produce too much or too little advertising from a social perspective depends on the effect of advertising on demand for the advertised good.

Equation (10.6) indicates that $V_a \geq p_a$; hence, $dT/dA \leq p_a \leq V_a$ because marginal revenue is not above price. Substitution of this inequality into equation (10.13) gives that $dS/dA \geq 0$ if $dp_x/dA \leq 0$. Therefore, no matter how advertising changes demand, equation (10.13) and the consumer first-order condition to maximize utility imply that the amount of advertising is insufficient if the equilibrium price of the advertised product falls. For if it falls, producers fail to include the higher amount consumers are willing to pay for the product advertised in their estimate of the gain from additional advertising.

Whether advertising lowers price of the product advertised is a remarkably simple test that can be applied in practice to determine whether there is too little advertising. And this criterion follows from the usual welfare analysis and consumer utility maximization without special assumptions about how advertising affects either demand for the product or consumer utility. In particular, it applies to the case where advertising is rationed and given away as well as when it is sold at a fixed price in whatever quantities consumers want; the case where advertising has negative marginal utility as well as when it has positive utility; and to advertising by competitive firms as well as by monopolists. This is a major implication of our approach that treats advertising as part of given metatastes, but it cannot be derived from a model where advertising shifts tastes.

Most discussions of advertising assume that it is given away to consumers ($dT/dA = 0$), and that advertisements do not directly provide utility ($V_A = 0$). Equation (10.13) then implies that advertising is excessive, optimal, or insufficient as it raises, does not change, or lowers the equilibrium price of the advertised good. This explains why Dixit and Norman (1978) conclude that advertising is generally excessive, for they essentially assume that $V_A = 0$, that advertising is not sold, and that advertising usually raises the price of advertised goods.

These assumptions are dubious, for advertising does affect the utility of consumers, and it is often sold—sometimes at a negative price. Therefore, with reasonable assumptions an increase in the equilibrium price does not necessarily imply that advertising is excessive. Our criterion, that advertising is insufficient if the equilibrium price *falls* does not require any special assumptions about the advertising market or the effect of advertising on consumer utility.

The surplus criterion can be generalized beyond the effects of advertising on the product advertised by including induced changes in the consumers' and producers' surplus in other markets. Equation (10.12) becomes

$$\frac{d\left(\sum_{j=1}^{m}\right) S_j}{d A_1} \gtreqless 0 \quad \text{as} \quad V_{A_1} + (p_1 - c_1)\frac{dx_1}{dA_1}$$

(10.14)

$$+ \sum_{i=2}^{m}(p_i - c_i)\frac{dx_i}{dA_1} \gtreqless c_{a_1}$$

where $S_j$ is the total surplus in the $j$th market, $x_1$ is the good advertised, $x_i$, $i = 2, \ldots, m$ are the other products affected by advertising for $x_1$, $p_j$, and $c_j$ are the price and marginal cost of $x_j$, and $dx_i/dA_1$ is the equilibrium change in $x_i$ induced by an increase in $A_1$. If the other products affected are perfectly competitive ($p_i = c_i$), equation (10.14) reduces to equation (10.12), and the previous discussion is fully applicable.

However, if the good advertised expands partly through substitution for a monopolized good, $x_2$, where $p_2 > c_2$ and $dx_2 < 0$, the advantage of expanding $x_1$ is partly negated by the disadvantage of contracting a monopolized substitute. A full analysis of the social optimality of advertising includes induced changes in the outputs of substitutes and complements as well as changes in the output of the advertised good.

One interesting application is to competitive advertising of brands, where advertising expands output of a brand partly or wholly at the expense of competing brands. From early discussions to more recent treatments (see, e.g., Pigou, 1920, pp. 197–199; Solow, 1967, p. 165; and

Scherer, 1980, p. 389), economists have generally agreed that brand advertising is largely worthless to society if it does not increase aggregate consumption of the brands. But our analysis shows that even this seemingly plausible conclusion does not necessarily follow from a consumer surplus analysis.

If $p_i - c_i = p_1 - c_1$, $i = 2, \ldots, m$, equation (10.14) differs from equation (10.12) simply by substituting the total change in outputs of all brands $(dX)$ for the change in the good advertised. If the total change $dX = 0$, then the criterion for excessive or insufficient advertising reduces simply to whether $V_{A_1} \lessgtr c_{a_1}$; i.e., whether the marginal value to consumers of the advertising exceeds or is less than its marginal cost. The relation between these marginal values and cost depends on whether advertising is sold, and how it shifts demand for the brand advertised.

If the total output of all brands is unaffected, equation (10.14) implies that advertising is excessive if the marginal utility of advertising is negative. For then, $V_{A_1} < 0 < c_{a_1}$. If the direct marginal revenue from advertising equals the marginal utility of the advertising (if $dT_1/dA_1 = V_{A_1}$), advertising by a firm is excessive under the frequently realized condition that the increased quantity demanded for its product exceed the increased demand for all brands. For then $V_A + dX/dA_1(p_x - c_x) < c_{a_1}$ (see equations 10.14 and 10.5 and the first two terms on the left-hand side of equation 10.3). However, with the usual assumption that advertising is rationed and is given away, the amount of advertising is insufficient when total brand output is unchanged as long as $V_{A_1} > x_1 \partial p_1/\partial A_1 = c_{a_1}$ (see equation 10.3); that is, if the increased utility from advertising by a firm exceeds the *marginal* increase in the demand for its product.

Our welfare analysis of advertising applies also to government efforts to persuade consumers to change behavior. Suppose that the government wants consumers to bring used bottles and cans to recycling centers. It produces advertisements that are complements in consumer utility functions with a more favorable attitude toward recycling. Even if these ads directly lower utility, and hence consumers must be compensated to accept them, they would indirectly raise utility if the externalities from throwing away bottles and cans are sufficiently strong. In equation (10.12), $x$ refers to proper disposal $(dx/dA > 0)$, $p_x - c_x > 0$ because the cost to consumers of proper disposal is less than the social gain (measured by $p_x$) and $V$ could be $< 0$. If $p_x - c_x$ is sufficiently positive, government efforts at persuasion could raise utility even when $V_A < 0$, and $c_a$ is not negligible.

As we indicated, the welfare analysis of advertising is similar to the welfare analysis of product quality and other complements, but there are some differences. Since advertisements are physically distinct from the products advertised, while quality is embodied in products, firms can more easily charge separately for advertisements than for quality, although the charge for ads is usually implicit in the cost of a package that includes other goods. For the same reason, advertisements are not likely to affect the marginal cost of the good advertised, whereas improvements in the quality of a product usually do raise the marginal cost of a larger quantity.

Although these and similar differences between advertising and quality are important, they do not explain the hostility to advertising. We believe the explanation is that economists are willing to abandon the principle of consumer sovereignty when evaluating advertising but not when discussing quality, although a few studies have criticized changes in quality (see, e.g., the well-known paper by Fisher, Griliches, and Kaysen, 1962). The taste-change interpretation of advertising abandons consumer sovereignty by ignoring the utility from advertising when evaluating its welfare effects. We have shown that respect for consumer sovereignty does not imply that the amount of advertising by profit-maximizing firms is necessarily welfare-maximizing, but it does cast doubt on most discussions of the welfare effects.

## 5. Negative Utility from Advertising on Radio and Television

"Free" radio and television do not charge audiences either for advertisements or programs. Advertisers usually pay for both the cost of preparing and using their ads, and for programming costs. Since radio and television could provide advertisements without programming, why do advertisers go to the expense of including costly programs?

There are several possible reasons, but we believe the main one is that utility from programs compensates the audience for tuning in and becoming exposed to the ads. Since consumers do not have to be compensated for utility-raising services, the inference must be that most ads on radio and television lower the utility of marginal viewers, after netting out the value of the time spent watching and listening. As it were, advertisers throw in free programming to generate the audience for utility-reducing ads. One can say either that advertising pays for the programming—the usual interpretation—or that programming compensates for the advertising, which is our preferred interpretation.

Advertisements that lower utility are less likely to be placed in newspapers, magazines, and other print media because readers can more easily ignore advertisements than can listeners or viewers. Therefore, the presumption is that the print media have a larger fraction of utility-raising ads, including those providing information, than do radio and television.

Although plausible, it is not true that advertisements must raise consumer utility if they increase demand for the goods advertised. For the effect of advertising on demand depends on the cross derivative in the utility function between advertising and advertised goods, while the effect on utility depends on the first derivative with respect to advertising.

Still, it may seem unlikely that most radio and television ads reduce utility since these ads constitute an important fraction of all advertising expenditures. But utility is necessarily reduced only to marginal viewers, and only after netting out the value of time spent viewing ads. And just as death, divorce, unemployment, and similar utility-reducing events often induce greater drinking, smoking, overeating, and similar changes in consumption, we believe so too do many advertisements lower utility and yet raise demand for the advertised goods. These ads produce anxiety and depression, stir up envious feelings toward the success and happiness of others, or arouse guilt toward parents or children (see Marchand, 1985).

Indeed, in some ways the assumption that many ads lower utility is easier to reconcile with consumer behavior than is the assumption that they raise utility. For consumers often do not appear to look forward to consuming advertisements, and rational consumers would not seek out even free advertising if it lowers their utility.

It may seem strange that firms can profit from advertisements that lower utility even when they have to fully compensate consumers for their loss, perhaps by including utility-raising programs along with the advertising. But suppose that advertising raises the marginal utility of the advertised good at the initial equilibrium quantity, reduces the marginal utility of the advertised good at some lower quantities, and possibly also lowers utility independently of consumption of that good. Such advertising may reduce utility overall, but the reduction could be small compared with the revenue from the higher price for the good due to the increase in marginal utilities. Essentially, such advertising would be profitable because it allows a firm to collect more of the consumer surplus from the advertised good (see the example in Becker and Murphy, 1990, p. 37).

# Norms and the Formation of Preferences

11

## 1. Introduction

Norms are those common values of a group which influence an individual's behavior through being internalized as preferences. Important norms have opposed murder and incest and supported honesty, aid to elderly parents, and deference to the upper classes. Less important norms cover tipping, manners, speech, and many other forms of behavior.

It is easy to appreciate the social contribution of many norms since they combat the tendency to free-ride by internalizing particular values in preferences. If a person does not free-ride at the expense of others when that is advantageous to him, it may be because norms against the behavior lower the utility from the free-riding.

Norms are recognized to be of the utmost significance in every society, but there is no generally accepted analysis of their growth and decay. Honesty, to take one example, enormously reduces the need to spend resources, both public and private, on the protection of property, and it simplifies relations among individuals. But how has this norm evolved everywhere?

In other words, how do honesty and other norms become internalized as part of an individual's preferences when self-interest is opposed to behavior implied by the norms? Marxists claim that the upper classes in effect "brainwash" lower classes to internalize behavior that benefits the upper classes, but how the brainwashing is accomplished has not been made clear. Although game-theoretical analysis of repeated behavior can generate norm-like behavior—as in analyses that rely on evolutionary stable strategies (see, e.g., Young, 1993)—this approach has not yet been able to explain why particular norms predominate in many cultures.

This chapter takes a different approach to explain how one class—usually the upper class—creates norms to influence the preferences of other classes. In this approach the upper class does not "brainwash" other classes, for they voluntarily allow their preferences to be influenced. But a member of the lower class must be compensated for such changes in his preferences if they lower his utility by discouraging behavior that would benefit him. The approach to the formation of norms in this chapter assumes that one class decides whether to "instill" particular norms in members of other classes, who in turn must decide whether to "allow" the norms to become part of their preferences.

## 2. Cooperation within the Upper Class

Consider a community prior to the widespread prevalence of honesty, respect for private property, and other norms. Families who own most of the wealth naturally want to protect their positions and to encourage honest and deferential behavior on the part of the other families. They would try to establish and enforce laws against stealing, and discourage uprisings against the economic and social order. They may hire police, guards, and private armies, and inflict punishment on transgressors.

These upper-class families would be more effective if they could overcome free-riding tendencies and act collectively. This may be easier at early stages of economic and social development, when the distribution of property is usually highly unequal, and relatively few families are at the top. Moreover, elite families often increase their ability to cooperate by arranging marriages among cousins and among children from different families in their class. These blood ties further reduce the incentives of the wealthy to free-ride on each other.

I assume, therefore, that the upper class can take effective collective action, partly because it contains a small number of families among which intermarriage is common. The wealthy families may act collectively to acquire laws and privileges that protect their properties and positions against theft, uprisings, and other harmful acts.

These types of actions have received much attention, but the upper class also creates norms that help protect its wealth and status against attack. This chapter discusses how the upper class inculcates favorable norms into the preferences of other classes. Although the upper class promotes these norms out of self-interest, these norms would not lower the welfare of other classes if these classes voluntarily accept the norms, possibly in "exchange" for other benefits.

## 3. "Churches" and the Formation of Norms

People often gather together to celebrate holidays or pray in church—
I call all such gatherings attendance at "church." Sermons and prayer help
a person come to terms with eventual death, and they allow socializing
with other families. Church activities also produce ethical beliefs and other
norms, like respect for elders and the sanctity of life.

There is considerable evidence that church attendance is correlated
with socially responsible behavior. For example, young persons who more
often attend church are less likely to commit crimes, especially when they
live in neighborhoods with many other church-goers (see Stark, 1994).
Greeley (1995) presents evidence that religious persons are, among other
things, more honest in dealing with the government, and more sympathetic
to the poor and others down on their luck.

People would not attend churches where they acquire norms that
lower their utility unless they are compensated with sufficient benefits.
Otherwise, they would stop going to church, or they would shift their
allegiance to churches with more congenial norms. Since the upper class
benefits from norms that help secure its economic and social position,
this class would be willing to subsidize clergy, buildings, and other ex-
penses of churches that help promote such norms. These subsidies can
make churches that promote norms favorable to the upper class more attractive to lower classes than churches that do not promote these norms
and are not subsidized.

In fact, churches have usually depended for most of their financial support on a small number of relatively rich families. In the United States "20
percent of church members provide more than 80 percent of the financial
support in most congregations" (Iannaccone, 1994, p. 1; also see Hoge,
1993), and contributions were probably even more skewed toward the rich
in the past.

To formalize the analysis in previous paragraphs, first recognize that
norms affect preferences, as in

$$(11.1) \qquad\qquad U = U(X, N, Y)$$

where $U$ is the utility function of lower-class members, $X$ are private goods
obtained by church attendance, $N$ are the norms created there, and $Y$ are
other goods. Sermons and other church activities raise $X$ and possibly also
$N$. I assume $dU/dN < 0$ to indicate that norms which help the upper class
typically make members of lower classes worse off.

Why would congregants listen to sermons and pray in churches that raise $N$, and hence lower their utility? If church attendance is voluntary, they would be willing to absorb utility-reducing norms only if private goods ($X$) are subsidized sufficiently. Congregants may try to resist absorbing values and norms that make them worse off, the way audiences try to avoid advertising that lowers their utility. I assume that congregants must absorb the norms produced by churches if they want to consume the private goods produced, just as audiences cannot fully avoid watching television advertisements when they watch subsidized programming (see Chapter 10).

All classes can be made better off from the creation of norms that favor the upper class if the other classes receive sufficient subsidies. If the subsidy to goods $X$ equals \$$S$ per congregant, and if a lower-class person loses the monetary equivalent of \$$C$ from absorbing $N$ norms, she would be made no worse off by attending churches which produce these norms if

$$(11.2) \qquad\qquad S(N) - C(N) \geq 0$$

Since the upper class acts collectively, it can reduce $S$ to the minimum level needed to induce congregants to absorb these norms:

$$(11.3) \qquad\qquad S(N) = C(N)$$

The upper class must gain enough from the norms to justify providing these subsidies. If $G(N)$ is the collective gain to the upper class from the behavior induced by the $N$ norms, and if $K(N)$ is the cost per congregant of producing and "advertising" the $N$ norms, the upper class would be willing to compensate congregants if

$$(11.4) \qquad\qquad G(N) \geq \{S(N) + K(N)\}L$$

where $L$ is the number of lower-class congregants. By Equation (11.3), this can be written as

$$(11.5) \qquad\qquad G(N) \geq \{C(N) + K(N)\}L$$

This last equation shows that the gain to the upper class from these norms must exceed the loss to other classes by enough to cover the cost of producing the norms ($K$).

No one is harmed when norms are created according to equations (11.3)–(11.5), since they add to the well-being of the upper class without making other classes worse off. Other classes *agree* to absorb harmful norms into their preferences because they receive enough compensation for doing that.

The enforcement of norms typically depends on negative reactions by peers toward individuals who deviate from "proper" behavior. Churches, schools, armies, and other organizations inculcate particular beliefs partly by relying on public displays of these beliefs that increase their hold over others. The major religions are organized around group prayer in churches, mosques, and temples because congregants become more confident about the existence of God and ethical beliefs when others display similar views. Schools use classes partly to increase the influence of students over each other, and group reinforcement of bravery, obedience, and other behavior is crucial to military doctrine.

To incorporate group reinforcement of norms, extend the utility function in equation (11.1) to include the norms of peers ($N_p$):

$$(11.6) \qquad\qquad U = U(X, Y, N, N_p)$$

An increase in peer "pressure" presumably lowers the marginal disutility from these norms to members of the group ($\partial^2 U/\partial N \partial N_p > 0$).

The upper class would save the cost of creating norms ($K(N)$) if lower classes agreed to obey these norms in return for a sufficiently large subsidy. But such "agreements" may be difficult to enforce, since members of these classes could promise to obey and then renege on their promises when that was advantageous. Norms reduce the likelihood of such opportunistic behavior because they are part of each person's preferences, and hence they cannot be ignored when it is profitable to do so.

I have lumped together all classes other than the upper class, but norms preferred by that class are not equally attractive to middle and bottom classes. The upper class may be able to "buy" the acquiescence of the middle class rather cheaply, because norms that favor the upper class may appeal also to many members of the middle class. After all, they too own property and have valuable human capital. By contrast, the cost of buying the bottom class's support could be prohibitive, since many members of that class may gain from crimes against property and an upheaval of the social order. The upper class may need to use force to put down attacks from that class.

Naturally, the upper class would prefer to have the power to *impose* norms and values on other classes through propaganda in compulsory schools and other forced activities (see Bowles and Gintis, 1976; and Lott, 1990). Members of other classes might be made worse off when force is used, since the upper class does not "buy" the negative effects of these norms on their utility. Force saves the resources $(S(N) + K(N))$ the upper class must spend to buy acquiescence. But since acquiring and using the power to force attendance at schools and other activities is also costly, it may be cheaper for the upper class to buy rather than force the conformity of other classes to particular norms.

A "functionalist" approach claims that only norms and other values which help a society function more effectively will evolve over time. My analysis has a functionalist flavor, for the norms voluntarily absorbed in churches and other activities help the upper class without harming others. But these norms are *biased* toward favoring the upper class, since I have assumed that only the upper class can act collectively. Even though many other norms also may be efficient, they would not emerge unless the upper class can arrange to be compensated by other classes for absorbing norms that harm its members.

Compensation from the bourgeoisie to the upper class, and perhaps to other classes as well, may explain why the bourgeoisie sometimes has benefited from favorable norms, including the prestige accorded business success in the United States during the nineteenth century, and the value placed on thriftiness (Richard Posner stressed to me the importance of bourgeoisie values). Wealthy merchants and manufacturers have promoted these values by subsidizing schools, churches, and other group activities, and by buying political influence.

## 4. Summary

This chapter argues that the upper class often has been able to generate norms that help maintain its economic and social privileges because this class has been in an especially good position to overcome free-riding and act collectively. These norms would be "functional" in the sense that they raise overall efficiency if other classes must be compensated for any reduction in utility due to the incorporation of the norms into their preferences. Some norms that raise overall efficiency may not emerge, however, if no group is able to act collectively to buy, or force, their incorporation into the preferences of groups that are made worse off by the norms.

## 12

Spouses and Beggars:
Love and Sympathy

## 1. Introduction

Love between a mother and her children is to be expected, given their genetic similarities and their physical and psychological "bonding" during the gestation period. But much other love, altruism, sympathy, and affection between persons develops through accidental encounters or through repeated and planned interactions over time. Many emotional attachments do not last, as continued interaction sometimes destroys the initial love or changes it into hatred and disdain.

Sexual and other intimacy between a man and a woman illustrate the intense emotions surrounding love. Every society recognizes the potential for good and bad of the attraction between the sexes, and tries to channel these feelings into satisfying and productive relations. These channels help determine who falls in love and the stability of their attachments.

The growth and decay of love and other emotions needs to be addressed by any theory of preference formation. This chapter considers the ebb and flow of these emotions when individuals maximize utility. Forward-looking individuals consider how their choices affect the probability of developing rewarding emotional relations. They also recognize, however, that emotions are often fickle, so they must prepare for the collapse of their love and sympathy.

## 2. Begging and Sympathy

I begin the discussion with contributions to beggars, a much simpler example than love between individuals (for interesting economic discussions of begging, see Newcomb, 1885; Mulligan, 1993; and Brecht, 1928). A beggar attempts to attract voluntary contributions by using his physical appearance and verbal requests to indicate that he is hungry and down on his luck. He hopes to create guilt, pity, or sympathy among passers-by, to induce them to part with a little of their wealth.

A person makes contributions to add to his own utility—otherwise he would not part with any wealth. But although contributions raise utility *ex post*, some persons are made worse off *ex ante* by encounters with beggars. They contribute only because the unpleasant appearance or persuasive appeals of beggars makes them feel uncomfortable or guilty. Newcomb noticed a century ago that "The fact that the benevolent gentleman may wish there were no beggars, and may be very sorry to see them, does not change the economic effect of his readiness to give them money" (1885, p. 527).

The following utility function illustrates the issues:

$$(12.1) \qquad\qquad U = U(X, C, S, B)$$

where $S$ is the degree of "sympathy" for a beggar after seeing him and hearing his pleas (measured by $B$), $C$ are contributions, and $X$ is the contributor's own consumption. Sympathy stimulates contributions if an increase in $S$ raises the (relative) marginal utility of $C$:

$$(12.2) \qquad\qquad \partial^2 U/\partial C \partial S > 0$$

This is why beggars who elicit more sympathy get larger contributions.

Sympathy is related to the quality of a beggar's appeal:

$$(12.3) \qquad\qquad S = S(B), \text{ with } dS/dB > 0$$

An effective beggar raises sympathy, which in turn raises contributions—by the complementarity in equation (12.2) between sympathy and contributions. But whether a potential contributor *wants* to encounter a beggar depends not on equation (12.2), or even on the production function in equation (12.3), but on how begging changes his preferences.

Encountering a beggar may lower utility because a person feels guilty or uncomfortable:

$$(12.4) \qquad\qquad \partial U/\partial B < 0$$

Conversely, it raises utility when meeting less fortunate individuals makes a person feel superior or lucky:

$$(12.5) \qquad\qquad \partial U/\partial B > 0$$

A person who enjoys beggars seeks them out when that is not too costly since the encounter makes him better off. However, Equation (12.4) expresses the analytically more interesting and more common situation when people do not want to encounter beggars, even though they may contribute handsomely after an encounter.

Beggars and these contributors engage in a game of strategy: beggars want to be seen by the contributors who want to avoid them. In effect, beggars gain utility at the expense of the contributors. Presumably, laws control where beggars can ply their trade to reduce contacts between beggars and reluctant contributors. But beggars try to go where they best appeal to their "victims," and free societies have great trouble controlling where they go. Similarly, persons who contribute out of guilt or discomfort try to outsmart beggars and avoid contact with them. By anticipating the negative effects of begging on their utility, guilty contributors may be able to avoid harmful shifts in their preferences.

## 3. Love and Marriage

In modern times, men and women generally marry only if they are in love, or develop other strong emotional bonds from sexual and other contacts. Much search, grooming, and other strategies go into meeting desirable spouses and companions. These strategies are highly sophisticated in many marriage "markets" found throughout the world.

To analyze the consequences of love and other emotions for preferences and behavior, represent the utility of female $f$ as

(12.6) $$U_f = (X_f, M_{fm}, A_{fm}, C_{fm})$$

where $M_{fm}$ is a variable that indicates whether or not $f$ is married to male $m$, $A_{fm}$ are the love and other bonds she feels toward $m$, and $C_{fm}$ are transfers from $f$ to $m$ if they marry. I assume that $A$ and $M$ are complements, so that a person is more likely to marry someone she loves:

(12.7) $$\partial^2 U / \partial M \partial A > 0$$

Note that equation (12.7) does not depend on the sign of $\partial U / \partial A$. A marriage can involve strong emotions and yet lower utility ($\partial U / \partial A < 0$). Masochistic and other "sick" reasons may push a person to marry someone who "abuses" her mentally or physically. Of course, she wants to *avoid encountering* such individuals, even though she would be willing to marry a man who behaved in this way after becoming "involved."

The rest of this chapter considers the more common situation where a person feels affection and love toward her spouse ($\partial U / \partial A > 0$). I also recognize that while love is necessary for marriage, most men and women also consider the effects of marriage on children, wealth, social status, and other "goods."

The marriage production function for these other goods ($Q$) can be expressed as:

$$(12.8) \qquad\qquad Q_{fm} = Q(Y_f, Y_m)$$

where the $Y$s are characteristics of men and women that determine the production of $Q$, and

$$(12.9) \qquad\qquad \partial Q / \partial Y > 0, \text{ and } \partial^2 Q / \partial Y_f Y_m \gtrless 0$$

To simplify I assume that $Q$ is a private good, so that

$$(12.10) \qquad\qquad Q_f + Q_m = Q_{fm}$$

where $Q_f$ and $Q_m$ are $f$'s and $m$'s marital incomes.

If love were not relevant for marriages—perhaps marriages are arranged by parents who do not care whether their children love their spouses—a perfect marriage market sorts high $Y$s with each other only if the cross-derivative in the production function is positive. That is, it sorts high $Y$s with each other only if $Y_m$ and $Y_f$ are complements in producing marital outputs. Conversely, high $Y$s marry low $Y$s if this second derivative is negative—if they are substitutes (see Becker, 1991, p. 114). Therefore, when love is unimportant, equilibrium marital sortings in a perfect market are determined only by the sign of $\partial^2 Q / \partial Y_f \partial Y_m$. Competition in the marriage market divides output between spouses in the equilibrium sorting according to their productivity in producing the output.

In modern times, however, love is usually a necessary condition for marriage. Love implies altruism: a person who is much better off than a spouse she loves helps him out with money and in other ways. These contributions reduce the inequality in their resources. I simplify the discussion by assuming that marital love is so strong that contributions to the poorer spouse equalize their incomes:

$$(12.11) \qquad\qquad Q_f^* = Q_m^* = \frac{1}{2} Q_{fm}$$

where $Q^*$ refers to incomes after spousal gifts.

What determines the sorting between men and women who do not marry unless they are in love, yet who also value marital goods? I do not distinguish degrees of love, so that either a couple loves each other or they do not. It might seem that if the probability of falling in love does not depend on personal characteristics, then the equilibrium set of matches would still be mainly determined by whether characteristics are complements or substitutes. For if, say, they are substitutes, if the derivative in equation (12.9) is negative, opposites would *tend* to marry even when they must be in love because opposites are no less likely to fall in love than are persons with similar characteristics.

The principal result of the model I have described is that this argument is wrong, even though it sounds plausible. Love can have a major effect on whether likes or unlikes marry even when the probability of falling in love does not depend on personal characteristics. If love equalizes the net incomes of spouses (as in equation 12.11), a person's income increases when his marital output increases. Then males and females with the best characteristics ($\hat{Y}_m \geq Y_m$ and $\hat{Y}_f \geq Y_f$) maximize their net incomes by marrying each other if they are in love—regardless of whether characteristics are complements or substitutes—because the maximum output in any marriage occurs when $\hat{Y}_m$ marries $\hat{Y}_f$. Yet if love were not important, and if characteristics are substitutes, $\hat{Y}_m$ would marry a woman with the lowest $Y$, and similarly for $\hat{Y}_f$.

If $\hat{Y}_f$ and $\hat{Y}_m$ marry each other, the same argument shows that men and women with the second highest $Y$s would marry each other if they are in love, again regardless of whether characteristics are complements or substitutes. Continuing along this line implies a perfectly positive marital sorting on personal characteristics when love is necessary for marriage, regardless of how male and female characteristics interact in the production function. Yet without love, personal characteristics would be negatively sorted if they are substitutes (see also the discussion in Becker, 1991, pp. 126–191, and Lam, 1988).

Therefore, love can completely change the direction of matches by family background, I.Q., and other characteristics. True, this example assumes that high-$Y$ men and high-$Y$ women fall in love, but this assumption does not require that persons with similar characteristics are *more likely* than opposites to fall in love. The argument implies that men and women with similar characters tend to be matched when likes and unlikes are equally likely to fall in love, or even when likes have only a moderately lower probability of falling in love with each other.

If high-characteristic men and women prefer to marry each other, they will structure their search to raise the likelihood of meeting each other. They will live in neighborhoods and join clubs and churches that have persons of their own background, they will go to the same schools, and so forth.

Of course, just as beggars try to encounter generous donors who do not want to meet them, some low $Y$s may try to meet high $Y$s in the hope they fall in love, marry, and receive transfers from their higher-income spouses. Indeed, if male and female characteristics are substitutes in marital outputs, low $Y$s might prefer high-$Y$ spouses even if they do not receive transfers because the incomes of low $Y$s before transfers would be higher than their incomes would be in marriages to high $Y$s. As an inducement, low $Y$s might even be willing to sign prenuptial agreements and make other promises to take minimal transfers from high-$Y$ spouses. But such agreements tend to be renegotiated after marriage because high $Y$s *want* to contribute to poorer, low-$Y$ spouses they love, and these spouses are willing to accept the gifts. Recognizing this beforehand, high $Y$s try to avoid low $Y$s and instead marry each other.

In effect, love limits the role of marginal products in matching men and women because it sharply curtails the divisions of marital outputs that are feasible. Becker and Murphy (1994) give a more general analysis of the relation between feasible price systems and the equilibrium sortings of different types into marriages, neighborhoods, and other categories.

Although modern societies have very strong positive sorting by education, family background, I.Q., race, and other characteristics (see Becker, 1991, p. 119), this does not necessarily mean that these characteristics are complements in producing marital output. The main result of this chapter is that love induces positive sortings even for characteristics that are substitutes. Although it is counterintuitive, the growing importance of love in marriage during the past couple of centuries might have *increased* the degree of positive sorting by family background and other personal and social characteristics.

## 4. Fickle Love and Divorce

"Marry in haste, repent in leisure" is ancient wisdom, a recognition that even the deepest and most passionate love frequently does not last. Maturation, knowledge that comes from living together, and inevitable frictions due to the many difficulties of life often transform love toward a spouse into indifference, loathing, disdain, and other unpleasant feelings.

Forward-looking persons, however deeply in love, force themselves to recognize that their love may not last. Expensive presents, dowries, and other gifts are commonly demanded up front while a spouse's love shines brightly. Prenuptial agreements that allocate assets, children, and other responsibilities are valuable when love dies and a couple seek divorce or separation.

If divorce is forbidden, forward-looking persons delay marriage until they believe their love has a reasonable chance of surviving the vicissitudes of life. At the same time, in choosing mates they also place less emphasis on fickle love, and greater emphasis on more durable characteristics. In addition, spouses are more likely to try to nurture their love when they cannot easily divorce since they must continue to put up with each other. Living together is hellish after love degenerates into bitterness and hatred. Love can be "nurtured" because its growth and decline is not exogenous but depends on the effort put into its preservation.

Obviously, the incentive to nurture love is weak when it is easy to divorce since a person who falls out of love can look for a more satisfying second marriage. Although divorced persons invariably claim they no longer love their former spouses, easy access to divorce may explain why they did not try to maintain their love.

Poorer performance in school and at other activities by children of divorced parents than by children with intact families (Beller and Chung, 1992) does not imply that divorce *causes* their performance to decline. For parents usually divorce only after they have been quarreling and creating other tensions in their household. Exposure to these tensions may be even worse for children than divorce.

But the endogeneity of love implies that even if quarreling and other tensions are worse for children than divorce, children may benefit if the obstacles to divorce are raised. Parents tend to quarrel more when they can readily divorce, since they would invest less in maintaining their love and a decent family atmosphere. Parents who are "stuck" with each other try harder to maintain their love, or at least to get along, than parents who can readily divorce. Children may grow up in a better atmosphere when their parents are induced to invest in maintaining cordial and even warm relations.

......................................

Acknowledgments

References

Index

# Acknowledgments

All figures were redrawn for this book by Roberto Marques.

CHAPTER 1

I appreciate the very helpful comments of Michael Aronson, Robert Barro, James Heckman, Casey Mulligan, Walter Oi, Tomas Philipson, Richard Posner, Paul Romer, Sherwin Rosen, and Cass Sunstein.

CHAPTER 2

The authors acknowledge helpful comments from Michael Bozdarich, Gilbert Ghez, James Heckman, Peter Pashigian, Sam Peltzman, Donald Wittman, and participants in the Workshop on Industrial Organization.

CHAPTER 4

The authors' research has been supported by the Lynde and Harry Bradley Foundation through the Center for the Study of the Economy and the State, University of Chicago, and by the Hoover Institution.

CHAPTER 5

Funding for this research was supported by a grant from the Bradley Foundation to the Center for the Study of the Economy and the State of the University of Chicago. The authors are indebted to Eugene M. Lewit, David Merriman, three anonymous referees, and the participants in seminars at the University of Chicago, Columbia University, Harvard University, the University of Kentucky, the Federal Trade Commission, the City University of New York Graduate School, Colgate University, Pennsylvania State University, and the State University of New York at Albany for helpful comments and suggestions. Thanks go to Frank Chaloupka, Brooks Pierce, Robert Tamura, Ahmet E. Kocagil, Geoffrey F. Joyce, Patricia De Vries, and Ismail Sirtalan for research assistance. This work has not undergone the review accorded official NBER publications; in particular, it has not been submitted for approval by the Board of Directors.

CHAPTER 6

An earlier version of this chapter was given as the Nancy Schwartz Lecture at Northwestern University, May 15, 1991. I have had helpful comments from Joseph Hotz, Kevin Murphy, Richard Posner, and Sherwin Rosen, and useful assistance from David Meltzer and M. Rebecca Kilburn. I am indebted to a grant from the Lynde and Harry Bradley Foundation to the Center for the Study of the Economy and the State, to the National Institute of Child Health and Development (Grant 5 R37 HD22054), and to the National Science Foundation (Grant SES–9010748) for support.

CHAPTER 7

This chapter is dedicated to the memory of George J. Stigler, who died almost exactly one year before this Nobel Lecture was delivered. Nobel Laureate, outstanding economist, very close friend and mentor, he would have been as happy as I was had he lived to see me deliver the 1992 Nobel Lecture in Economic Sciences. I have had valuable comments from James Coleman, Richard Posner, Sherwin Rosen, Raaj Sah, Jose Scheinkman, Richard Stern, and Stephen Stigler.

CHAPTER 8

Over the years I have received helpful comments on a succession of drafts from numerous persons, especially my colleagues at the University of Chicago and the National Bureau of Economic Research. I received very useful comments on the draft prepared for publication from Robert Barro, Isaac Ehrlich, Sam Peltzman, and George Stigler, and valuable research assistance from Walter Wessels. My research has been supported by a grant to the NBER from the National Institute of Child Health and Human Development, National Institutes of Health, U.S. Department of Health, Education, and Welfare. This chapter is not an official NBER publication since it has not been reviewed by the NBER Board of Directors.

CHAPTER 9

I am indebted for helpful comments to Ted Bergstrom, Bruno Frey, David Friedman, Milton Harris, Eugene Kandel, Edward Lazear, Kevin M. Murphy, Sherwin Rosen, and George Stigler and to the participants in a Seminar on Rational Choice in the Social Sciences at the University of Chicago and to the Lynde and Harry Bradley Foundation and the Hoover Institution for support.

CHAPTER 10

The authors benefited from useful comments by William Comanor, David Friedman, Paul Milgrom, Richard Posner, Sherwin Rosen, Andrei Shleifer, George Stigler, and two excellent referees, from the discussion at an Economic and Legal Organization Workshop of the University of Chicago, and from research assistance by David Meltzer and M. Rebecca Kilburn. Our research has been supported by the Lynde and Harry Bradley Foundation through the Center for the Study of the Economy and the State.

CHAPTER 11

I have benefited from very helpful comments on an earlier draft of this chapter by Robert Cooter, Bruno Frey, Casey Mulligan, Kevin M. Murphy, and Richard Posner.

CHAPTER 12

The ideas in this paper were developed jointly with Kevin M. Murphy, but he is not responsible for any errors.

# References

Aaron, Henry J. 1994. "The Distinguished Lecture on Economics in Government: Public Policy, Values and Consciousness." *Journal of Economic Perspectives* 8: 1–17.

Adams, James D. 1974. "Asset Transfers at Deathtime." Paper presented at Workshop in Applications of Economics, Department of Economics, University of Chicago.

Adler, Stephen J., and Alix M. Freedman. 1990. "Tobacco Suit Exposes Ways Cigarette Firms Keep the Profits Fat." *Wall Street Journal,* March 5, p. 1.

Akabayashi, Hideo. 1995. "The Role of Incentives in the Function of Formation of Family Background: Theory and Evidence." Unpublished memorandum, University of Chicago.

Akerlof, George A. 1980. "A Theory of Social Custom, of Which Unemployment May Be One Consequence." *Quarterly Journal of Economics* 94: 749–775.

——— 1991. "Procrastination and Obedience." *American Economic Review* 81: 1–19.

Alchian, Armen A., and W. R. Allen. 1967. *University Economics.* 2d ed. Belmont, CA: Wadsworth.

Appelbaum, Elie. 1982. "The Estimation of the Degree of Oligopoly Power." *Journal of Econometrics* 19: 287–299.

Aristotle. 1962. *Nicomachean Ethics.* Indianapolis: Bobbs-Merrill Company.

Arrow, Kenneth J. 1972. "Models of Job Discrimination." In *Racial Discrimination in Economic Life,* ed. Anthony H. Pascal. Lexington, MA: Lexington Books.

——— 1973. "The Theory of Discrimination." In *Discrimination in Labor Markets,* ed. Orley Ashenfelter and Albert Rees. Princeton, NJ: Princeton University Press.

Arrow, Kenneth J., and Frank H. Hahn. 1971. *General Competitive Analysis.* San Francisco: Holden-Day.

Arrow, Kenneth J., and Mordecai Kurz. 1970. *Public Investment, the Rate of*

*Return, and Optimal Fiscal Policy*. Baltimore: Johns Hopkins University Press (for Resources for the Future).

Bain, Joe S. 1968. *Industrial Organization*. 2d ed. New York: Wiley.

Baltagi, Badi H., and Dan Levin. 1986. "Estimating Dynamic Demand for Cigarettes Using Panel Data: The Effects of Bootlegging, Taxation and Advertising Reconsidered." *Review of Economics and Statistics,* 68: 148–155.

Barnett, Harold J. 1966. Comment on "Supply and Demand for Advertising Messages," by Lester Telser. Both in *American Economic Review Proceedings,* 56: 457–466, 467–470.

Barro, Robert J. 1974. "Are Government Bonds Net Wealth?" *Journal of Political Economy* 82: 1095–1117.

Barro, Robert J., and Xavier Sala-i-Martin. 1992. "Convergence." *Journal of Political Economy* 100: 223–251.

Beccaria, Cesare, marchese di. 1986. *On Crimes and Punishments*. Translation of *Dei delitti e delle pene* (1797), by David Young. Indianapolis: Hackett.

Becker, Gary S. [1957] 1971. *The Economics of Discrimination*. 2d ed. Chicago: University of Chicago Press.

———— 1961. "Notes on an Economic Analysis of Philanthropy." Working Paper, National Bureau of Economic Research.

———— 1962. "Investment in Human Capital: A Theoretical Analysis." *Journal of Political Economy* 70: 9–49.

———— [1964] 1975. *Human Capital*. 2d ed. New York: Columbia University Press, for the National Bureau of Economic Research.

———— 1965. "A Theory of the Allocation of Time." *Economic Journal* 75: 493–517.

———— 1968a. "Crime and Punishment: An Economic Approach." *Journal of Political Economy* 76: 169–217.

———— 1968b. "Interdependent Preferences: Charity, Externalities, and Income Taxation." Manuscript, University of Chicago.

———— 1974. "A Theory of Marriage: Part II." *Journal of Political Economy* 82:11–26.

———— [1981] 1991. *A Treatise on the Family*. Enlarged ed. Cambridge, MA: Harvard University Press.

Becker, Gary S., and Barry R. Chiswick. 1966. "Education and the Distribution of Earnings." *American Economic Review Papers and Proceedings* 56: 358–369.

Becker, Gary S., Michael Grossman, and Kevin M. Murphy. 1987. "An Empirical Analysis of Cigarette Addiction." Paper presented at the Workshop in Applications, University of Chicago, May 18.

———— "An Empirical Analysis of Cigarette Addiction." 1990. Working Paper No. 3322, National Bureau of Economic Research.

———— 1991. "Rational Addiction and the Effect of Price on Consumption." Working Paper, Center for the Study of the Economy and the State, University of Chicago.

Becker, Gary S., Elisabeth M. Landes, and Robert T. Michael. 1977. "An Economic Analysis of Marital Instability." *Journal of Political Economy* 85: 1141–1187.

Becker, Gary S., and Vicente Madrigal. 1995. "The Formation of Values with Habitual Behavior." Unpublished memorandum, Stern School of Business, New York University.

Becker, Gary S., and Casey B. Mulligan. 1995. "On the Endogenous Determination of Time Preference." Working Paper No. 98, Center for the Study of the Economy and the State, University of Chicago; Discussion Paper 94-2, Economics Research Center/NORC, University of Chicago.

Becker, Gary S., and Kevin M. Murphy. 1986. "A Theory of Rational Addiction." Working Paper no. 41, Center for the Study of the Economy and the State, University of Chicago.

——— 1990. "A Simple Theory of Advertising as a Good." Working Paper No. 58, Center for the Study of the Economy and the State, University of Chicago.

——— 1994. "Optimal Social and Private Sorting among Categories When the Composition of Members Matters." Manuscript, University of Chicago.

Becker, Gary S., Kevin M. Murphy, and Robert Tamura. 1990. "Human Capital, Fertility, and Economic Growth." *Journal of Political Economy* 98: S12–S37.

Becker, Gary S., and George J. Stigler. 1974. "Law Enforcement, Malfeasance, and Compensation of Enforcers." *Journal of Legal Studies* 3: 1–18. Reprinted in *Chicago Studies in Political Economy,* by George J. Stigler. Chicago: University of Chicago Press, 1988.

Becker, Gary S., and Nigel Tomes. 1986. "Human Capital and the Rise and Fall of Families." *Journal of Labor Economics* 4: S1–S39.

Beller, Andrea H., and Seung Sin Chung. 1992. "Family Structure and Educational Attainment of Children: Effects of Remarriage." *Journal of Population Economics* 5: 39–59.

Benham, Lee. 1972. "The Effect of Advertising on the Price of Eyeglasses." *Journal of Law and Economics* 15: 337–352.

Bentham, Jeremy. 1789. *Principles of Morals and Legislation.* Oxford: Clarendon.

——— 1931. *Theory of Legislation.* New York: Harcourt, Brace.

——— 1952. "The Philosophy of Economic Science." In *Jeremy Bentham's Economic Writings,* vol. 1, ed. W. Stark. New York: Franklin.

Bergstrom, Theodore C. 1989. "A Fresh Look at the Rotten Kid Theorem—and Other Household Mysteries." *Journal of Political Economy* 97: 1138–1159.

Blau, Peter M. 1968. "Interaction: Social Exchange." In *International Encyclopedia of the Social Sciences,* vol. 7, ed. D. E. Sills. New York: Macmillan.

Blumer, H. C. 1968. "Fashion." In *International Encyclopedia of the Social Sciences,* vol. 5, ed. D. E. Sills. New York: Macmillan.

Böhm-Bawerk, Eugen von. 1959. *Capital and Interest,* vol. 2. Trans. George D. Huncket and Hans F. Sennholz. South Holland, IL: Libertarian Press.

Bond, Eric W., and N. Edward Coulson. 1989. "Externalities, Filtering and Neighborhood Change." *Journal of Urban Economics* 26: 231–249.

Bond, Ronald S., et al. 1980. "Effects of Restrictions on Advertising and Commercial Practices in the Professions." Staff Report, Federal Trade Commission, Washington, D.C., September.

Boserup, Ester. 1987. "Inequality Between the Sexes." In *The New Palgrave: A Dictionary of Economics,* ed. John Eatwell, Murray Milgate, and Peter Newman. New York: Stockton.

Boulding, Kenneth E. 1973. *The Economy of Love and Fear.* Belmont, CA: Wadsworth.

Bover, Olympia. 1991. "Relaxing Intertemporal Separability: A Rational Habits Model of Labor Supply Estimated from Panel Data." *Journal of Labor Economics* 9: 85–100.

Bowles, Samuel, and Herbert Gintis. 1976. *Schooling in Capitalist America: Educational Reform and the Contradictions of Economic Life.* New York: Basic Books.

Boyer, Marcel. 1978. "A Habit Forming Optimal Growth Model." *International Economic Review* 19: 585–609.

—— 1983. "Rational Demand and Expenditures Patterns Under Habit Formation." *Journal of Economic Theory* 31: 27–53.

Brady, D., and R. D. Friedman. 1947. "Savings and the Income Distribution." In *Studies in Income and Wealth.* Conference on Research in Income and Wealth, vol. 10. New York: Cambridge University Press for the National Bureau of Economic Research.

Brecht, Bertolt. 1928. *Dreigroschenoper.* Published in English as *The Threepenny Opera,* trans. Hugh Mac Diarmid. London: Methuen, 1973.

Brenner, Reuven. 1983. *History: The Human Gamble.* Chicago: University of Chicago Press.

Cain, Bruce E., John Ferejohn, and Morris Fiorina. 1987. *The Personal Vote: Constituency Service and Electoral Independence.* Cambridge, MA: Harvard University Press.

Cain, Glen G. 1986. "The Economic Analysis of Labor Market Discrimination: A Survey." In *Handbook of Labor Economics,* vol. 1, ed. Orley Ashenfelter and Richard Layard. Handbooks in Economics Series, no. 5. New York: Elsevier Science.

Cass, David. 1965. "Optimum Growth in an Aggregative Model of Capital Accumulation." *Review of Economic Studies* 32: 233–240.

Chaloupka, Frank. 1991. "Rational Addictive Behavior and Cigarette Smoking." *Journal of Political Economy* 99: 722–742.

Coleman, James S. 1990. *Foundations of Social Theory.* Cambridge, MA: Harvard University Press.

Comanor, William S. 1985. "Vertical Price-Fixing, Vertical Market Restrictions, and the New Antitrust Policy." *Harvard Law Review* 98: 983–1002.

Comanor, William S., and Thomas A. Wilson. 1974. *Advertising and Market Power*. Cambridge, MA: Harvard University Press.

Cook, Philip J., and George Tauchen. 1982. "The Effect of Liquor Taxes on Heavy Drinking." *Bell Journal of Economics* 13: 379–390.

Crime Commission. 1967a. *Crime and Its Impact: An Assessment*. Task Force Report. Washington, DC: United States Government Printing Office.

———— 1967b. *The Challenge of Crime in a Free Society*. Task Force Report. Washington, DC: United States Government Printing Office.

Davids, Anthony, and Bradley B. Falkoff. 1975. "Juvenile Delinquents Then and Now: Comparisons of Findings from 1959 and 1974." *Journal of Abnormal Psychology* 84: 161–164.

Denison, Edward F. 1962. *Sources of Economic Growth in the United States*. Washington, DC: Commission on Economic Development.

De Tray, Dennis. 1973. "Child Quality and the Demand for Children." *Journal of Political Economy* 81: 70–95.

Dixit, Avinash, and Victor Norman. 1978. "Advertising and Welfare." *Bell Journal of Economics* 9: 1–17.

Donegan, Nelson H., Judith Rodin, Charles P. O'Brien, and Richard L. Solomon. 1983. "A Learning-Theory Approach to Commonalities." In *Commonalities in Substance Abuse and Habitual Behavior,* ed. Peter K. Levinson, Dean R. Gerstein, and Deborah Maloff. Lexington, MA: Heath.

Dorfman, Robert, and Peter O. Steiner. 1954. "Optimal Advertising and Optimal Quality." *American Economic Review* 44: 826–836.

Douglas, Mary. 1983. "Identity: Personal and Socio-Cultural." *Uppsala Studies in Cultural Anthropology* 5: 35–46.

Duesenberry, James S. 1949. *Income, Savings, and the Theory of Consumer Behavior*. Cambridge, MA: Harvard University Press.

———— 1960. "Comment on 'An Economic Analysis of Fertility.'" In *Demographic and Economic Change in Developed Countries: A Conference of the Universities—National Bureau Committee for Economic Research*. Princeton, NJ: Princeton University Press, for the National Bureau of Economic Research.

Dunkin, Amy, Michael Oneal, and Kevin Kelly. 1988. "Beyond Marlboro Country." *Business Week*, August 8, pp. 54–58.

Edgeworth, Francis Y. 1922. "Equal Pay to Men and Women for Equal Work." *Economic Journal* 32: 431–457.

Ehrlich, D., I. Guttman, P. Schönbach, and J. Mills. 1957. "Postdecision Exposure to Relevant Information." *Journal of Abnormal Psychology* 54: 98–102.

Ehrlich, Isaac. 1973. "Participation in Illegitimate Activities: A Theoretical and Empirical Investigation." *Journal of Political Economy* 81: 521–565.

———— 1975. "The Deterrent Effect of Capital Punishment: A Question of Life and Death." *American Economic Review* 65: 397–417.

Ehrlich, Isaac, and Gary S. Becker. 1972. "Market Insurance, Self-Insurance, and Self-Protection." *Journal of Political Economy* 80: 623–648.

Ehrlich, Isaac, and Lawrence Fisher. 1982. "The Derived Demand for Advertising: A Theoretical and Empirical Investigation." *American Economic Review* 72: 366–388.

Elkins, David J., and Richard E. P. Simeon. 1979. "A Cause in Search of Its Effect; or, What Does Political Culture Explain?" *Comparative Economics* 11: 127–145.

Elster, Jon. [1979] 1984. *Ulysses and the Sirens: Studies in Rationality and Irrationality*. Rev. ed. Cambridge: Cambridge University Press.

Epstein, Larry G., and Stanley E. Zin. 1991. "Substitution, Risk Aversion, and the Temporal Behavior of Consumption and Asset Returns: An Empirical Analysis." *Journal of Political Economy* 99: 263–286.

Farrell, Christopher, and Michael Mandel. 1992. "Uncommon Sense." *Business Week*, October 26, pp. 36–37.

Farrell, Joseph, and Garth Saloner. 1988. "Coordination through Committees and Markets." *Rand Journal of Economics* 19: 235–252.

Farrell, Philip, and Victor R. Fuchs. 1982. "Schooling and Health: The Cigarette Connection." *Journal of Health Economics* 1: 217–230.

Fawcett, Millicent G. 1918. "Equal Pay for Equal Work." *Economic Journal* 28: 1–6.

Ferson, Wayne, and George Constantinides. 1991. "Habit Persistence and Durability in Aggregate Consumption: Empirical Tests." *Journal of Financial Economics* 29: 199–240.

Fethke, Gary, and Raj Jagannathan. 1991. "Monopoly Pricing with Habit Formation." Working Paper 91-10, Department of Economics, University of Iowa.

Fisher, Franklin M., Zvi Griliches, and Carl Kaysen. 1962. "The Costs of Automobile Model Changes since 1949." *Journal of Political Economy* 70: 433–451.

Fisher, Franklin M., and John J. McGowan. 1979. "Advertising and Welfare: Comment." *Bell Journal of Economics* 10: 726–727.

Fisher, Irving. 1926 *Mathematical Investigations in the Theory of Value and Price*. New Haven: Yale University Press.

Frank, Robert H. 1985. *Choosing the Right Pond: Human Behavior and the Quest for Status*. New York: Oxford University Press.

Friedman, Milton. 1957. *A Theory of the Consumption Function*. Princeton, NJ: Princeton University Press.

Galbraith, John K. 1958. *The Affluent Society*. Boston: Houghton-Mifflin.

Geroski, Paul A. 1983. "Some Reflections on the Theory and Application of Concentration Indices." *International Journal of Industrial Organization* 1: 79–94.

Gintis, Herbert. 1974. "Welfare Criteria with Endogenous Preferences." *The Economics of Education* 15: 415–430.

Goldin, Claudia. 1990. *Understanding the Gender Gap: An Economic History of American Women*. Series on Long-Term Factors in Economic Development.

New York: Oxford University Press, for the National Bureau of Economic Research.

Granovetter, Mark. 1985. "Economic Action and Social Structure: The Problem of Embeddedness." *American Journal of Sociology* 91: 481–510.

Greeley, Andrew. 1995. *Religion as Poetry*. New Brunswick, NJ: Transaction Publishers.

Grossman, Gene M., and Carl Shapiro. 1984. "Informative Advertising with Differentiated Products." *Review of Economic Studies* 51: 63–81.

Grossman, Michael. 1971. "The Economics of Joint Production in the Household." Report 7145, Center for Mathematical Studies in Business Economics, University of Chicago.

Grossman, Sanford J., and Oliver D. Hart. 1983. "An Analysis of the Principal-Agent Problem." *Econometrica* 51: 7–45.

Hansen, Lars Peter, and Kenneth J. Singleton. 1983. "Stochastic Consumption, Risk Aversion, and the Temporal Behavior of Asset Returns." *Journal of Political Economy* 91: 249–265.

Harris, Jeffrey E. 1980. "Cigarette Smoking among Women and Men in the United States, 1900–1979." In *1980 Surgeon General's Report on Smoking and Health: The Health Consequences of Smoking for Women*. Washington, DC: United States Department of Health, Education, and Welfare.

—— 1987. "The 1983 Increase in the Federal Cigarette Excise Tax." In *Tax Policy and the Economy*, vol. 1, ed. Lawrence H. Summers. Cambridge, MA: MIT Press.

Hausman, Jerry A. 1978. "Specification Tests in Econometrics." *Econometrica* 46: 1251–1271.

Heaton, John. 1991. "An Empirical Investigation of Asset Pricing with Temporally Dependent Preference Specifications." Manuscript. Massachusetts Institute of Technology.

Hernandez, Donald. 1992. *When Households Continue, Discontinue, and Form*. Washington, DC: United States Bureau of the Census.

Hicks, John R. 1965. *Capital and Growth*. Oxford: Clarendon Press.

Hirschman, Albert O. 1992. *Rival Views of Market Society and Other Recent Essays*. Cambridge, MA: Harvard University Press.

Hoge, Dean. 1993. "Theoretical Approaches for Explaining Levels of Financial Giving by Church Members." Unpublished memorandum, Catholic University, Washington, DC.

Horstman, Ignatius J., and Glenn MacDonald. 1987. "Recurrent Advertising." Chicago: Economic Research Center/NORC Discussion Paper Series, No. 87-11.

Hotz, V. Joseph, Finn E. Kydland, and Guilherme L. Sedlacek. 1988. "Intertemporal Preferences and Labor Supply." *Econometrica* 56: 335–360.

Houthakker, H. S., and Lester D. Taylor. 1966. *Consumer Demand in the United States, 1929–1970*. Cambridge, MA: Harvard University Press.

Hugo, Victor. 1909. *Les Miserables* [1862], *Saint Denis,* book II, chapter I. Trans. Charles E. Wilbour. New York: J. M. Dent and Sons.

Hume, David. 1748. *An Enquiry Concerning Human Understanding.* Reprint (ed. Anthony Flew), LaSalle, IL: Open Court, 1988.

Hurwitz, Mark A., and Richard E. Caves. 1988. "Persuasion or Information? Promotion and the Shares of Brand Name and Generic Pharmaceuticals." *Journal of Law and Economics.* 31: 299–320.

Hutt, William H. 1964. *The Economics of the Colour Bar: A Study of the Economic Origins and Consequences of Racial Segregation in South Africa.* London: Deutsch, for the Institute of Economic Affairs.

Iannaccone, Laurence R. 1984. "Consumption Capital and Habit Formation with an Application to Religious Participation." Ph.D. dissertation, University of Chicago.

——— 1986. "Addiction and Satiation." *Economics Letters* 21: 95–99.

——— 1994. "Skewness Explained: A Rational Choice Model of Religious Giving." Paper presented at the Society for Scientific Study of Religion, Albuquerque, NM, November.

Ippolito, Richard A., R. Dennis Murphy, and Donald Sant. 1979. *Staff Report on Consumer Responses to Cigarette Health Information.* Washington, DC: Federal Trade Commission.

Jefferson, Thomas. 1785. Letter to Peter Carr, August 19. In *The Writings of Thomas Jefferson,* vol. 5, ed. A. A. Lipscomb. Washington, DC: Thomas Jefferson Memorial Association, 1905.

Johnson, Harry G. 1952. "The Effect of Income-Redistribution on Aggregate Consumption with Interdependence of Consumers' Preferences." *Economica* 19: 131–147.

Jones, Stephen R. G. 1984. *The Economics of Conformism.* Cambridge, MA: Blackwell.

Kahneman, Daniel, Jack L. Knetsch, and Richard Thaler. 1986. "Fairness as a Constraint on Profit Seeking: Entitlements in the Market." *American Economic Review* 76: 728–741.

——— 1990. "Experimental Tests of the Endowment Effect and the Coase Theorem." *Journal of Political Economy* 98: 1325–1348.

Kahneman, Daniel, and Amos Tversky. 1986. "Rational Choice and the Framing of Decisions." *Journal of Business* 59: S251–S278.

Kaldor, Nicholas V. 1949. "The Economic Aspects of Advertising." *Review of Economic Studies* 18: 1–27.

Kandel, Eugene. 1990. "Intertemporal Pricing in the Book Publishing Industry." Manuscript, Simon School of Management, University of Rochester.

Kandel, Eugene, and Edward P. Lazear. 1992. "Peer Pressure and Partnerships." *Journal of Political Economy* 100: 801–817.

Kihlstrom, Richard E., and Michael H. Riordan. 1984. "Advertising as a Signal." *Journal of Political Economy* 92: 427–450.

Klein, Ben, and Kevin M. Murphy. 1988. "Vertical Restraints as Contract Reinforcement Mechanism." *Journal of Law and Economics* 31: 265–297.

Klein, Frederick C. 1992. "Two New Pitchers Put Reds on a Roll." *Wall Street Journal,* July 7, p. A8.

Kydland, Finn E., and Edward C. Prescott. 1982. "Time to Build and Aggregate Fluctuations." *Econometrica* 50: 1345–1370.

Lam, David. 1988. "Marriage Markets and Assortative Mating with Household Public Goods: Theoretical Results and Empirical Implications." *Journal of Human Resources* 23: 462–487.

Landes, William M., and Richard A. Posner. 1975. "The Private Enforcement of Law." *Journal of Legal Studies* 4: 1–46.

Leibenstein, Harvey. 1950. "Bandwagon, Snob, and Veblen Effects in the Theory of Consumers' Demand." *Quarterly Journal of Economics* 64: 183–207.

Lewit, Eugene M. 1982. "The Interstate Market for Smuggled Cigarettes." Paper presented at the annual meetings of the American Economic Association, 28–30 December.

Lewit, Eugene M., and Douglas Coate. 1982. "The Potential for Using Excise Taxes to Reduce Smoking." *Journal of Health Economics* 1: 121–145.

Lewit, Eugene M., Douglas Coate, and Michael Grossman. 1981. "The Effects of Government Regulation on Teenage Smoking." *Journal of Law and Economics* 24: 545–569.

Lindbeck, Assar, and Jörgen W. Weibull. 1988. "Altruism and Time Consistency: The Economics of Fait Accompli." *Journal of Political Economy* 96: 1165–1182.

Linder, Staffan Burenstam. 1970. *The Harried Leisure Class.* New York: Columbia University Press.

Lipset, Seymour M., and R. Bendix. 1959. *Social Mobility in Industrial Societies.* Berkeley: University of California Press.

Lott, John R., Jr. 1990. "An Explanation for Public Provision of Schooling: The Importance of Indoctrination." *Journal of Law and Economics* 33: 199–231.

Loury, Glenn C. 1992. "Incentive Effects of Affirmative Action." *Annals of the American Academy of Political and Social Science* 523: 19–29.

Lucas, Robert E., Jr. 1988. "On the Mechanics of Economic Development." *Journal of Monetary Economics* 22: 3–42.

Lundahl, Mats. 1992. *Apartheid in Theory and Practice: An Economic Analysis.* Boulder, CO: Westview.

McElroy, Marjorie B., and Mary Jean Horney. 1981. "Nash-bargained Household Decisions: Toward a Generalization of the Theory of Demand." *International Economic Review* 22: 333–349.

McPherson, Michael. 1974. "The Effects of Public on Private College Enrollment." Ph.D. dissertation, University of Chicago.

Madison, James. 1787. Federalist Paper no. 49. In *The Federalist Papers,* ed. I. Kramnick. Hammondsworth: Penguin, 1987.

Mankiw, N. Gregory, Julio J. Rotemberg, and Lawrence H. Summers. 1985. "Intertemporal Substitution in Macroeconomics." *Quarterly Journal of Economics* 100: 225–251.

Marchand, Roland. 1985. *Advertising the American Dream: Making Way for Modernity 1920–1940.* Berkeley: University of California Press.

Marshall, Alfred. 1962. *Principles of Economics.* 8th ed. London: Macmillan.

Marx, Karl. 1906. *Capital.* 3d ed., vol I. Trans. Samuel Moore and Edward Aveling. Chicago: Charles H. Kerr.

Max, Daniel. 1992. "An Extremely Brief History of *A Brief History of Time.*" *Lingua Franca: The Review of Academic Life* 2 (June–July): 23.

Meltzer, David. 1992. "Mortality Decline, the Demographic Transition and Economic Growth." Ph.D. dissertation, University of Chicago.

Menninger, Karl. 1966. *The Crime of Punishment.* New York: Viking.

Michael, Robert T., and Gary S. Becker. 1973. "On the New Theory of Consumer Behavior." *Swedish Journal of Economics* 75: 378–396.

Mill, John Stuart. 1872. *A System of Logic.* 8th ed. London: Longman, Green, Reader and Dyer.

Mincer, Jacob. 1962. "Labor Force Participation of Married Women." In *Aspects of Labor Economics.* Universities–National Bureau Committee for Economic Research, no. 14. Princeton, NJ: Princeton University Press, for the National Bureau of Economic Research.

——— 1974. *Schooling, Experience, and Earnings.* New York: Columbia University Press, for the National Bureau of Economic Research.

Mobilia, Pamela. 1990. "An Economic Analysis of Addictive Behavior: The Case of Gambling." Ph.D. dissertation, City University of New York.

Moffitt, Robert. 1992. "Incentive Effects of the U.S. Welfare System: A Review." *Journal of Economic Literature* 30: 1–16.

Mullahy, John. 1985. "Cigarette Smoking: Habits, Health Concerns, and Heterogeneous Unobservables in a Macro-economic Analysis of Consumer Demand." Ph.D. dissertation, University of Virginia.

Mulligan, Casey. 1993. "On Intergenerational Altruism, Fertility, and the Persistence of Economic Status." Ph.D. dissertation, University of Chicago.

——— 1995. "Pecuniary and Nonpecuniary Incentives to Work in the U.S. During World War II." Population Research Center Working Paper 95-3, University of Chicago.

Murphy, Kevin M., and Finis Welch. 1992. "The Structure of Wages." *Quarterly Journal of Economics* 107: 285–326.

Myrdal, Gunnar. 1944. *An American Dilemma: The Negro Problem and Modern Democracy.* New York: Random House.

National Research Council. Panel of Research on Deterrent and Incapacitative Effects. 1978. *Deterrence and Incapacitation: Estimating the Effects of Criminal Sanctions on Crime Rates,* ed. Alfred Blumstein, Jacqueline Cohen, and Daniel Nagin. Washington, DC: National Academy of Science.

Nelson, Charles R., and Richard Startz. 1990. "The Distribution of the Instrumental Variables Estimator and Its $t$-Ratio When the Instrument Is a Poor One." *Journal of Business* 63: S125–S140.

Nelson, Philip. 1974. "Advertising as Information." *Journal of Political Economy* 82: 729–754.

Newcomb, Simon. 1885. *Principles of Political Economy*. New York: Harper.

Oi, Walter Y. 1962. "Labor as a Quasi-fixed Factor." *Journal of Political Economy* 70: 538–555.

O'Neill, June. 1985. "The Trend in the Male-Female Wage Gap in the United States." *Journal of Labor Economics* 3: S91–S116.

Orphanides, Athansios, and David Zervos. 1995. "Rational Addiction with Learning and Regret." *Journal of Political Economy* 103: 739–758.

Panteleoni, M. 1898. *Pure Economics*. Clifton, NJ: Kelley.

Parsons, Donald O. 1978. "Intergenerational Wealth Transfers and the Educational Decisions of Male Youth." *Quarterly Journal of Economics* 92: 521–524.

Parsons, Talcott. 1968. "Social Interactions." In *International Encyclopedia of the Social Sciences*, vol. 7, ed. D. S. Sills. New York: Macmillan.

Peele, Stanton. 1985. *The Meaning of Addiction: Compulsive Experience and Its Interpretation*. Lexington, MA: Lexington.

Peltzman, Sam. 1973. "The Effect of Government Subsidies-in-Kind on Private Expenditures: The Case of Higher Education." *Journal of Political Economy* 81: 1–27.

Phelps, Edmund S. 1972. "The Statistical Theory of Racism and Sexism." *American Economic Review* 62: 659–661.

Philipson, Tomas. 1993. "Social Welfare and Measurement of Segregation." *Journal of Economic Theory* 60: 322–334.

Phlips, Louis. 1974. *Applied Consumption Analysis*. Amsterdam: North-Holland.

Pigou, Arthur C. 1903. "Some Remarks on Utility." *Economic Journal* 13: 19–24.

——— 1920. *The Economics of Warfare*. London: Macmillan and Company.

Polinsky, A. Mitchell, and Steven Shavell. 1984. "The Optimal Use of Fines and Imprisonment." *Journal of Public Economics* 24: 89–99.

Pollak, Robert A. 1970. "Habit Formation and Dynamic Demand Functions." *Journal of Political Economy* 78: 745–763.

——— 1976. "Habit Formation and Long-Run Utility Functions." *Journal of Economic Theory* 13: 272–297.

Porter, Robert H. 1986. "The Impact of Government Policy on the U.S. Cigarette Industry." In *Empirical Approaches to Consumer Protection Economics*, ed. Pauline M. Ippolito and David T. Scheffman. Washington, DC: Federal Trade Commission.

Posner, Richard A. 1986. *Economic Analysis of Law*. 3d ed. Boston: Little, Brown.

——— 1995. *Aging and Old Age*. Chicago: University of Chicago Press.

Psacharopoulos, George. 1985. "Returns to Education: A Further International Update and Implication." *Journal of Human Resources* 20: 583–604.

Robins, Lee N., John E. Helzer, Michi Hesselbrook, and Eric Wish. 1980. "Vietnam Veterans Three Years After Vietnam: How Our Study Changed Our View of Heroin." In *The Yearbook of Substance Use and Abuse,* vol. 2, ed. Leon Brill and Charles Winick. New York: Human Sciences.

Rogers, Alan R. 1994. "Evolution of Time Preference by Natural Selection." *American Economic Review* 84: 460–481.

Romer, Paul M. 1986. "Increasing Returns and Long-Run Growth." *Journal of Political Economy* 94: 1002–1037.

——— 1994. "Preferences, Promises, and the Politics of Entitlement." Unpublished memorandum, University of California, Berkeley.

Ryder, Harl E., Jr., and Geoffrey M. Heal. 1973. "Optimum Growth with Intertemporally Dependent Preferences." *Review of Economic Studies* 40: 1–33.

Samuelson, Paul A. 1954. "The Pure Theory of Public Expenditures. *Review of Economics and Statistics* 36: 387–389.

——— 1956. "Social Indifference Curves." *Quarterly Journal of Economics* 70: 1–22.

Sanders, Seth. 1991. "A Dynamic Model of Welfare Participation." Ph.D. dissertation, University of Chicago.

Schelling, Thomas C. 1978. *Micromotives and Macrobehavior*. New York: Norton.

——— 1984a. *Choice and Consequence*. Cambridge, MA: Harvard University Press.

——— 1984b. "Self-Command in Practice, in Policy, and in a Theory of Rational Choice." *American Economic Review* 74(1): 1–11.

Scherer, Frederic M. 1980. *Industrial Market Structure and Economic Performance*. 2d ed. Boston, MA: Houghton-Mifflin.

Schneider, Lynne, Benjamin Klein, and Kevin M. Murphy. 1981. "Governmental Regulation of Cigarette Health Information." *Journal of Law and Economics* 24: 575–612.

Schoeck, Helmut. 1966. *Envy*. New York: Harcourt, Brace and World.

Schultz, Theodore W. 1963. *The Economic Value of Education*. New York: Columbia University Press.

Schwartz, R. 1970. "Personal Philanthropic Contributions." *Journal of Political Economy* 78: 1264–1291.

Sen, Amartya. 1977. "Rational Fools: A Critique of the Behavioral Foundations of Economic Theory." *Philosophy and Public Affairs* 6: 317–344.

Shapiro, Carl. 1982. "Consumer Information, Product Quality, and Seller Reputation." *Bell Journal of Economics* 13: 20–35.

Shoup, C. 1966. *Federal Estate and Gift Taxes*. Washington, DC: Brookings Institution.

Showalter, Mark H. 1991. "Monopoly Behavior with Intertemporal Demands." Ph.D. dissertation, Massachusetts Institute of Technology.

Smith, Adam. 1937. *The Wealth of Nations,* ed. Edwin Cannan. New York: Modern Library.

———— 1976. *The Theory of Moral Sentiments.* Indianapolis: Liberty Classics.

Soffer, O. 1990. "Before Beringia: Late Pleistocene Bio-social Transformations and the Colonization of Northern Eurasia." In *Chronostratigraphy of the Paleolithic in North Central, East Asia and America.* Novosibirsk: Academy of Sciences of the U.S.S.R.

Solow, Robert M. 1967. "The New Industrial State or Son of Affluence." *Public Interest* 9: 100–108.

Spence, Michael. 1976. "Product Selection, Fixed Costs, and Monopolistic Competition." *Review of Economic Studies* 43: 217–235.

Spinnewyn, Frans. 1981. "Rational Habit Formation." *European Economic Review* 15: 91–109.

Stark, Rodney. 1994. "Religion as a Context: Hellfire and Delinquency One More Time." Unpublished memorandum, University of Washington.

Stigler, George J. 1949. "Lecture 1: The Economists and Equality." In *Five Lectures on Economic Problems.* London: Longmans, Green and Co.

———— 1970. "The Optimum Enforcement of Laws." *Journal of Political Economy* 78: 526–536.

Sumner, Daniel A. 1981. "Measurement of Monopoly Behavior: An Application to the Cigarette Industry." *Journal of Political Economy* 89: 1010–1019.

Sunstein, Cass. 1993. "Endogenous Preferences, Environmental Law." *Journal of Legal Studies* 22: 217–254.

Taussig, Michael. 1965. "The Charitable Contribution in the Federal Personal Income Tax." Ph.D. dissertation, Massachusetts Institute of Technology.

Telser, Lester G. 1962. "Advertising and Cigarettes." *Journal of Political Economy* 70: 471–499.

———— 1964. "Advertising and Competition." *Journal of Political Economy* 72: 537–562.

Thompson, Michael, Richard Ellis, and Aaron Wildavsky. 1990. *Cultural Theory.* Boulder, CO: Westview Press.

Tirole, Jean. 1988. *The Theory of Industrial Organization.* Cambridge, MA: MIT Press.

Tobacco Tax Council. 1986. *The Tax Burden on Tobacco: Historical Compilation,* vol. 20. Richmond, VA: Tobacco Tax Council.

———— [Various years.] *Municipal Tax Surveys.* Richmond, VA: Tobacco Tax Council.

Tocqueville, Alexis de. 1969. *Democracy in America,* vol. II. New York: Anchor Books.

Townsend, Joy L. 1987. "Cigarette Tax, Economic Welfare and Social Class Patterns of Smoking." *Applied Economics* 19: 355–365.

United States Bureau of the Census. 1973. 1970 Census of Population. Volume 1, Characteristics of the Population, part 1: "United States Summary," section 1. Washington, DC: United States Government Printing Office. [Comparable sources used for data from the 1960 and 1980 Census of Population.]

——— 1985. Current Population Reports: Population Estimates and Projections, Series P-25, No. 970. Washington, DC: United States Government Printing Office. [Also No. 957, 1984; No. 460, 1971; No. 304, 1965.]

United States Bureau of Economic Analysis. [Various years.] *Survey of Current Business*. Washington, DC: United States Government Printing Office.

United States Sentencing Commission. 1992. *Federal Sentencing Guidelines Manual*. Washington, DC: Government Printing Office.

Veblen, Thorstein. 1934. *The Theory of the Leisure Class*. New York: Modern Library.

Vickery, W. S. 1962. "One Economist's View of Philanthropy." In *Philanthropy and Public Policy*, ed. F. Dickinson. New York: National Bureau of Economic Research.

Warner, Kenneth E. 1986. *Selling Smoke: Cigarette Advertising and Public Health*. Washington, DC: American Public Health Organization.

Weizsäcker, Carl C. von. 1971. "Notes on Endogenous Changes of Tastes." *Journal of Economic Theory* 3: 345–372.

Williamson, Oliver E. 1985. *The Economic Institutions of Capitalism: Firms, Markets, Relational Contracting*. New York: Free Press.

Winston, Gordon C. 1980. "Addiction and Backsliding: A Theory of Compulsive Consumption." *Journal of Economic Behavior and Organization* 1: 295–324.

Wordsworth, William. 1822. "Reflections." *Ecclesiastical Sonnets*, pt. II, Sonnet 28. In *The Poetical Works of Wordsworth*, rev. Paul D. Sheats. Boston: Houghton-Mifflin, 1982.

Wu, De-Min. 1973. "Alternative Tests of Independence between Stochastic Regressors and Disturbances." *Econometrica* 41: 733–750.

Yaari, Menahem E. 1977. "Consistent Utilization of an Exhaustible Resource, or How To Eat an Appetite-Arousing Cake." Working paper, Center for Research on Mathematical Economics and Game Theory, Hebrew University, Jerusalem.

Young, Peyton. 1993. "The Evolution of Conventions." *Econometrica* 61: 57–84.

# Index